# the About.com guide to

# SOUTHERN COOKING

All you need to prepare 225 delicious
home cooked favorites

Diana Rattray

Adams Media
Avon, Massachusetts

# About **About**.com

About.com is a powerful network of 500 Guides—smart, passionate, accomplished people who are experts in their fields. About .com Guides live and work in more than twenty countries and celebrate their interests in thousands of topics. They have written books, appeared on national television programs, and won many awards in their fields. Guides are selected for their ability to provide the most interesting information for users, and for their passion for their subject and the Web. The selection process is rigorous—only 15 percent of those who apply actually become Guides. The following are some of the most important criteria by which they are chosen:

- High level of knowledge/passion for their topic
- Appropriate credentials
- Keen understanding of the Web experience
- Commitment to creating informative, actionable features

Each month more than 48 million people visit About.com. Whether you need home repair and decorating ideas, recipes, movie trailers, or car buying tips, About.com Guides can offer practical advice and solutions for everyday life. Wherever you land on About.com, you'll always find content that is relevant to your interests. If you're looking for "how to" advice on refinishing your deck, About.com will also show you the tools you need to get the job done. No matter where you are on About.com, or how you got there, you'll always find exactly what you're looking for!

# About Your Guide

**DIANA RATTRAY,** an avid home cook, recipe collector, and confessed foodie, lives in Mississippi. Diana has long been fascinated with cooking and has had a passion for recipes ever since she can remember. Diana's grandfather, a baker and chef who cooked at restaurants, resorts, and farms in various Maine towns, was certainly an inspiration, as was her mother, who let her help with the family cooking and baking from a very young age.

On the Internet, Diana has been a member and participant in food forums and recipe mailing lists for many years. Southern food and cooking has been Diana's passion since moving to Mississippi in 1995, and in 1997 she was fortunate enough to be invited to grow and develop that interest as the Southern Cuisine Guide for About.com. As a Guide, Diana continues to develop and write new recipes and has written many articles about the wonderful and varied dishes of the South.

## Acknowledgments

Thanks: To my grandfather, Edward Bernard, who introduced me to the wonderful world of cooking with his passion to cook for everyone. To my mother, Grace Rattray, for taking the time and letting me cook with her. To my mother-in-law, Dorothy Lawhon, for answering so many of my questions, and finally to my Southern husband, Loy Lawhon, for tasting and testing whatever I made, whether he was hungry or not.

## ABOUT.COM

CEO & President
*Scott Meyer*

COO
*Andrew Pancer*

SVP Content
*Michael Daecher*

VP Marketing
*Lisa Abourezk*

Director, About Operations
*Chris Murphy*

Senior Web Designer
*Jason Napolitano*

## ADAMS MEDIA

### Editorial

Publishing Director
*Gary M. Krebs*

Associate Managing Editor
*Laura M. Daly*

Development Editor
*Katie McDonough*

### Marketing

Director of Marketing
*Karen Cooper*

Assistant Art Director
*Frank Rivera*

### Production

Director of Manufacturing
*Susan Beale*

Associate Director of Production
*Michelle Roy Kelly*

Senior Book Designer
*Colleen Cunningham*

About.com® is a registered trademark of About, Inc.

Published by Adams Media, an F+W Publications Company
57 Littlefield Street
Avon, MA 02322
www.adamsmedia.com

ISBN 10: 1-59869-096-5
ISBN 13: 978-1-59869-096-5

Printed in China.

J I H G F E D C B A

Library of Congress Cataloging-in-Publication Data
is available from the publisher.

This publication is designed to provide accurate and authoritative information with regard to the subject matter covered. It is sold with the understanding that the publisher is not engaged in rendering legal, accounting, or other professional advice. If legal advice or other expert assistance is required, the services of a competent professional person should be sought.

—From a *Declaration of Principles* jointly adopted by a Committee of the American Bar Association and a Committee of Publishers and Associations

Many of the designations used by manufacturers and sellers to distinguish their product are claimed as trademarks. Where those designations appear in this book and Adams Media was aware of a trademark claim, the designations have been printed with initial capital letters.

*This book is available at quantity discounts for bulk purchases. For information, please call 1-800-872-5627.*

# How to Use This Book

Each About.com book is written by an About.com Guide—an expert with experiential knowledge of his or her subject. While the book can stand on its own as a helpful resource, it can also be coupled with the corresponding About.com site for even more tips, tools, and advice to help you learn even more about a particular subject. Each book will not only refer you back to About .com, but it will also direct you to other useful Internet locations and print resources.

All About.com books include a special section at the end of each chapter called Get Linked. Here you'll find a few links back to the About.com site for even more great information on the topics discussed in that chapter. Depending on the topic, these could be links to such resources as photos, sheet music, quizzes, recipes, or product reviews.

About.com books also include four types of sidebars:

- **Ask Your Guide:** Detailed information in a question-and-answer format
- **Tools You Need:** Advice about researching, purchasing, and using a variety of tools for your projects
- **Elsewhere on the Web:** References to other useful Internet locations
- **What's Hot:** All you need to know about the hottest trends and tips out there

Each About.com book will take you on a personal tour of a certain topic, give you reliable advice, and leave you with the knowledge you need to achieve your goals.

# CONTENTS

# Introduction from Your Guide

*My own experience with Southern cooking began with a move from New Hampshire to Mississippi ten years ago.* After my initial shock at not being able to find such things as split-top hot dog rolls and the relief that came with the revelation that lard was no longer a major ingredient here, I became fascinated with the differences in dishes and ingredients and delighted with the new tastes I found here. I'll never forget my first meal; it was a sampler of sorts, and included fried chicken, fried green tomatoes, freshly cooked black-eyed peas, fried okra slices, chicken and dumplings, hot buttered biscuits, and that delicious Southern cornbread. Though there are many wonderful regional food specialties and dishes throughout the nation, nothing in the United States is quite like Southern cuisine.

As I began tasting these foods and new versions of old foods, I found that I wanted to learn to cook them myself, not only to please my husband, who is a native Southerner, but also to satisfy my own culinary curiosity. I passed a milestone when my husband approved of my fried green tomatoes, and another one when he liked my fried chicken, but my greatest achievement in Southern cooking came when my mother-in-law approved of my cornbread.

Southern cuisine spans quite a large area and incorporates a variety of influences. The states with the richest history include Louisiana, Mississippi, Alabama, Georgia, Kentucky, Tennessee, Arkansas, Florida, North Carolina, and South Carolina. You'll also find Southern food traditions in parts of Texas and Oklahoma, Missouri, Virginia and West Virginia, and even Maryland.

African-Americans have certainly had as much influence on Southern cuisine as any other culture or nationality, but you'll also find Spanish and Caribbean influences in Florida; French in Louisiana and South Carolina; English, Scots, and Irish throughout the area; Moravian in North Carolina; German in Kentucky and parts of Tennessee; and the list goes on. Of course, the Native American influence is as pervasive in the South as anywhere else in the Americas. Without their influence, there would be no corn or hominy or grits, no pumpkin, squash, tomatoes, potatoes, chili peppers, peanuts, sweet potatoes, many types of beans, or a long list of other foods.

Through the years, the basics have changed little, though with the availability of more ingredients and population changes in many of the larger cities, there is much more experimentation, something all Southern cooks dearly love. Drop in on a conversation between the most Southern of cooks; they'll be talking about their Chicken Cordon Bleu right along with their pinto beans and greens, and grilled tuna as well as catfish and hush puppies. Ask ten Southern cooks how they make their cornbread, and you'll get ten slightly different answers, but no complete recipe. The one thing they all have in common is the claim that their own personal recipe is the "best." Southern favorites, such as barbecue, vary widely according to which state you live in. In some cases, such as with North Carolina barbecue sauces and a regional Kentucky mutton barbecue, it can actually vary from one section of the state to another.

The Southern Foodways Alliance is one organization dedicated to preserving the heritage of our unique cuisine, making sure through writings, events, chefs and cooking demonstrations, that it passes on from one generation to the next. Even with the changes that come with passing time and differing people and markets, traditional favorites will be remembered, and treasured recipes will hopefully change only slightly, depending on the region and the cook.

With this cookbook, I hope to do my own small part to preserve our Southern food culture in bringing you a taste of many of the basics, some best-loved foods and recipes from regions throughout the South, along with some of my personal favorites.

## Chapter 1

# Beverages

**ASK YOUR GUIDE:**

Where did bourbon originate?
▶ **PAGE 5**

What's the best way to juice lemons and other citrus fruits?
▶ **PAGE 7**

What is the best way to peel peaches?
▶ **PAGE 9**

How do I make sweetened whipped cream?
▶ **PAGE 10**

How do I scald milk?
▶ **PAGE 11**

▶ It's always a good idea to have a nonreactive pot and skillet in your arsenal of cooking tools. Certain acidic foods can react to some materials, including aluminum, copper, and iron. Good nonreactive pot and skillet materials include glass, stainless steel, enamel or an enamel-lined pan (with no chips), or glazed ceramic.

## Southern-Style Iced Tea
MAKES 1 QUART

*When I moved to the South, I quickly learned that if I want unsweet-ened tea, I should say so! Sweetened or not, iced tea has been a South-ern tradition since the nineteenth century, around the time ice became available to most people.*

3 cups water
3 teaspoons (heaping) fresh orange pekoe bulk tea
4 cups cold water

1. Put 3 cups water in a nonreactive saucepan and bring to a boil over high heat. Reduce heat to low and add the tea. Cover and let simmer for 5 to 8 minutes.
2. Strain into a large pitcher; add 4 cups cold water. Refrigerate to chill thoroughly.

## Orange Cooler

SERVES 6

*Easy, nutritious, and delicious, this is a drink the kids will love. A sprig of mint, a straw, and a long iced-tea spoon make this drink look extra special.*

3 cups cold orange juice
6 large scoops orange sherbet
Ginger ale, chilled
Sprigs fresh mint for **garnish**, optional

1. Pour ½ cup of orange juice into each of 6 tumblers. Add a generous scoop of orange sherbet to each glass, then fill with cold ginger ale.
2. Stir slightly and serve with iced-tea spoons and straws. Garnish with a sprig of mint, if desired.

ELSEWHERE ON THE WEB

▶ The Florida Department of Citrus has an informative Web site at www .floridajuice.com. You'll find information on orange nutrition and health benefits, special promotions, and a very good variety of recipes and ideas using Florida oranges and grapefruit and their juice. Another excellent site is the Sunkist site, at www .sunkist.com, which has a super recipe database, some unique health tips—including refreshing citrus spa treatments and using citrus to relieve stress—nutritional facts, and fun for kids.

ELSEWHERE ON THE WEB

▶ Linda Larsen, the Busy Cooks Guide for About.com, has a wonderful recipe for a mixture of brown sugar and spices that you can make ahead of time and use to mull apple cider or wine for the holidays. To see the recipe, just go to http://busycooks .about.com and search for "Mulling Mix." This would also make a super holiday gift. Wrap some mix in cellophane and tie it off with a bow, then tuck it in a pretty mug with a cinnamon stick and a tag with preparation instructions.

## Hot Spiced Cider
MAKES 2 QUARTS

*This is an easy and delicious drink, perfect for cold winter nights and holiday gatherings. If you're having an adult get-together or New Year's Eve party, offer this with a little rum or bourbon.*

    2 quarts apple cider
    ¼ cup packed brown sugar
    8 whole cloves
    6 whole allspice berries
    1 cinnamon stick
    ⅛ teaspoon freshly grated nutmeg
    Dash salt
    Cinnamon sticks (1 for each serving)

1. Combine all ingredients in a large saucepan. Bring to a boil over medium-high heat.
2. Strain and serve hot in mugs, with cinnamon sticks, if desired.

## Bourbon Vanilla Milk Punch
SERVES 8

*A wonderful combination of flavors, this bourbon milk punch makes a beautiful beverage for a summer party or get-together. I would serve this punch at a relaxing summer cookout with good friends and neighbors.*

2 quarts vanilla ice cream
1 cup good-quality Kentucky bourbon
2 tablespoons vanilla
Freshly grated nutmeg, for garnish

1. In a blender, combine the ice cream, bourbon, and vanilla. Blend until smooth.
2. Pour into cups or small tumblers and grate a little nutmeg over each serving.

ASK YOUR GUIDE

***Where did bourbon originate?***

▶ Bourbon is actually as American as apple pie. It's whiskey in a distinctly Southern blend, made with at least 51 percent corn, along with rye and other grains. Bourbon evolved in the late 1700s in Bourbon County, Virginia, an area that would later become part of Kentucky. Today, bourbon is produced exclusively in Kentucky and is exported all over the world.

► You'll want to serve the traditional julep on Derby Day, but you might want to try another combination of flavors for a holiday gathering or a hot summer's day. Here are two of my favorite variations on the traditional mint julep from my About.com site. The first is a Strawberry Julep, at http://about.com/southern food/strawberryjulep, made with fresh strawberries, sugar, and bourbon. The second is a Georgia Mint Julep at http://about .com/southernfood/georgia mintjulep, made with brandy and peach brandy, along with sugar and a garnish of fresh mint.

# Kentucky Mint Julep
MAKES ABOUT 20

*Serve mint juleps in a traditional silver julep cup, if you have one—otherwise, a glass will do just fine! Stir the ice a bit to frost the julep cup, or serve in frosted glasses.*

> 2 cups granulated sugar
> 2 cups water
> ¼ cup fresh mint leaves
> Crushed ice
> Kentucky bourbon, about 2 ounces per serving

1. In a saucepan, combine sugar and water; heat over medium-low heat until hot and clear. Remove from heat. Put mint leaves in a cup and bruise by gently pressing leaves against sides of cup with a spoon. Stir leaves into syrup and let steep for about 20 to 25 minutes.
2. Fill a julep cup or glass with crushed ice, then add 1 tablespoon of the syrup and 2 ounces of bourbon.
3. Garnish each serving with fresh mint sprigs and serve with a short straw.

## Mint Citrus Cooler
MAKES 3 QUARTS

*This is a beautiful citrus beverage for a special summer occasion or gathering. You can also make a big pitcher-full for a family cookout.*

1 ½ cups granulated sugar
2 ½ cups water
1 cup fresh mint leaves
Juice of 2 medium oranges
Juice of 6 medium lemons
1 heaping tablespoon orange **zest**, grated fine
Thin-sliced lemon and orange for garnish
Fresh mint sprigs for garnish, optional

1. In a saucepan, combine sugar and water. Bring to a boil over medium-high heat. Reduce heat to medium-low and simmer for 5 minutes. Remove from heat and let cool for 10 minutes.
2. Place 1 cup mint leaves in a bowl; add the slightly cooled syrup, orange juice, lemon juice, and orange zest. Cover and let steep for about 1 hour. Strain into a 1-quart container. Cover and refrigerate until serving time.
3. For each tall glass, mix ⅓ cup syrup with ⅔ cup cold water. Add a few ice cubes, a thin orange or lemon slice, and a sprig of mint.

ASK YOUR GUIDE

*What's the best way to juice lemons and other citrus fruits?*

▶ To get the most juice from your oranges and lemons, have them at room temperature and roll them on the counter under your palm for a few seconds before squeezing. If the lemons or oranges are still cold, microwave on HIGH power for about 20 to 30 seconds, then let stand for a minute or two before squeezing.

## Cranberry Party Punch

MAKES 1 GALLON

*Here's a festive and flavorful fruit punch for the holidays, perfect for a party or family gathering. This recipe can be doubled quite easily if you're expecting a crowd.*

6 cups cranberry juice
4 ½ cups apple juice
¾ cup fresh lemon juice, about 5 to 6 small lemons
1 lemon, sliced thin
1 can (8 ounces) pineapple tidbits with juice
6 cups club soda

1. Combine cranberry juice, apple juice, and lemon juice. Add lemon slices and pineapple tidbits.
2. Chill thoroughly, then pour into a punch bowl. Add club soda just before serving, along with ice cubes or an ice ring.

**WHAT'S HOT**

▶ For a party, you might want to make a beautiful cranberry ice ring to go in this punch. Fill a 3- to 4-cup ring mold with fresh cranberries and lemon slices, then cover with water and freeze for about 6 hours, or until solid. Dip the mold in lukewarm water to remove the ring and put it in the punch bowl for an extra-special festive look.

## Georgia Peach Shake

SERVES 4

*This delicious peach shake hits the spot on a hot summer day, and it's a great way to use those juicy ripe peaches. The kids will adore it!*

> 2 cups sliced fresh peaches
> ½ cup pineapple juice
> ½ cup sugar
> 1 quart vanilla ice cream
> 1 ½ cups milk

1. Using an electric blender, blend sliced peaches, pineapple juice, and sugar until smooth. Add ice cream and blend until soft and blended; pour in milk and pulse just until combined.
2. Pour into tall chilled glasses and serve with straws.

ASK YOUR GUIDE

***What is the best way to peel peaches?***

▶ I usually use a sharp paring knife to peel peaches, but if you need perfectly smooth peeled peaches, plunge them into boiling water for a few seconds then immerse quickly in ice water. Under running water, use your fingers to scrape or peel the skin away. Cut peaches in half to remove the pit, then slice or dice. Peeling peaches this way is especially nice for recipes that use whole peaches or uniform halves or slices.

ASK YOUR GUIDE

### How do I make sweetened whipped cream?

▶ To make sweetened whipped cream, whip 1 cup of heavy whipping cream until almost stiff, then add about 3 to 4 tablespoons of powdered sugar and 1 teaspoon vanilla. Beat until the whipped cream holds peaks. I like my whipped cream with at least 3 tablespoons of sugar, but you might try with different amounts if you don't want it too sweet. Be careful not to whip the cream too long or you'll end up with butter!

## Strawberry Ice Cream Soda
SERVES 2

*This is an ice cream soda you'll make again and again. The whole family will be asking for this one, and not only during hot weather months. Luckily, fresh strawberries are available almost year-round these days!*

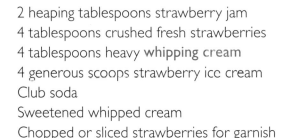

2 heaping tablespoons strawberry jam
4 tablespoons crushed fresh strawberries
4 tablespoons heavy whipping cream
4 generous scoops strawberry ice cream
Club soda
Sweetened whipped cream
Chopped or sliced strawberries for garnish

1. In each of 2 tall 16-ounce glasses, put 1 heaping tablespoon jam, 2 tablespoons crushed strawberries, 2 tablespoons whipping cream, and 1 generous scoop of strawberry ice cream. Fill each glass about ⅔ full with club soda, then add another generous scoop of strawberry ice cream.
2. Top each soda with a dollop of whipped cream and sliced or chopped strawberries. Serve with a long iced tea spoon and a straw.

## Old-Fashioned Hot Cocoa

SERVES 4

*If you have a utensil or machine specially made for frothing, fill cups about ¾ of the way and make that beautiful foamy top. You could almost skip the marshmallows.*

> 3 tablespoons unsweetened cocoa powder
> ¼ cup granulated sugar
> 4 cups milk
> ¼ teaspoon vanilla
> Miniature marshmallows or marshmallow creme

1. In a small bowl, combine the cocoa and sugar, blending well.
2. In a saucepan, heat milk to scalding. Stir about ½ cup of the hot milk into the cocoa and sugar mixture, then pour the hot cocoa mixture into the hot milk in saucepan. Stir until well blended, then stir in vanilla.
3. Serve in cups with mini marshmallows or a dollop of marshmallow creme.

ASK YOUR GUIDE

### How do I scald milk?

▶ Many recipes call for scalded milk just because that was how bacteria was killed before the days of pasteurization. You still might want to heat or scald milk if you need to dissolve sugar in it or melt butter or other fat, or if you use raw milk. Scald milk by heating it in a saucepan over low heat, stirring occasionally, just until small bubbles begin to form around the inside edge of the pan. The milk will form a slight skin on top, which you will notice when you stir, and it will begin to steam.

## Get Linked

*At my Southern Food site on **About.com**, you can find more information on beverages. Here are some links to resources that might help you.*

**A SOUTHERN TRADITION: ICED TEA**

This article offers a little tea history and takes a look at the tradition of iced tea in the South. You'll also find several recipes, including teas and drinks using teas, punch recipes, coolers, and other popular beverages.

 http://about.com/southernfood/icedtea

**ICE CREAM BEVERAGES**

This is a list of several beverages made with ice cream, including milkshakes and ice cream sodas, flips and coolers, and other old-fashioned favorites.

 http://about.com/southernfood/icecreamdrinks

## Chapter 2

# Appetizers and Breads

**ASK YOUR GUIDE:**

What snacks are good choices for dipping with this recipe?
▶ **PAGE 17**

What's the trick to making perfect hard-cooked eggs?
▶ **PAGE 18**

What's the best way to soften a package of cream cheese?
▶ **PAGE 20**

How can I make my biscuits lighter?
▶ **PAGE 26**

Why are they called hush puppies?
▶ **PAGE 28**

How many fritters can I fry at once?
▶ **PAGE 29**

▶ A food processor is one tool that no cook—and definitely no Southern cook!—should be without. Your food processor will save you time in many recipes, and it can come in especially handy for this recipe. Combine the ingredients in the bowl of a food processor fitted with a metal blade. Pulse in short bursts until the mixture is just blended and clumping together.

## Spicy Cheese Straws
MAKES 5 TO 6 DOZEN

*A Southern favorite, these cheese straws are spicy and delicious. Roll them into straw shapes or cut into narrow strips and gently turn to make cheese twists.*

14 tablespoons butter, at room temperature
3 cups grated sharp Cheddar cheese
1 ¾ cups all-purpose flour, plus more for rolling
⅛ teaspoon salt
½ teaspoon ground cayenne pepper, or to taste
1 teaspoon Worcestershire sauce

1. Preheat oven to 300°F.
2. In a large mixing bowl, combine the flour, salt, and cayenne pepper. Using two knives or a pastry blender, cut butter, cheese, and Worcestershire sauce into the flour mixture until thoroughly blended.
3. Working with a small amount of dough at a time, roll into long tube about the width of a straw and cut in desired lengths. Or, roll dough out on a floured surface to a thickness of about ⅛ to ¼ inch. Cut into strips, and gently twist.
4. Arrange straws or twists on ungreased baking sheets. Bake for 20 to 25 minutes, or until the straws are crisp and just lightly browned.
5. Remove the straws and let cool.

## Crab-Stuffed Mushrooms
MAKES 20

*This is a delicious appetizer to fix for a Derby Day party, New Year's Eve, the Super Bowl, or just about any occasion.*

20 large mushrooms (about 1 pound)
6 tablespoons butter
4 green onions, chopped fine
2 tablespoons minced red bell pepper
4 ounces crabmeat
1 cup fresh bread crumbs, processed until fine
½ teaspoon Creole seasoning or seasoned salt
Dash ground black pepper
2 tablespoons freshly grated Parmesan cheese, optional

1. Preheat oven to 350°F.
2. Wash mushrooms. Trim ends then twist to separate them from the caps. Chop the stems finely and set aside.
3. Melt 2 tablespoons butter; brush over the mushroom caps. Lightly butter a shallow 8- or 9-inch baking dish or spray with a no-stick cooking spray.
4. Melt remaining 4 tablespoons butter in a skillet. Add the chopped mushroom stems, chopped green onions, and minced red bell pepper. Sauté until vegetables are tender.
5. Combine vegetables with bread crumbs, crabmeat, and seasonings. Fill mushrooms, mounding slightly. Arrange in one layer in the baking dish. Sprinkle each mushroom with a little Parmesan cheese, if desired.
6. Bake until the mushrooms are tender and stuffing is hot, about 15 to 20 minutes.

**WHAT'S HOT**

▶ Here's a great time-saving tip: Don't throw away day-old bread or rolls—use them to make homemade bread crumbs! Just chop up the bread into smaller chunks, then run it through your food processor. Season as you like, and then freeze crumbs in small bags. Just pull what you need out of the freezer when you're ready to use it in a recipe. Some seasonings you might add to homemade bread crumbs include Parmesan cheese, dried parsley flakes, oregano and basil, garlic powder, onion powder, paprika, seasoned salt, or herb seasoning.

## Benedictine Dip or Spread

MAKES ABOUT 1 ½ CUPS

*This light-green cucumber dip is a Kentucky tradition, named for Jennie Benedict, who ran a tearoom in Louisville, Kentucky, in the early 1900s. I usually serve this as a dip with fresh vegetables.*

1 large cucumber, peeled
½ small onion
8 ounces cream cheese, **softened**
1 tablespoon mayonnaise
Dash salt
Green food coloring, optional
1 to 2 tablespoons sour cream or **heavy cream**, optional

1. Grate cucumber and onion into a colander; drain well, pressing to remove all excess moisture.
2. Blend cream cheese and mayonnaise with mixer or food processor; add salt, grated cucumber, and onion. If desired, stir in a few drops of green food coloring.
3. To make sandwiches, spread bread slices with mayonnaise, then a layer of Benedictine. To use as a dip for vegetables, stir in a little heavy cream or sour cream to thin slightly.

## Spicy Cheese Dip

MAKES 7 TO 8 CUPS

*This easy slow-cooker cheese dip is always a hit, and it's very flexible. I like to add a little diced hot pepper or ground cayenne to give it some extra heat.*

2 pounds pasteurized processed cheese food, cut into **cubes**
8 ounces cream cheese, cut into cubes
1 small can (4 ounces) chopped mild green chile pepper
1 envelope (1.25 ounces) taco seasoning mix
16 ounces chunky salsa or Mexican-style diced tomatoes

1.  Combine all ingredients in a 3- to 5-quart **slow cooker**.
2.  Cover and cook on LOW setting, stirring occasionally, until cheese is melted and mixture is hot.
3.  Serve warm from the slow cooker or a chafing dish. Stir occasionally to keep smooth.

ASK YOUR GUIDE

**What snacks are good choices for dipping with this recipe?**

▶ Serve this flavorful dip with your favorite tortilla chips, bread cubes, or assorted crackers, or serve it as a dip with a variety of fresh vegetables. For a heartier dip, add about 8 ounces of lean ground beef or sausage, browned and drained. I like it spicy, so I usually add minced jalapeño peppers or ground cayenne. This dip is easy to double for a big party.

*What's the trick to making perfect hard-cooked eggs?*

▶ For perfect hard-cooked eggs, put eggs in a single layer in a large saucepan and cover with at least 1 inch of cold water. Cover the pan and bring to a rolling boil over high heat. Remove from heat and let stand, covered, for 15 minutes, or 18 minutes for extra-large. Immediately run cold water over the eggs or cool in ice water. To peel, crack lightly then roll on the counter to make cracks all around. Start peeling at the large end, where there will be a slight air pocket. Hold the egg under cold running water while peeling.

# Deviled Eggs with Mustard
SERVES 12

*Honestly, it seems everyone loves deviled eggs. These have just a touch of mustard, and you can top them with an olive slice, a piece of pickle, or a sprinkle of paprika to give them a little color.*

12 hard-cooked eggs
2 to 3 tablespoons mayonnaise (enough to moisten yolks)
1 teaspoon prepared mustard, or to taste
1 scant teaspoon salt
3 to 4 tablespoons sweet pickle relish, or to taste, optional
Ground paprika, optional
Olive slices or chopped pickles, optional

1. Cut hard-cooked eggs in half lengthwise. Remove and mash the yolks; combine with mayonnaise, mustard, salt, and the sweet pickle relish.
2. Refill centers of the egg whites with the yolk stuffing mixture.
3. Garnish the stuffed eggs with a sprinkling of ground paprika, olive slices, or chopped pickle.

## Creamy Crab Dip
MAKES ABOUT 2 CUPS

*This flavorful dip is wonderful with assorted crackers or chips.*

6 ounces cream cheese (2 small packages), softened
1 cup sour cream
2 tablespoons green onion, chopped
Dash ground cayenne pepper
½ teaspoon ground paprika
1 envelope (about ½ ounce) ranch-style dressing mix
8 ounces crabmeat
Salt and pepper, to taste
1 tablespoon chopped green onion or parsley, for garnish

1. Beat cream cheese with sour cream until well blended. Blend in the 2 tablespoons chopped green onion, cayenne, paprika, and dressing mix. Stir in crabmeat.
2. Taste and **adjust seasonings** with salt and pepper, if desired.
3. Sprinkle chopped green onion or parsley over the dip. Chill until serving time.

**WHAT'S HOT**

▶ Do you ever find that canned crabmeat has an unpleasant metallic taste? Before using, soak the crabmeat in ice water for about 5 to 10 minutes. Remove from the water and blot gently with paper towels to dry before using in a recipe. Canned crabmeat is notorious for having small pieces of shell, and you should always pick it over gently before using, taking care not to break up the larger lumps.

## Dried Beef and Cheese Dip
SERVES 10

*My mother-in-law makes a dip similar to this one every Christmas Eve. It's festive and delicious!*

> 4 ½ ounces dried beef (2 small jars), minced
> 1 pound cream cheese, softened
> 8 ounces sour cream
> ¼ cup chopped red bell pepper
> ¼ cup chopped green bell pepper
> 3 tablespoons onion, grated or minced fine, or sliced green onions
> 1 cup pecans, chopped

1. Preheat oven to 300°F.
2. Combine minced beef with cream cheese and sour cream, blending well. Stir in chopped red and green bell pepper, and grated onion.
3. Spread mixture in a 1 ½-quart baking dish; sprinkle the chopped pecans evenly over top.
4. Bake for 25 to 30 minutes, until thoroughly heated.
5. Serve with assorted crackers or chips.

# Tangy Glazed Sausage Bites
MAKES 5 TO 6 DOZEN

*These tangy sausage bites are a great alternative to meatballs. They're perfect for a game party, New Year's Eve, or any other special occasion.*

2 pounds bulk pork sausage
2 eggs, slightly beaten
1 cup fine dry bread crumbs, plain
½ cup milk
1 teaspoon ground sage
½ teaspoon leaf thyme, crumbled
1 cup water
⅔ cup ketchup
¼ cup brown sugar, packed
2 tablespoons vinegar
2 tablespoons soy sauce

1. In a large bowl, combine the sausage, beaten eggs, bread crumbs, milk, sage, and thyme. With an electric mixer or food processor, beat until well blended.
2. With wet hands, shape mixture into balls about 1 to 1 ¼ inch in diameter.
3. In a large skillet, arrange a batch of sausage balls in a single layer; **brown** on all sides. This will take about 12 to 15 minutes for each batch. When all sausage bites are browned, pour off excess fat and return to the skillet, or transfer to a large saucepan or Dutch oven.
4. Combine remaining ingredients; pour over sausage. Cover and simmer for 15 minutes, stirring occasionally.
5. Serve hot from slow cooker or chafing dish, with toothpicks for spearing the sausage bites.

**TOOLS YOU NEED**

▶ I find that using a stand mixer or food processor for meat mixtures such as the one in this recipe is quicker and more efficient than mixing with a spoon and much less messy than using your bare hands. Try using your mixer for the next meatloaf, burger mixture, or meatball recipe you fix. Keep in mind that overmixing can make meatloaf tough and rather compact, so mix just until ingredients are well combined.

## Cheddar Sausage Balls

MAKES 36

*This is a popular appetizer in the South, and it is delicious served with dips. I like a mayonnaise-mustard dip with these, but a sweet-and-sour sauce would also be a great choice.*

I pound bulk breakfast sausage, mild or spicy
2 cups sharp Cheddar cheese, **shredded** fine
3 cups biscuit baking mix
½ cup green onion, minced fine

1. Preheat oven to 350°F.
2. Combine all ingredients in a large bowl; mix well with hands or a heavy-duty electric mixer.
3. Shape mixture into 1-inch balls; arrange on a large jelly-roll pan or baking pan.
4. Bake for 12 to 15 minutes, or until bottoms are browned.
5. Serve with your favorite dips.

# Barbecued Chicken Wings

MAKES 48 PIECES

*These chicken wings are sure to please your guests. If you like a spicier flavor, add a little ground cayenne to the sauce.*

24 chicken wings
2 tablespoons prepared mustard
⅓ cup cider vinegar
1 cup ketchup
¾ cup molasses
3 tablespoons vegetable oil
1 tablespoon Worcestershire sauce
½ teaspoon salt
¼ teaspoon ground black pepper
¼ teaspoon garlic powder

1. Preheat broiler to 500°F. Line a broiler pan with foil; brush with some oil to keep wings from sticking.
2. Cut each chicken wing through joints to make three pieces; discard the tip portion.
3. In a saucepan, combine remaining ingredients; blend well and bring to a boil. Remove from heat.
4. Arrange wing pieces on foil-lined pan. Reserve about ⅓ cup of the sauce in a small serving bowl; refrigerate until serving time. Use remaining sauce for basting.
5. **Broil** chicken wings about 6 inches from heat for 12 minutes, turning frequently. Brush wings with sauce; turn and brush the other side. Continue broiling and turning, basting occasionally, for about 10 minutes longer, removing smaller pieces earlier as needed to keep them from burning.

**WHAT'S HOT**

▶ Instead of discarding the tips of the wings, put them in a food storage bag, and then seal and freeze for up to six months. When you need to make homemade chicken broth, add the wing tips along with any other chicken pieces, vegetables, and seasonings, and then strain them out of the finished broth. Use the broth in soup or any other recipe calling for chicken broth.

▶ Always keep cornmeal in the pantry—cornbread is an essential side to greens, black-eyed peas, pinto beans, and chili. Although an iron skillet isn't absolutely necessary for this recipe, it makes the best, crustiest cornbread. If you don't have a skillet, use a nine-inch square baking pan and heat in the oven with oil before filling with batter.

## Southern Skillet Cornbread
MAKES 1 10-INCH SKILLET

*Most Southern cooks make cornbread so often they don't need a recipe. Here's my favorite recipe for buttermilk cornbread. This **batter** can also be used for corn sticks or muffins.*

> 1 tablespoon vegetable oil, for skillet
> 2 ½ cups cornmeal, white or yellow
> 1 cup all-purpose flour
> 2 teaspoons salt
> 2 teaspoons baking powder
> 1 scant teaspoon baking soda
> 2 large eggs
> 1 cup milk
> 1 cup buttermilk
> 2 tablespoons vegetable oil or melted butter

1. Preheat oven to 375°F. Place 1 tablespoon of the vegetable oil in skillet and place in the oven.
2. In a large bowl, combine the cornmeal, flour, salt, baking powder, and soda.
3. In another bowl, **whisk** together the eggs. Lightly whisk in milk, buttermilk, and oil or melted butter.
4. Pour milk and egg mixture into the dry ingredients. Mix just until dry ingredients are moistened.
5. Using pot holders, carefully take the hot skillet from the preheated oven; swirl gently to coat sides with the oil. Pour batter into the hot oil. Return to oven and bake for 35 minutes, or until lightly browned on top.
6. Remove and let cool slightly on a rack. Cut into wedges or squares.

## Savory Bacon Cheddar Muffins
MAKES 10 TO 12

*Delicious, savory muffins are wonderful with fruit for breakfast, or you can serve them with chili, baked beans, or a hearty vegetable soup.*

12 slices bacon (about 8 ounces)
1 ¼ cups all-purpose flour
¼ cup white or yellow cornmeal
2 ½ teaspoons baking powder
½ teaspoon baking soda
3 green onions, sliced fine
½ cup shredded sharp Cheddar cheese
1 large egg
1 cup milk
2 tablespoons melted butter

1. Preheat oven to 375°F.
2. Cook bacon until crisp; drain well and crumble.
3. Combine the drained bacon with flour, cornmeal, baking powder and soda, sliced green onions, and Cheddar cheese.
4. In another bowl, whisk milk with egg and melted butter. Blend milk and egg mixture into the dry ingredients, mixing just until all dry ingredients are moistened.
5. Fill muffin cups about ¾ full. Bake for 25 to 30 minutes, until a toothpick inserted in center of a muffin comes out clean.

**WHAT'S HOT**

▶ Nowadays, people seem to be much busier, and they need to do everything more quickly. Southern cooks like to take their time with their recipes, but they also appreciate a good shortcut. If you need to make this recipe in a hurry, substitute ¾ cup of purchased crumbled real bacon or use diced cooked smoked ham in place of the bacon.

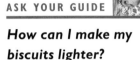
**How can I make my biscuits lighter?**

▶ Southern flours are typically lower in protein and gluten than most all-purpose flours. If you can find a brand milled in the South, give it a try. For light and flaky biscuits, also remember to cut the fats in with care, leaving some small pea-sized pieces. Handle the biscuits as little as possible to get the dough to clump together, then lightly pat—do not roll—into a circle before cutting.

# Perfect Buttermilk Biscuits
MAKES 10 TO 12

*These delicious biscuits won't disappoint you. Be sure not to overmix, and use your hands to gently* **knead** *and pat the dough into a circle.*

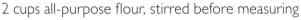

2 cups all-purpose flour, stirred before measuring
2 ½ teaspoons baking powder
¼ teaspoon baking soda
1 teaspoon salt
¼ cup **lard** or vegetable shortening, chilled
2 tablespoons butter, chilled
¾ cup buttermilk

1. Heat oven to 450°F. Adjust oven rack to center position.
2. In a large bowl, combine flour, baking powder, soda, and salt. **Cut in** chilled lard or shortening and butter until you have pieces the size of small peas. Make a well in the center of the dry ingredients, and pour in buttermilk. With a wooden spoon, gently blend dry ingredients into the buttermilk, just until mixture is clumping together. If necessary, add a few more teaspoons of buttermilk.
3. Transfer dough to a lightly floured board and knead gently just 4 or 5 times. Pat out in a circle about 8 inches in diameter and ½ inch thick. Using a 2 ½-inch biscuit cutter, cut out and place on ungreased baking sheet. Bake on center oven rack for about 10 to 12 minutes, until tops are browned.

## Angel Biscuits

MAKES 24

*Yeast, along with baking powder, makes these a light and airy favorite.*

1 package active dry yeast ($\frac{1}{4}$ ounce)
$\frac{1}{4}$ cup warm water (about 110°)
2 cups buttermilk, at room temperature
5 to 5 $\frac{1}{4}$ cups all-purpose flour
$\frac{1}{4}$ cup granulated sugar
2 teaspoons baking powder
1 teaspoon baking soda
1 tablespoon salt
$\frac{3}{4}$ cup shortening, chilled
4 tablespoons butter, chilled
Melted butter for brushing tops

1. Dissolve the yeast in the $\frac{1}{4}$ cup of warm water. Set aside.
2. In a mixing bowl, combine flour, sugar, baking powder, baking soda, and salt; stir to blend. Cut in shortening until mixture resembles coarse meal, with some small pea-size pieces remaining. Stir in yeast mixture and buttermilk, blending well.
3. Turn dough out onto a floured surface; knead a few times with floured hands, adding a little more flour if needed. Pat into a circle about $\frac{1}{2}$-inch thick. Cut out rounds with 2 $\frac{1}{2}$-inch biscuit cutter. Place biscuits on a lightly greased baking sheet. Put the scraps of dough together, pat out, cut, and repeat until all of the dough is used. Cover uncooked biscuits with a dish cloth and let rise in a draft-free place for about 30 to 45 minutes.
4. Bake at 400°F for about 15 to 20 minutes, until tops are browned. Remove from oven and brush with melted butter while biscuits are still hot.

**WHAT'S HOT**

▶ Flavored butters can make a great alternative to butter and preserves or jelly. Soften 4 ounces of butter to room temperature then stir until smooth and creamy. Stir in 1 heaping teaspoon of fine-grated orange zest and about 4 teaspoons of fresh orange juice. Put the butter on a sheet of waxed paper or foil, roll up in the shape of a cylinder, and then chill until firm.

**Why are they called hush puppies?**

▶ One interesting legend about hush puppies takes us back to Civil War days. According to this popular story, Southerners would sit beside a campfire at meal-time. If Yankee soldiers came near, they would toss their dogs some of the little corn-meal breads with the com-mand, "Hush, puppies."

# Hush Puppies
MAKES 24

*These **hush puppies** are delicious with fried catfish! If you don't have **Creole** seasoning, use ½ teaspoon seasoned salt and ½ teaspoon seasoned pepper. If you have **bacon drippings**, replace part of the butter with a teaspoon or two of that.*

> 2 cups cornmeal
> 1 cup all-purpose flour
> 1 ½ teaspoons baking powder
> ½ teaspoon baking soda
> ½ teaspoon salt
> 1 teaspoon Creole seasoning
> 2 eggs, beaten
> ½ cup buttermilk
> ½ cup milk
> 2 tablespoons melted butter
> ½ cup chopped green onion
> Oil for **deep frying**

1. Heat oil to 375°F in deep fryer or a deep, heavy skillet.
2. Combine cornmeal, flour, baking powder, soda, salt, and sea-soning blend.
3. In another bowl, lightly beat eggs with the buttermilk, milk, and melted butter. Stir milk and egg mixture into the dry ingredients, just until moistened. **Fold** in green onions.
4. Carefully drop by teaspoonfuls into hot oil; do not crowd. Hush puppies will puff up and come to the surface. **Fry** until golden brown and cooked through. Check the first few for timing and adjust size if the hush puppies are browning but still soft in the center.

## Ham and Corn Fritters

MAKES 12 TO 15

*These fluffy* **fritters** *are a great way to use leftover ham. You can also try them with a little diced* **country ham** *or crumbled bacon. I like to serve these fritters with beans or a hearty vegetable soup.*

ASK YOUR GUIDE

2 eggs, slightly beaten
¾ cup milk
1 cup cream-style corn
2 teaspoons baking powder
2 cups all-purpose flour
¼ cup cornmeal
1 teaspoon salt
½ cup chopped green onion
¾ cup ham, diced fine
Oil for deep frying

1. Heat oil to 375° in deep fryer or deep kettle.
2. Lightly whisk eggs; stir in milk and cream-style corn. Stir in the flour, cornmeal, baking powder, and salt, stirring just until moistened. Fold in the chopped green onion and diced ham.
3. Using 2 tablespoons, drop scant tablespoons of batter into the hot oil; fry until golden brown, about 4 minutes. Check the first few to make sure centers are cooked thoroughly and adjust timing or size if necessary.

### How many fritters can I fry at once?

▶ Fry the fritters in small batches to maintain the temperature of the oil. In a deep fryer, I fry five or six small fritters at a time, but use the temperature of the oil as your guide if you're using a deep skillet or heavy pot. The temperature shouldn't dip too low with any batch, and you should let the oil come back to temperature between batches.

## Get Linked

*Here are some great links to my* **About.com** *site for more crowd-pleasing appetizer recipes.*

**PARTY SNACKS**

Here's a page with dozens of party snacks and finger foods, including sugared, spiced, and peppered pecans and other nuts, party snack-mix recipes, cheese snacks, appetizer puffs, popcorn balls, potato chips, and more.

 http://about.com/southernfood/partysnacks

**HOLIDAY APPETIZERS**

This page is filled with some of my favorite appetizers for any special occasion. You'll find delicious meatballs and cocktail franks, several of my favorite dips, nachos, the very popular vegetable pizza, tortilla roll-ups, recipes for chicken wings, cheese bites, stuffed mushrooms and celery, and many more.

 http://about.com/southernfood/holidayapps

**DIP RECIPES**

Here's a page of delicious dip recipes, including a smoked oyster dip, mushroom dip, ham dips, guacamole, several cheese dips, popular artichoke dips, and many more.

 http://about.com/southernfood/dips

## Chapter 3

# Breakfast

**ASK YOUR GUIDE:**

How can I add a twist to the classic French toast recipe?
▶ **PAGE 34**

Are there any variations on the classic coffee cake?
▶ **PAGE 36**

What are quick breads?
▶ **PAGE 37**

Can this breakfast bake be made in advance like others?
▶ **PAGE 41**

Is there any secret to making buttered bread crumbs?
▶ **PAGE 42**

Can I vary this recipe for a little more kick?
▶ **PAGE 44**

## Light and Fluffy Pancakes
SERVES 4 TO 6

*These have long been my favorite pancakes, made light and fluffy with beaten egg whites. I sometimes add chopped pecans to this batter for an extra crunch.*

2 cups all-purpose flour
2 tablespoons granulated sugar
½ teaspoon salt
1 teaspoon baking powder
½ teaspoon baking soda
1 cup buttermilk
¾ cup milk
2 large eggs, separated
¼ cup melted butter
Vegetable oil

1. In a mixing bowl, combine the flour, sugar, salt, baking powder, and baking soda. In another bowl, whisk together buttermilk, milk, egg yolks, and melted butter. Blend the wet ingredients into the dry until all ingredients are just moistened.
2. Beat egg whites in another bowl until stiff peaks form. Fold into the batter until well incorporated.
3. Heat a small amount of oil in a large skillet over medium heat. When the oil is hot enough for a drop of water to sizzle and pop, scoop pancake batter onto the skillet in about ¼-cup portions, spreading slightly. When edges begin to look a little dry and bubbles are popping (after about 2 to 3 minutes), turn over and cook the other side until browned (about 2 minutes longer).
4. Serve hot with butter and your favorite syrup.

# Apple Cinnamon Waffles

SERVES 6

*The aroma of these wonderful cinnamon-scented waffles will summon everyone to the breakfast table. I use Golden Delicious apples in this recipe, but you could use Fuji, Granny Smith, or whatever you have on hand.*

2 cups all-purpose flour
3 teaspoons baking powder
¼ teaspoon ground cinnamon
1 tablespoon sugar
½ teaspoon salt
3 eggs, separated
1 ½ cups whole milk
4 tablespoons melted butter
1 ½ cups chopped apple

1. Sift flour before measuring. Sift again into a mixing bowl with baking powder, cinnamon, sugar, and salt; set aside.
2. In a medium bowl, beat egg yolks; stir in milk and melted butter. Pour into dry ingredients and whisk until smooth and well blended. Stir in chopped apple.
3. Beat egg whites until stiff peaks form. Gently fold whites into the apple batter until blended.
4. Spoon batter into each section of a hot waffle iron. Cook until crispy and browned.

**WHAT'S HOT**

▶ Did you know you can make waffles in big batches and freeze for those busy mornings? Just cool the cooked waffles and seal in plastic freezer bags; freeze for up to six months. To reheat, bake on a baking sheet for about 5 minutes in a 325°F oven or heat in the toaster.

**How can I add a twist to the classic French toast recipe?**

▶ There's a variety of French toast recipes on my About .com site, from delicious basic French toast and French toast sticks to overnight French toast and fruit and berry versions. Visit http://about.com/southern food/frenchtoast. You'll even find a few favorite recipes from our forum members.

## Pain Perdu (French Toast)
SERVES 4

*French bread, a little sugar, and vanilla make this baked* **pain perdu**, *a Louisiana version of French toast, extra special.*

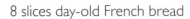

8 slices day-old French bread
2 eggs, slightly beaten
2 tablespoons sugar
⅓ cup milk
A few drops vanilla extract
Dash cinnamon, optional
8 tablespoons melted butter
Syrup or honey

1. Preheat oven to 400°F. Lightly butter a large jelly roll pan or baking sheet with sides.
2. Remove crusts from bread; set bread aside.
3. In a bowl, beat eggs with sugar, milk, vanilla, and cinnamon, if using. Pour mixture into a shallow baking dish or pie plate. Put a few bread slices in the dish and let soak for several seconds, turning once. Place soaked bread slices on the prepared baking sheet; repeat with remaining bread. Spoon any remaining egg mixture over the bread.
4. Bake for 15 to 20 minutes, turning after the first 10 minutes to brown on both sides. Serve immediately with melted butter and your favorite syrup or honey, or lighten them up with a light **drizzle** of butter and a sprinkling of powdered sugar.

# Disappearing Peach Muffins
MAKES 12

*If you prefer another kind of fruit, diced fresh pears or nectarines instead of peaches would both work well in this recipe.*

1 ½ cups ripe peaches, diced
2 teaspoons lemon juice
1 ½ cups all-purpose flour
½ cup brown sugar, firmly packed
2 teaspoons baking powder
¼ teaspoon salt
1 teaspoon ground cinnamon
½ cup melted butter
¼ cup milk
1 large egg
½ cup pecans or walnuts, chopped fine, optional
1 tablespoon sugar mixed with ½ teaspoon cinnamon

1. Heat oven to 400°F. Toss the diced peaches with lemon juice. Set aside. Line 12 standard muffin cups with paper or foil liners, or **grease** and flour the muffin cups.
2. Combine flour, brown sugar, baking powder, salt, and 1 teaspoon cinnamon in a large mixer bowl. In another bowl, whisk together butter, milk, and egg. Stir milk mixture into the dry ingredients and blend until all ingredients are just moistened. Fold in diced peaches, along with the chopped nuts, if using.
3. Spoon into muffin cups, filling each about ⅔ to ¾ full; sprinkle each muffin with a little of the cinnamon sugar.
4. Bake for 25 to 30 minutes, or until a cake tester inserted in center of a muffin comes out clean. Cool for 3 minutes in pan on rack, then remove muffins to a rack to cool completely.

WHAT'S HOT

▶ If you'd like to have cinnamon sugar on hand for sprinkling on muffins, French toast, cakes, and other goodies, combine ½ cup sugar with 1 tablespoon of cinnamon and store in a small canning jar or cleaned spice shaker. You'll be amazed at how often you reach for that jar.

## Buttermilk Streusel Coffee Cake
SERVES 12

*I've seen this and similar recipes posted on our About.com forum by many different people. It's a delicious and popular coffee cake.*

1 cup granulated sugar
½ cup butter, softened
2 eggs
1 cup whole buttermilk or sour cream
2 teaspoons vanilla extract
2 cups all-purpose flour
1 teaspoon baking powder
1 teaspoon baking soda
½ teaspoon salt
1 ½ teaspoons ground cinnamon
3 tablespoons granulated sugar
½ cup pecans, chopped

1. Heat oven to 350°F. Combine sugar and butter in mixing bowl; cream with electric mixer until light. Add eggs, one at a time, beating after each addition. Beat in buttermilk and vanilla. Sift together the flour, baking soda, baking powder, and salt; stir into creamed mixture.
2. In a small bowl, combine the cinnamon, sugar, and chopped nuts; set aside.
3. Grease and flour a 10-inch tube pan. Pour half of the batter into the tube cake pan. Sprinkle with half of the cinnamon-sugar-pecan mixture. Spoon the remaining batter over the pecan mixture, and then sprinkle with the remaining pecan mixture.
4. Bake for 35 to 40 minutes. Cool in pan on rack; carefully loosen and remove sides and bottom.

**ASK YOUR GUIDE**

***Are there any variations on the classic coffee cake?***

▶ Of course! I have always loved coffee cakes and used to make them regularly for neighborhood get-togethers. Here are two of my favorite coffee cake recipes: Easy Orange Crumb Cake (at http://about.com/southernfood/orange crumbcake) and Apple Streusel Coffee Cake (at http://about.com/southern food/applestreusel).

## Fabulous Peach Bread

MAKES 1 LOAF

*Peach schnapps gives this bread an incredible burst of flavor, but flavorful peach nectar can be used as a nonalcoholic substitute. Serve this bread with plain or flavored butter for brunch, breakfast, or dessert.*

3 cups fresh peaches, diced
¼ cup peach schnapps or peach nectar
1 teaspoon vanilla extract
4 ounces butter, softened
1 cup granulated sugar
3 large eggs
2 ¾ cups all-purpose flour
1 ½ teaspoons baking powder
½ teaspoon baking soda
1 teaspoon salt
1 ½ teaspoons ground cinnamon

1. Heat oven to 350°F. Grease and flour a 9" × 5" × 3" loaf pan.
2. In a saucepan, combine the diced peaches with peach schnapps or peach nectar; simmer for 5 minutes, or until peaches are tender. Remove from heat and stir in vanilla; set aside.
3. In a mixing bowl with an electric mixer, cream butter and sugar. Add eggs, one at a time, beating after each addition.
4. In another bowl, combine the flour, baking powder, baking soda, salt, and cinnamon. With a wooden spoon, stir dry ingredients into the creamed mixture, alternating with the peach mixture.
5. Spread batter in prepared pan. Bake for 55 to 65 minutes, or until a wooden pick inserted near center comes out clean. Cool in pan on rack for 10 minutes. Remove from pan and cool completely.

ASK YOUR GUIDE

***What are quick breads?***

▶ Quick breads are usually leavened with baking powder and/or baking soda, along with heat and eggs. In addition to typical quick breads that are baked in loaf pans, pancakes, muffins, and fried dough or fritters might also fall in this category.

# Beignets

MAKES ABOUT 4 DOZEN

*These are very close in texture and flavor to some wonderful **beignets** we sampled in the New Orleans French Market District. Sprinkle hot beignets heavily with powdered sugar and serve with coffee.*

**ELSEWHERE ON THE WEB**

▶ Debra Weber, the About.com Guide to French Cuisine, has a delicious recipe for a smaller batch of Creole-style New Orleans beignets. Check out http://about.com/frenchfood/beignets.

1 envelope active dry yeast
1 ½ cups warm water, 105°F to 110°F
½ cup granulated sugar
1 teaspoon salt
2 eggs, beaten
1 cup evaporated milk
7 cups all-purpose flour, plus more for rolling
¼ cup shortening, room temperature
Oil for deep frying
Powdered sugar

1. In a large bowl, sprinkle yeast over warm water. Stir and let stand for 5 minutes. Add the sugar, salt, eggs, and evaporated milk. Whisk to blend well. Add 4 cups of flour and beat until smooth. Beat in shortening, then gradually blend in remaining flour until a soft dough has formed. Cover and refrigerate for at least 4 hours.
2. Heat oil in deep fryer to 360°F.
3. Roll out dough on a well-floured surface to about ⅛-inch thickness. Cut into 2 ½-inch squares.
4. Fry in hot fat, a few at a time, until golden brown on both sides, turning a few times. Drain on paper towels, then sprinkle generously with powdered sugar.

# Banana Fritters

MAKES 12

*Are your bananas getting a little overripe? Try making tasty banana fritters instead of banana bread. Sprinkle these fritters with a little cinnamon sugar and serve with vanilla sauce or maple syrup.*

1 ⅔ cups all-purpose flour
2 teaspoons baking powder
2 tablespoons powdered sugar
¼ teaspoon salt
⅔ cup milk
1 large egg
3 bananas, mashed
1 teaspoon lemon juice
Oil for deep frying
Powdered sugar or syrup

1. Sift flour, baking powder, 2 tablespoons powdered sugar, and salt into a mixer bowl; set aside.
2. In a separate bowl, combine milk and eggs. Whisk to blend well. Add milk mixture to the dry ingredients. Fold in mashed bananas. Batter should mound up in a spoon. If too thick, add a small amount of milk, or add flour if too thin.
3. Heat oil in deep fryer or deep heavy skillet to 375°F.
4. Drop batter by tablespoons into the hot oil, cooking about 4 to 6 at a time. As fritters brown on the bottom, turn to brown on the other side. With a slotted spoon, move the fritters to paper towels to drain. Keep warm.
5. Just before serving, sprinkle with cinnamon sugar or powdered sugar and serve with syrup, if desired.

**TOOLS YOU NEED**

▶ An electric deep fryer is a nice appliance to have, and many have temperature controls, filters, and baskets. If you don't have an electric deep fryer, a heavy kettle will work fine, but you should use a deep-fat thermometer for best results. Use one spoon to hold the batter and another to push the batter carefully into the hot fat, and have a slotted metal spoon ready to transfer the fritters to paper towels.

## Mississippi Breakfast Bake
SERVES 4

*This all-in-one breakfast* casserole *is such a snap to make, and you can prepare it the night before. Just refrigerate overnight and pop it in the oven when you get up in the morning. It's a great breakfast for a holiday or busy weekend.*

4 slices bread, crusts removed
1 pound breakfast sausage
3 green onions, sliced, including green parts
1 small tomato, seeded and diced
1 cup shredded Cheddar cheese
Salt and pepper
6 large eggs
1 cup milk
¼ teaspoon salt
¼ teaspoon Creole seasoning or seasoned salt
⅛ teaspoon ground black pepper
Dash paprika

1. Brown sausage in a skillet, breaking up chunks and stirring frequently. Drain well. Tear bread into pieces; spread over the bottom of a buttered 2-quart baking dish. Evenly layer the browned sausage over the bread, then layer with the green onion, diced tomato, and cheese. Sprinkle with salt and pepper.
2. In a medium bowl, combine eggs, milk, and remaining seasonings. Whisk until well blended. Pour evenly over the cheese layer. Bake immediately, or cover and refrigerate overnight.
3. If refrigerated overnight, take the casserole out of the refrigerator about 30 minutes before baking. Bake in a preheated 350°F oven for 40 to 45 minutes, or until set in center.

**ELSEWHERE ON THE WEB**

▶ One thing I love about breakfast bakes is their adaptability. Breakfast casseroles can easily be altered to suit your own tastes with different combinations of chopped vegetables or meats, a different variety of cheese, or your own choice of herbs and seasonings. This easy Fiesta Egg Bake is a meat-free and spicy version of the typical breakfast casserole: http://about.com/southernfood/fiestaeggbake.

## Bacon-and-Egg Casserole
SERVES 4 TO 6

*This easy and convenient breakfast bake is similar to a delicious break-fast casserole my Kentucky sister-in-law makes when the family gets together. She usually leaves the meat out and serves it with a warm fruit compote and easy sweet rolls or cinnamon buns.*

10 slices bacon, diced
5 slices bread, lightly buttered
1 cup shredded Cheddar or Monterey Jack cheese
6 eggs, lightly beaten
2 cups milk
1 teaspoon salt
1 teaspoon dry mustard
½ teaspoon ground paprika

1. Cook bacon in a large skillet; transfer to paper towels to drain.
2. Heat oven to 350°F. Lightly butter a 2-quart baking dish.
3. Tear buttered bread into small pieces. Layer torn bread, diced bacon, and cheese in the prepared baking dish. In a bowl, whisk together the eggs, milk, salt, mustard, and paprika; pour over bread mixture.
4. Bake for 40 to 45 minutes, or until casserole is puffy and a knife inserted near center comes out clean.

ASK YOUR GUIDE

**Can this breakfast bake be made in advance like others?**

▶ Absolutely! This casserole can be made in advance, which is such a convenience for busy households. Prepare it the night before, then refrigerate overnight. In the morning, take the casserole out of the refrigerator about 1 hour and 15 minutes before serving time. Let the casserole sit at room temperature for 30 minutes at room temperature. Preheat the oven to 350°F, and then bake the casserole as directed.

**Is there any secret to making buttered bread crumbs?**

▶ To make buttered bread crumbs for a casserole topping, tear or crumble day-old bread into small pieces, or whirl in the food processor, then drizzle the crumbs (about ½ to 1 cup) with a few tablespoons of melted butter. Like most toppings, you can personalize. A bread crumb topping on many casseroles would be delicious with a few tablespoons of Parmesan or other grated cheese, or you might toss the bread crumbs with a little sliced green onion, parsley, or other seasonings.

# Hard-Cooked Egg Casserole
SERVES 4

*Hard-cooked eggs are baked with a flavorful sherry cheese sauce.*

8 eggs
4 tablespoons butter
4 tablespoons flour
¾ cup chicken broth
1 ¼ cups milk
½ cup shredded sharp Cheddar cheese
¼ cup freshly grated Parmesan cheese
2 tablespoons sherry
¼ teaspoon Worcestershire sauce
Dash Tabasco sauce
Salt and pepper
Soft buttered bread crumbs, about ½ cup
Chopped fresh parsley or green onions for garnish

1. In a saucepan, cover eggs with water. Cover and bring to a rolling boil. Remove from heat and let stand for 20 minutes.
2. In a medium saucepan over low heat, melt butter. Stir flour into the butter, cooking and stirring until well blended and bubbly, about 1 minute. Gradually add chicken broth and milk, stirring constantly. Continue to cook, stirring constantly, until thickened. Stir in Cheddar and Parmesan cheeses, sherry, Worcestershire sauce, and Tabasco. Continue to stir until cheese is melted. Add salt and pepper to taste. Set sauce aside.
3. Heat oven to 300°F. Drain eggs and peel; place in a baking dish. Pour sauce over the eggs and sprinkle with the buttered bread crumbs. Bake for 15 to 20 minutes, or until heated through. Sprinkle with chopped parsley or green onion.

# Fluffy Garden Omelet

SERVES 1

*This is a delicious two-egg omelet, filled with a perfect combination of cheese, vegetables, and seasonings. You could easily add a little cooked sausage or sautéed mushrooms to the filling.*

2 eggs
2 tablespoons milk
¼ teaspoon salt
Few drops Worcestershire sauce
Dash Creole seasoning, optional
Dash freshly ground black pepper
2 teaspoons butter
2 to 3 tablespoons Cheddar cheese, shredded fine
1 tablespoon green onion, chopped
1 tablespoon tomato, seeded and diced

1. Beat eggs until frothy; whisk in the milk, salt, Worcestershire sauce, seasoning blend, and black pepper.
2. Heat a nonstick 8-inch skillet over medium heat; add butter and move around pan to melt. When butter is hot, pour eggs into the pan and reduce heat to medium-low. Cook the omelet slowly, gently lifting edges with a spatula several times to let uncooked egg run underneath. When the omelet is almost cooked but still shiny on top, cover and cook for 1 or 2 minutes longer or until the surface is almost dry.
3. Sprinkle the cheese, green onion, and tomato over the top of the omelet. Fold over and continue cooking to let cheese melt. Remove from heat and serve immediately.

WHAT'S HOT

▶ If you aren't sure how fresh your eggs are, try this trick. Fill a deep bowl with cold water, enough to cover an egg, then place the egg in the water. If the egg lies on its side on the bottom, it's very fresh. If the egg stands up and bobs a bit on the bottom, it isn't quite as fresh. If it floats to the surface, you shouldn't use it. Fresh eggs are best in many recipes, but eggs that are about a week old are easier to peel when hard-cooked in the shell.

## Eggs Benedict with Tomato Slices
SERVES 6

*Garnish each plate of hot Eggs Benedict with a tomato slice.*

2 egg yolks
1 teaspoon fresh lemon juice
½ cup butter
¼ cup boiling water
Dash salt
Dash ground red pepper

3 medium tomatoes
6 slices Canadian bacon
½ teaspoon salt
3 large eggs
6 English muffins, split, toasted
Butter

1. In the top of a double boiler, whisk egg yolks with lemon juice. Add about 3 tablespoons of the butter. Place the pan over simmering water and cook, whisking constantly, until butter has melted and sauce has begun to thicken. Add 3 more tablespoons of butter. Stir until butter has melted; then add remaining 2 tablespoons of butter. Gradually whisk in the boiling water. Continue cooking over simmering water, stirring constantly, until mixture thickens. Remove from heat and stir in a dash of salt and ground red pepper. Set aside.

2. Slice off tomato ends and cut in half. Place tomato halves and Canadian bacon on rack of a broiler pan. Broil about 4 inches from heat for 3 minutes, or until the meat begins to brown.

3. Meanwhile, pour about 2 inches of water into a large skillet, along with ½ teaspoon of salt. Bring water to the boiling point; reduce heat to maintain a light simmer. Carefully break an egg into a cup, then slip into water. Repeat with remaining eggs. Continue to simmer, basting with the water, for 3 to 5 minutes, or until whites are thoroughly cooked and yolks are hot.

4. Toast and butter English muffins. Top each muffin half with a slice of Canadian bacon, a poached egg, and Hollandaise sauce.

## Confetti Scrambled Eggs

SERVES 4

*This recipe is a flavorful version of everyday scrambled eggs. Allowing two eggs per person, you can easily adjust this recipe up or down.*

8 large eggs
4 tablespoons milk or **half-and-half**
½ teaspoon salt
⅛ teaspoon freshly ground black pepper
2 tablespoons butter
1 large tomato, seeded and diced
1 heaping tablespoon green onion tops, sliced thin
4 tablespoons ham, chopped fine, optional

1. In a medium bowl, whisk eggs, milk, salt, and pepper together until well blended.
2. Melt butter in a heavy skillet over medium-low heat. When the butter is sizzling hot, pour in the egg mixture. Reduce heat slightly. As the egg mixture begins to look set on bottom and sides of skillet, fold over toward the center with a spatula. Repeat until eggs are almost set, then fold in the tomato, green onion tops, and ham if using. Heat through and serve hot.

**TOOLS YOU NEED**

▶ I always use a heavy non-stick skillet for scrambled eggs, and a good flexible spatula is a must. You'll also find it's helpful to heat the skillet before adding the butter. For light and fluffy scrambled eggs, use a whisk and beat the egg mixture vigorously. This will add more air to the mixture.

## Get Linked

*At my Southern Food site on **About.com**, you can find many more breakfast recipes. Here are a few of the best links to resources that might help you.*

**EGG RECIPES**

A big variety of egg recipes, including omelets, breakfast casseroles, quiche recipes, French toast recipes, breakfast skillets, several for scrambled eggs, hard-cooked eggs, and more.

 http://about.com/southernfood/eggrecipes

**MUFFINS**

Here's a page full of muffin recipes, including sweet potato muffins, strawberry muffins, cranberry-orange muffins, delicious blueberry muffins, apple-cinnamon muffins, banana muffins, and dozens more.

 http://about.com/southernfood/muffinrecipes

**PANCAKES AND WAFFLES**

Pancakes are easy to make, and kids love them. Here are several recipes for pancakes and waffles, from basic pancakes and sour cream waffles to chocolate waffles and sweet potato pancakes.

 http://about.com/southernfood/pancakeswaffles

## Chapter 4

# Soups and Salads

## About

**ASK YOUR GUIDE:**

Why is a roux so important to gumbo?
▶ PAGE 51

Is there any type of canned salmon I should use for soups?
▶ PAGE 54

Can I use canned beans in this recipe?
▶ PAGE 56

Can this salad be made with broccoli florets?
▶ PAGE 65

Could I use fresh strawberries in this recipe?
▶ PAGE 68

I'm trying to lower the fat in my family's diet. How could I lighten this recipe?
▶ PAGE 69

## Chicken Tortilla Soup

SERVES 4

*It's really easy to fry strips of fresh corn tortillas for this recipe, but you can use purchased tortilla chips in a pinch. This is a very flavorful soup the whole family will enjoy.*

4 cups chicken broth
Juice of 1 lime
1 can (14.5 ounces) diced tomatoes, with juice
1 teaspoon jalapeño pepper, chopped fine, optional
1 can (4 ounces) chopped mild green chile pepper
2 tablespoons fresh cilantro, chopped
2 green onions, white and green, chopped
1 medium carrot, diced or sliced thin
¾ cup fresh or frozen corn kernels (thawed if frozen)
1 ½ cups cooked chicken, diced
¼ teaspoon freshly ground black pepper
Salt, to taste
Vegetable oil
3 corn tortillas, cut into ½-inch wide strips
½ cup shredded Monterey Jack cheese or a Mexican blend

*Chicken Tortilla Soup (continued)*

1. In a large saucepan or Dutch oven, combine chicken broth, tomatoes, lime juice, jalapeño pepper, mild chile peppers, cilantro, green onion, carrots, and corn. Cook over medium heat for 40 minutes. Add the diced chicken and cook for 5 minutes longer. Taste and add salt and pepper to taste.
2. In a deep skillet or saucepan, heat about 1 inch of vegetable oil to 360°F. Add tortilla strips to the hot oil in small batches, frying for just a few seconds, until crispy.
3. To serve, top each bowl of soup with a several crisp tortilla strips and a sprinkling of shredded cheese. Serve remaining tortilla strips on the side.

**ELSEWHERE ON THE WEB**

▶ This taco soup for a crowd is a quick and easy recipe from Jean Brandau's Huntsville, Alabama, site. It's made with ground beef, beans, Mexican-style corn, taco seasonings, tomatoes, and other ingredients. Visit http://about.com/huntsville/tacosoup for the recipe.

## Chicken and Sausage Gumbo
SERVES 6

*This is a relatively easy version of **gumbo**, but it is one of our favorites and it certainly won't disappoint. If you're new to making **roux**, just remember to stir constantly and take great care not to burn it. If you get nervous as it gets darker, stop at a lighter color and go from there.*

4 skinless boneless chicken breasts
4 skinless boneless chicken thighs
Salt and pepper
1 ½ teaspoon Creole seasoning
12 ounces smoked sausage, cut into ½-inch pieces
½ cup vegetable oil
½ cup all-purpose flour
½ cup green bell pepper, chopped
½ cup red bell pepper, chopped
1 cup onion, chopped
3 ribs celery, chopped
3 medium cloves garlic, minced
6 cups chicken broth
1 can (14.5 ounces) diced tomatoes with purée
½ teaspoon dried leaf thyme, crumbled
Salt and freshly ground black pepper, to taste
1 cup sliced fresh or frozen **okra** (thawed if frozen)
4 green onions, sliced thin
2 tablespoons fresh parsley, chopped
Hot cooked rice

1. Trim chicken of fat and cut into small pieces; sprinkle with salt and pepper then toss with ½ teaspoon of the Creole seasoning.

*Chicken and Sausage Gumbo (continued)*

2. Heat 1 tablespoon of oil in a heavy skillet over medium heat; add chicken. Continue to cook, stirring, until browned. Transfer to a dish and set aside. Brown sliced sausage; add to chicken.

3. Put chopped onion, bell pepper, and chopped celery in a bowl; set aside.

4. In a large, heavy saucepan or Dutch oven, heat the remaining oil; add the flour. Cook, stirring constantly, until the roux reaches a deep blonde color, about the color of dark peanut butter. You can do this over medium to medium-high heat, but stir constantly and watch carefully. It cannot burn, or you will have to start from scratch. The heat control of a gas range makes this a little easier to keep the heat high and adjust as you near the color you're looking for. If you're not a novice to roux-making, you might want to make a darker roux. If you are a novice, you can keep it a bit lighter.

5. When roux has reached the color you want, add the chopped onions, bell pepper, and celery and stir briskly. Continue to cook, stirring constantly, for about 3 to 4 minutes. Add the garlic, chicken broth, tomatoes, seasonings, chicken, and sausage. Bring to a boil, then cook for about 1 hour, skimming fat off the top as needed.

6. Add okra and cook for about 20 minutes longer. Add chopped green onions and parsley and cook for 10 minutes longer.

7. To serve, mound about ½ cup of hot cooked rice in a bowl then spoon the gumbo around it. Serve with a warm crusty French bread with plenty of butter.

**ASK YOUR GUIDE**

*Why is a roux so important to gumbo?*

▶ In general, a roux is usually made to thicken a sauce or soup. As a roux becomes darker in color, its thickening properties diminish, but the roux becomes more flavorful. A roux for cream soup will generally be made quite light, since its purpose is to thicken the soup. A gumbo roux, meant to add complex flavor, is almost always cooked to a deep blonde or dark reddish brown. Many gumbos get their thickening from the addition of okra, or filé powder might be added just before serving, after the gumbo is removed from the heat.

## Old-Fashioned Vegetable Beef Soup

SERVES 6

*I think we all crave a version of this wonderful soup, no matter where we're from. Beef shanks make this soup more flavorful, if you can find them. If you can't, use about a pound of good stew beef.*

2 pounds meaty beef shanks
6 cups water
1 can (10 ½ ounces) condensed beef broth
1 teaspoon salt
1 cup onion, chopped
3 ribs celery, chopped
¼ teaspoon freshly ground black pepper
1 small bay leaf
1 large can (28 ounces) diced tomatoes with juice
2 cups shredded cabbage
2 medium carrots, sliced thin
2 medium potatoes, diced
1 teaspoon sugar
2 teaspoons Worcestershire sauce

1. In a large stockpot, combine beef shanks, water, broth, salt, onions, celery, pepper, and the bay leaf. Cover and simmer for 2 to 2 ½ hours.
2. Remove shanks and chop meat. Return meat to the pot. Add remaining ingredients and simmer for about 45 minutes longer, or until vegetables are tender. Taste and adjust seasonings. Remove bay leaf.
3. Serve with crusty bread and butter along with a tossed salad.

# Grilled Burger Soup

SERVES 4 TO 6

*This soup makes a wonderful lunch, and it's hearty enough to serve as a main dish with crusty bread and a salad.*

12 to 16 ounces lean ground beef
Vegetable oil
4 cups beef broth
1 can (14.5 ounces) diced tomatoes
2 medium carrots, diced
1 medium onion, chopped
3 ribs celery, sliced thin
1 large potato, peeled and cubed
⅛ teaspoon freshly ground black pepper
1 tablespoon fresh parsley, chopped
½ cup corn kernels
¼ cup frozen peas, optional
Salt and pepper, to taste

1. Form ground beef into burger patties. **Grill** the burgers in a stovetop grill pan, on charcoal or gas grill, in a skillet or under broiler, using a little oil in the pan or broiler rack.
2. In a large stockpot, combine beef broth with tomatoes, carrots, onion, celery, potato, and pepper. Bring to a boil. Reduce heat to low, cover, and simmer for 30 to 45 minutes, or until vegetables are tender.
3. Cut cooked burgers into small pieces; add to the soup. Add parsley, corn, and peas, if using. Cover and continue cooking for about 15 minutes longer.
4. Serve in cups or bowls with crusty bread and a fresh tossed salad.

**TOOLS YOU NEED**

▶ I love my stovetop grill pan, and I use it almost weekly to cook fish, pork chops, burgers, lamb chops, and lots of other foods. A big plus is that you can sear some nice grill marks on the meat or chicken, and then pop the whole thing in the oven to finish cooking. Of course, if you can run out to the backyard and use the grill any time you want, that's a very good thing!

**Is there any type of canned salmon I should use for soups?**

▶ Pink salmon is fine for soups, but you could use a red salmon or you might even want to poach or grill fresh salmon fillets or steaks, flake it, and use that. Most canned salmon will include some very soft bones and even a little skin, but it's usually not necessary to remove that. If you do want to remove small bones, handle the salmon gently so you'll still have some nice big chunks for your soup.

## Hearty Salmon and Cheddar Chowder
SERVES 8

*My family loves this flavorful chowder as a first course or for lunch with a sandwich.*

2 tablespoons butter
½ cup celery, sliced thin
2 tablespoons all-purpose flour
⅛ teaspoon freshly ground pepper
3 cups milk
2 cups potatoes, cooked, diced
1 cup frozen peas and carrots, cooked, drained
14 to 16 ounces canned salmon
2 cups shredded Cheddar cheese or American cheese

1. In a large saucepan over medium-low heat, melt butter. Add celery; sauté until tender. Stir in flour and pepper; continue cooking, stirring constantly, until smooth and bubbly.
2. Gradually stir in milk. Continue to cook, stirring constantly, until bubbly and thickened.
3. Stir in the cooked diced potatoes, peas and carrots, and flaked salmon. Heat through. Add cheese, gently stirring just until melted.

## Old-Fashioned Corn Chowder
SERVES 6 TO 8

*This is truly a comfort food for me, and this version is one of my favorites. Serve this as a main dish with crusty bread or crackers, or make it for lunch.*

8 slices bacon, diced
1 medium onion, chopped
2 tablespoons all-purpose flour
2 cups potatoes, diced
2 cups chicken broth
3 small cans (8 ounces each) cream-style corn
1 teaspoon salt
3 green onions, sliced thin
1 tablespoon fresh parsley, chopped
2 cups half-and-half
Salt and freshly ground black pepper, to taste

1. Cook diced bacon in a Dutch oven or large heavy saucepan. Add onion and cook for 1 minute. Stir in flour until well blended. Add diced potato. Gradually stir in chicken broth and bring to a boil, stirring constantly. Reduce heat to low and simmer for about 10 to 12 minutes, until potatoes are tender.
2. Add corn, salt, green onion, and parsley. Simmer for about 1 minute. Add half-and-half; heat through. Taste and add salt and pepper, as desired.
3. Serve with crackers or crusty bread.

**ELSEWHERE ON THE WEB**

▶ Corn chowder can be the old-fashioned variety, like this recipe, or it might be made with seafood, poultry, meat, or even Ramen noodles! Here are two out-of-the-ordinary corn chowders: Ramen Corn Chowder from Linda Larsen, with Ramen noodles, cream-style corn, cheese, and more, at http://about.com/busy cooks/ramencornchowder; and Slow Cooked Potato Corn Chicken Chowder with chicken, cheese, potatoes, and corn, from Dianne Hadaway at http://about.com/singleparents/potcornchick chowder.

**Can I use canned beans in this recipe?**

▶ Absolutely! I often used canned bean in recipes, especially if I'm short on time. Use two 15-ounce cans of beans, drained then rinsed. Skip the first step and cook for about 30 to 45 minutes, or until vegetables are tender. Finish the soup as directed in the final two steps. Did you know you can freeze cooked beans for up to three months? Cook dried beans for about 20 to 30 minutes less than the suggested cooking time, so they're not quite done. Freeze in 1- to 2-cup portions and cover with water or broth, leaving a headspace of about 1 inch. Just thaw and use in a cooked recipe or finish cooking to use in other dishes.

# Ham and Bean Soup
SERVES 8

*This old-fashioned ham and white bean soup is a dish I really enjoy. I usually use navy beans in this soup, but it's delicious with Great Northern beans as well.*

1 pound dried Great Northern beans or navy beans
8 cups water
1 ham hock or meaty ham bone
1 large onion, chopped
¼ teaspoon pepper
1 small bay leaf
2 medium carrots, diced
½ cup celery, chopped
2 cups ham, diced
½ teaspoon salt
1 can (8 ounces) tomato sauce

1. Rinse beans and discard any that are discolored as well as any stones you find. Cover with the water in a large pot. Bring to a boil; boil for 2 minutes. Remove from heat, cover, and let stand for 1 hour.
2. Add ham bone or ham hock, onion, pepper, bay leaf, diced carrot, and celery. Bring to a boil. Reduce heat to low, cover, and simmer for about 1 to 1 ½ hours. Add water as necessary.
3. Remove ham bone or ham hock. Trim meat from bone and chop; return meat to the beans. Add the diced ham, salt, and tomato sauce. Simmer for about 30 minutes.
4. Remove bay leaf before serving. Serve hot, with fresh cornbread or warm crusty bread.

# Alabama Peanut Soup

SERVES 4

*This is a creamy peanut soup, and the taste is just heavenly. Garnish with a bit of sliced green onion along with ground peanuts for a memorable presentation.*

2 ribs celery, chopped
¼ cup onion, chopped
4 tablespoons butter
3 tablespoons all-purpose flour
4 cups chicken broth, warm
1 ¼ cups peanut butter
½ cup heavy cream
2 teaspoons lemon juice
½ teaspoon salt
¼ teaspoon celery salt
Sliced green onion, for garnish
Ground peanuts, for garnish

1. In a large saucepan over medium heat, sauté the celery and onion in the butter for 5 minutes, or until tender. Add the flour, stirring until blended and bubbly. Stir in the warm chicken broth. Simmer over low heat for 30 minutes, stirring occasionally.
2. Stir in the peanut butter, heavy cream, lemon juice, salt, and celery salt. Cook soup, stirring constantly, until hot.
3. If you would like a smooth soup, blend in batches until smooth. Ladle into soup bowls and sprinkle with sliced green onion and ground peanuts.

**WHAT'S HOT**

▶ This is a delicious Southern soup with a rich history. George Washington Carver, an African-American botanist who worked with the Tuskegee Institute in Alabama actually created this soup, along with hundreds of recipes using peanuts. His peanut soup, called Tuskegee Soup, included a little sherry and some oysters. It's a delicious and unique soup to serve as a first course, and your guests will be delighted.

## Crab and Shrimp Bisque
SERVES 4 TO 6

*Tomato paste adds color and flavor to this seafood* **bisque** *recipe. I like to use a combination of crabmeat and shrimp, but lobster would be very good in this bisque as well.*

3 tablespoons butter
2 tablespoons green onion, chopped fine
2 tablespoons celery, chopped fine
3 tablespoons all-purpose flour
2 ½ cups whole milk
½ teaspoon freshly ground pepper
1 tablespoon tomato paste
1 cup heavy cream
8 ounces crabmeat
8 ounces lobster meat, chopped, or small cooked shrimp
2 tablespoons dry sherry

1. In a large saucepan over medium-low heat, melt butter. Add green onion and celery; sauté until tender. Blend in the flour. Cook, stirring constantly, for 1 minute.
2. Gradually stir milk into the saucepan. Cook, stirring constantly, until bubbly and thickened. Add the pepper, tomato paste, and cream. Stir until smooth.
3. Stir in crabmeat, shrimp or lobster, and the sherry. Bring to a simmer.
4. Serve hot as a first course or serve for lunch with a sandwich.

**ELSEWHERE ON THE WEB**

▶ Here are a few more delicious seafood soups: Debra Weber's delicious lobster bisque at http://about .com/frenchfood/lobster bisque, with fresh-cooked lobster meat and broth, a little sherry and white wine, butter, cream, and seasonings; and Kim's Country Clam Chowder from New England for Visitors, Guide Kim Knox Beckius, at http:// about.com/gonewengland/ clamchowder, made with fresh chopped clams, bacon, potatoes, milk, cream, and seasonings.

## Seven-Layer Salad
SERVES 12

*My mother-in-law makes this delicious salad every Thanksgiving, and it's a very popular salad throughout the South.*

6 cups lettuce, chopped
Salt and pepper
6 hard-cooked eggs, peeled and sliced
2 cups frozen peas, thawed
8 ounces bacon, cooked and crumbled
2 cups shredded mild Cheddar cheese
1 cup mayonnaise
3 tablespoons granulated sugar
½ cup green onions with green tops, sliced thin
Ground paprika

1. Place 3 cups of the lettuce in bottom of large bowl or serving dish; sprinkle with salt and pepper. Layer sliced hard-cooked eggs over and sprinkle with more salt and pepper. Continue to layer vegetables in this order: peas, remaining lettuce, crumbled bacon, and shredded cheese, along with light sprinklings of salt and pepper.
2. Combine mayonnaise and sugar; spread over top, spreading to edge of bowl to cover entire salad.
3. Cover and chill overnight or up to 24 hours. Toss the salad lightly before serving. Garnish with the sliced green onion and a sprinkling of ground paprika.

**TOOLS YOU NEED**

▶ Save the paper towels and get a salad spinner. A salad spinner is a plastic bowl with a removable plastic strainer inside. You activate the top of the spinner to make the inner strainer spin inside the outer bowl. The action pulls excess water from the vegetables and leaves it in the outer bowl. It's a great tool to own, because you can rinse lettuce and other vegetables in the basket then simply spin to dry. Dressing will adhere much better to dry leaves and vegetables, so you'll have a much more flavorful salad.

## Perfect Potato Salad
SERVES 8

*This is my family's favorite version of potato salad. If you can get new potatoes, it doesn't get much better than that.*

3 pounds potatoes
6 hard-cooked eggs, peeled and chopped
¼ cup red onion, chopped
½ cup celery, chopped
¾ cup mayonnaise, or to taste
1 to 2 tablespoons prepared mustard
Salt and pepper, to taste
Thin-sliced cucumber, optional

1. Peel potatoes; cut in half or quarter. If using new potatoes, just scrub and cut them in half or quarter. Cover with water and boil just until tender, about 15 to 20 minutes. Drain and let cool completely.
2. Cut cooled potatoes into small cubes. In a large bowl, combine potatoes with the chopped eggs, chopped onion, and chopped celery. Add mayonnaise, mustard, and salt and pepper. Gently stir until combined and ingredients are well moistened, adding more or less to suit your taste.
3. If desired, garnish with sliced cucumbers.

**WHAT'S HOT**

▶ A waxy variety of potato makes the best salad because they hold their shape quite well. Potato varieties that work well in salads, gratins, and potato scallops include Yellow Finn, boiling potatoes, red-skinned potatoes, round whites, purple potatoes, new potatoes, and the Baby Dutch. Good mashing potatoes include Yukon gold, Caribe, Russet, and long whites. Russet potatoes also make superb whole baked potatoes and French fries.

## Hearty Chopped Salad

SERVES 6

*A delicious chopped salad I ordered at a restaurant was the inspiration for this recipe. Serve this as a main-dish salad or with soup or a sandwich.*

1 cup cooked ham, diced
1 large head romaine lettuce, chopped
⅓ cup purple onion, diced
½ cup pecans or roasted peanuts, chopped
½ cup cooked garbanzo beans or red kidney beans
1 medium cucumber, peeled, seeded, and diced
2 medium tomatoes, seeded and diced
1 cup Havarti or Cheddar cheese, diced
1 tablespoon fresh parsley, chopped
¼ cup balsamic vinegar
1 teaspoon honey-Dijon mustard
½ cup extra-virgin olive oil
Salt and freshly ground black pepper
Tortilla chips

1. Heat a skillet; spray with vegetable cooking spray or a little butter then brown ham. Combine ham with the chopped lettuce, onion, pecans, garbanzo beans or kidney beans, cucumber, tomato, cheese, and parsley; toss to mix well.
2. In a measuring cup or small bowl, combine the balsamic vinegar and honey mustard. Gradually whisk in the olive oil; season with salt and pepper to taste.
3. Arrange tortilla chips on individual salad plates. Top with a mound of salad and serve with dressing on the side.

**ELSEWHERE ON THE WEB**

▶ Here are two more delicious chopped salad combinations: This Breakthrough Salad, from Linda Larsen, is a chopped vegetable salad with tomatoes, peppers, endive, herbs, and a tarragon-lemon dressing and sour cream garnish. Here's a link to Linda's recipe: http://about.com/busycooks/breakthroughsalad. And what could be easier than this light Chopped Tomato Salad from Fiona Haynes? It's made with fresh tomatoes, yellow bell pepper, red onion, and cilantro. Check it out at http://about.com/lowfatcooking/tomatosalad.

## Creamy Cabbage Slaw
SERVES 8

*My husband likes very basic coleslaw with mayonnaise, salt, and pepper, but I like mine a little tangier and sweeter. This is my favorite version.*

1 medium head green cabbage, shredded
1 medium carrot, shredded
1 tablespoon minced or grated onion
1 ¼ cups mayonnaise
⅓ cup sugar
¼ cup vinegar
¼ teaspoon celery seed, or to taste
¼ teaspoon ground black pepper, or to taste
Salt, to taste

1. In a large bowl, combine shredded cabbage, carrot, and minced or grated onion.
2. In a medium bowl, combine the mayonnaise, sugar, vinegar, and celery seed. Whisk to blend well. Taste and add salt and pepper, to taste. If too sweet for your taste, add a little more mayonnaise.
3. Add dressing to cabbage mixture and stir until well moistened.
4. Refrigerate the slaw for at least 2 hours, until thoroughly chilled.

**WHAT'S HOT**

▶ Here are some helpful coleslaw tips: When it comes to shredding cabbage for coleslaw, cut the cabbage in quarters first and remove the core. For the crispest slaw, soak the shredded cabbage in ice water for 20 to 30 minutes before preparing. Coleslaw will develop more flavor if refrigerated for at least an hour before serving. You can use a blender for mixing the dressing, but a clean jar with a screw-on top will do an excellent job and cleanup is a breeze. Just shake ingredients until well blended and then pour over the vegetables.

## Tangy Coleslaw with Cooked Dressing
SERVES 8

*This particular coleslaw makes a great topping for **pulled pork** sandwiches. It's tangy and delicious, and lighter than the mayonnaise version.*

1 medium green cabbage
1 medium purple onion
1 cup granulated sugar
1 teaspoon salt
1 teaspoon dry mustard
1 teaspoon celery seed
1 cup vinegar
⅔ cup vegetable oil

1. Shred cabbage into a large bowl. Quarter the purple onion then slice thin. Add to the shredded cabbage.
2. Combine remaining ingredients in a saucepan; bring to a boil. Pour the hot dressing over cabbage mixture; toss.
3. Chill thoroughly before serving.

**WHAT'S HOT**

▶ I love a cooked tangy slaw on pulled pork sandwiches, and it would also be great on corned beef. My slow-cooker pulled pork recipe is very popular, easy to prepare, and incredibly delicious. Check it out at http://about.com/southernfood/pulledpork. Serve the pulled pork on split buns with a topping of coleslaw. These sandwiches are wonderful with Barbecue Baked Beans (page 177) and Perfect Potato Salad (page 60).

## Wilted Spinach Salad with Bacon
SERVES 4

*I've seen this popular salad with the name "killed salad." I see it on the menu at most of the local restaurants—it's the bacon drippings that give it such great flavor.*

2 tablespoons bacon drippings
2 tablespoons all-purpose flour
¼ cup minced **sweet onion**
1 cup water
½ teaspoon dry mustard
2 tablespoons vinegar
1 pound fresh spinach, cleaned and chopped
Salt and pepper, to taste
1 hard-cooked egg, sliced thin, optional

1. Heat bacon drippings in a large saucepan. Stir in flour until smooth. Add minced onion, stirring until well blended.
2. Add water, dry mustard, and vinegar. Cook over low heat, stirring constantly, until thickened and smooth.
3. Put spinach in a large bowl; pour hot dressing over the spinach. Toss to mix. Season the salad with salt and pepper, to taste.
4. Garnish with sliced hard-cooked eggs, if desired.

## Broccoli Salad with Raisins and Pecans

SERVES 8

*This classic broccoli salad is a great dish to take along to a potluck or family dinner.*

8 ounces bacon
1 bunch fresh broccoli
¼ cup purple onion, chopped
½ cup raisins
1 cup mayonnaise
3 tablespoons vinegar
2 tablespoons granulated sugar
¾ cup pecans, chopped coarse

1.  In a large skillet, cook bacon over medium heat until browned and crisp. Drain on paper towels. Crumble into a cup or bowl, cover, and refrigerate.
2.  Cut broccoli into small, bite-size pieces.
3.  In a serving bowl, combine broccoli, the chopped onion, and raisins. In a separate bowl, combine mayonnaise, vinegar, and sugar. Whisk to blend well. Pour dressing over the broccoli mixture and stir to combine. Refrigerate for 2 to 4 hours.
4.  Just before serving, add the crumbled bacon and pecans. Toss to combine.

ASK YOUR GUIDE

**Can this salad be made with broccoli florets?**

▶ Broccoli florets are great in this salad, and you can buy them all separated and cleaned in the produce section of the supermarket. Use 1 pound of broccoli florets, or about 4 to 5 cups. I sometimes combine broccoli and cauliflower florets for a little color and texture contrast and use sunflower seeds or peanuts instead of pecans. I've also replaced the raisins with dried cranberries, and the salad was delicious.

▶ One of my favorite ways to serve fresh tomatoes is unbelievably simple, but it's so delicious. Slice tomatoes thin and arrange the slices on a serving plate. Sprinkle the tomatoes lightly with salt and pepper, and then top with sliced (chiffonade) or chopped fresh basil. Let the tomatoes sit at room temperature for about 15 to 20 minutes. Serve as is or with a vinaigrette or your favorite prepared salad dressing. Enjoy!

## Bacon, Lettuce, and Tomato Salad
SERVES 4

*This classic combination makes a great sandwich, but it also makes for a super salad. Use a French dressing, **vinaigrette**, or your own favorite dressing.*

6 slices bacon
2 medium tomatoes, quartered
4 cups mixed salad greens
French dressing or your favorite dressing
Salt and freshly ground black pepper, to taste
3 hard-cooked eggs, quartered

1. In a skillet over medium heat, cook bacon until browned and crisp. Transfer to paper towels and crumble. Reserve 1 tablespoon of bacon drippings.
2. In a serving bowl, combine the tomatoes, crumbled cooked bacon, reserved drippings, and salad greens. Toss with dressing. Add salt and pepper, to taste. Arrange quartered hard-cooked eggs on top of the salad.

# Black-Eyed Pea Salad with Basil Dressing
SERVES 6

*Use fresh basil in this delicious, nutritious salad for the best flavor. Serve this salad on your New Year's Day table for good luck.*

3 cups cooked black-eyed peas
¼ teaspoon salt
½ cup purple onion, chopped fine
½ cup celery, chopped fine
¼ cup red bell pepper, chopped fine
¼ cup yellow bell pepper, chopped fine
¼ cup apple cider vinegar
3 tablespoons fresh basil, chopped
3 medium cloves garlic, crushed
1 ½ teaspoons granulated sugar
¼ teaspoon freshly ground black pepper
¼ teaspoon salt
1 cup olive oil

1. In a serving dish, combine the black-eyed peas, ¼ teaspoon salt, chopped onion, celery, and red and yellow bell pepper. The yellow pepper makes the salad a little more colorful, but you can use all red. Toss and set aside.
2. In a small deep bowl, combine the vinegar, fresh basil or 1 tablespoon dried basil, garlic, sugar, ground black pepper, ¼ teaspoon salt. Slowly whisk in oil until well blended.
3. Pour dressing over the black-eyed pea mixture and toss to combine. Cover and refrigerate for at least 2 hours. Garnish with a few fresh basil leaves before serving, if desired.

ELSEWHERE ON THE WEB

▶ Hoppin' John (page 174) is one of my New Year's Day traditions, but any way you serve your New Year's black-eyed peas, they should bring you good luck throughout the New Year. Here's a popular black-eyed pea dip, Texas Caviar, from Linda Larsen. It's made with black-eyed peas, onion and green pepper, garlic, tomatoes, and salad dressing. Check it out at http://about.com/busycooks/texascaviar.

**Could I use fresh strawberries in this recipe?**

▶ Absolutely, and they are usually more flavorful! Toss about 3 cups of cleaned and sliced strawberries with ¼ cup of granulated sugar and let stand for at least 30 minutes. Let the gelatin mixture cool slightly before adding the fresh strawberries, then chill and finish the recipe as directed.

## Dot's Strawberry Pretzel Salad
SERVES 10

*This is my mother-in-law's recipe, and it is delicious. Make it for a holiday dinner or take the salad along to a potluck dinner or summer get-together. Don't forget to take a copy of the recipe, because you'll be asked for it.*

2 cups crushed pretzels
¾ cup melted butter
1 cup plus 3 tablespoons sugar, divided
1 package (6 ounces) strawberry-flavored gelatin
2 cups boiling water
2 packages (10 ounces each) frozen strawberries
1 package (8 ounces) cream cheese
1 container (8 ounces) **whipped topping**
Fresh strawberries and whipped topping for garnish

1. Heat oven to 400°F.
2. Combine crushed pretzels with melted butter and 3 tablespoons sugar. Press mixture evenly over the bottom of a 9" × 13" baking pan. Bake for 8 minutes. Set aside to cool.
3. Add the strawberry-flavored gelatin to the boiling water. Add frozen strawberries, stirring until strawberries are thawed. Chill until slightly thickened.
4. In a large bowl, beat cream cheese with the remaining 1 cup sugar. Fold in whipped topping. Spread over the cooled pretzel layer.
5. Spoon the partially thickened gelatin mixture over the cream cheese layer. Garnish with fresh strawberries and more whipped topping, if desired.

# Millionaire Fruit Salad

SERVES 8

*This delicious fruit salad is an old-fashioned classic, with a few updates. I love this salad with an Easter ham dinner, but you'll find it's a great fit with other holiday dinner menus.*

1 small package (3 ounces) cream cheese, softened
3 tablespoons half-and-half or light cream
¼ cup mayonnaise
2 tablespoons fresh lemon juice
2 tablespoons granulated sugar
1 can (8 ounces) pineapple tidbits, drained
1 small container (8 ounces) peach chunks, drained
1 can (11 ounces) mandarin orange sections, drained
½ cup drained halved maraschino cherries
½ cup seedless grapes, halved
½ cup pecans, chopped coarse
1 cup miniature marshmallows
1 cup heavy whipping cream

1. In a large bowl, combine cream cheese with 3 tablespoons half-and-half, mayonnaise, lemon juice, and granulated sugar. Beat until smooth.
2. Stir in pineapple tidbits, peach chunks, orange sections, cherries, grapes, pecans, and marshmallows.
3. In another bowl, beat 1 cup whipping cream until stiff. Fold into the fruit mixture until well blended. Transfer to an 8-inch square baking dish.
4. Chill or freeze this fruit salad before serving.

ASK YOUR GUIDE

**I'm trying to lower the fat in my family's diet. How could I lighten this recipe?**

▶ There are many products on the market these days that can take the place of higher-fat foods. I would suggest using light cream cheese and mayonnaise and substituting fat-free or reduced-calorie whipped topping for the heavy whipped cream. You could even replace the sugar with Splenda and cut back on the pecans or leave them out altogether.

## Get Linked

*At my Southern Food site on **About.com**, you can find many more soup and salad recipes. Here are a few of the best links to resources that might help you.*

**CHEESE SOUP RECIPES**

Here's a variety of cheese soup recipes, including a broccoli cheese soup, a cheese soup with beer, a chile cheese soup, and many more.

 http://about.com/southernfood/cheesesoups

**PASTA SALADS**

Here you'll find several pasta salads, including tuna macaroni salad, salmon pasta salad, delicious macaroni salads, pasta salads with ham, and others.

 http://about.com/southernfood/pastasalads

**BEAN SALADS**

This list includes some delicious bean salad recipes, including black bean salad, lima bean salad, bean and bacon salad, a macaroni and bean salad, green bean salad, and several multi-bean salads.

 http://about.com/southernfood/beansalads

## Chapter 5

# Sandwiches

**ASK YOUR GUIDE:**

Where did the po' boy sandwich get its name?
▶ **PAGE 73**

Are there other ways to make plain old chicken salad more interesting?
▶ **PAGE 77**

## Pimiento Cheese Sandwiches
MAKES 1 CUP

*The pimiento cheese sandwich is a classic here in the South. Use this delicious cheese spread as is or add a few tomatoes and a little bacon or sliced ham to the sandwich.*

**TOOLS YOU NEED**

▶ This cheese mixture can be mixed by hand, but you'll find that a food processor makes preparation of this spread a breeze, from shredding the cheese to mixing it all together. Some other delicious add-ins you could consider include a little Parmesan cheese, a small amount of minced jalapeño pepper, and some coarsely ground black pepper. This spread recipe is very easy to double or triple for party sandwiches.

1 small jar (2 ounces) diced pimientos, drained
1 cup sharp Cheddar cheese, shredded fine
¼ cup mayonnaise
2 teaspoons lemon juice
⅛ teaspoon salt
Dash garlic powder
Few drops hot sauce, optional
Sliced white or whole wheat bread

1. Drain and mash pimientos.
2. In a large bowl, combine the pimientos, shredded cheese, mayonnaise, lemon juice, salt, garlic powder, and hot sauce, if using. Mix all ingredients with hands or a fork until well blended.
3. Refrigerate until ready to serve. Spread on sliced bread to make sandwiches.

# New Orleans–Style Roast Beef Po' Boy

SERVES 4

*Use good French bread and your favorite meat or seafood for these delicious sandwiches. Roast beef makes a classic* po' boy, *but fried oysters, shrimp, ham, and sausage are other popular fillings.*

4 French bread rolls or 2 baguettes
Mayonnaise
1 cup shredded lettuce
1 pound roast beef, sliced thin
1 cup thick beef gravy
2 medium tomatoes, sliced thin
Dill pickle slices, optional

1. Split rolls lengthwise. If using baguettes, cut into 12-inch lengths then split lengthwise.
2. Warm or toast the split French bread in the oven or under the broiler.
3. Spread bottom half of bread with mayonnaise, then layer with shredded lettuce, sliced roast beef, the gravy, then the tomato slices and dill pickles, if using. Top with the top piece of bread. Repeat with remaining bread.
4. Serve with potato chips, French fries, or potato salad.

ASK YOUR GUIDE

**Where did the po' boy sandwich get its name?**

▶ The po' boy, or poor boy, sandwich is a New Orleans version of the submarine sandwich. There are more than a few stories on how the name came about, but one of them is that the sandwich was created in the 1920s by New Orleans grocers Benny and Clovis Martin. During a transit workers' strike, they purportedly gave sandwiches away or charged the "poor boys" on strike only five cents. The French term *pourboire,* which means "for drinks," is another possibility. Some believe the French expression was used by begging children, and the children were given sandwiches made with French bread.

▶ I have another recipe for The Hot Brown on my site, and it comes from Kentucky Chef Nick Sundberg. Nick, who was chef at the Beaumont Inn at the time he offered the recipe, feels his version is closer to the original than many recipes: http://about.com/southern food/hotbrown. Another similar recipe is this Hot Brown Special, made quick and easy with cream of mushroom soup instead of homemade sauce. Check it out at http://about.com/ southernfood/hotbrown special.

# Kentucky Hot Brown
SERVES 6

*This hot turkey sandwich was created by Louisville's Brown Hotel in the 1920s. This is a version with a Parmesan cheese sauce, but it is also frequently made with Cheddar cheese.*

5 tablespoons butter
⅔ cup all-purpose flour
1 ½ cups chicken broth
1 ½ cups milk
½ teaspoon salt
⅛ teaspoon freshly ground black pepper
1 cup freshly grated Parmesan cheese
12 slices bread
12 slices roast turkey
Ground paprika
12 slices tomato
12 slices bacon, cut in half crosswise, cooked
Freshly grated Parmesan cheese, for garnish, optional

1. Heat oven to 400°F. In a saucepan over medium-low heat, melt the butter. Blend in flour, stirring until incorporated. Gradually whisk in broth, then slowly add milk, whisking until smooth. Stir in salt, pepper, and Parmesan cheese. Reduce heat to low and cook, stirring, for 5 minutes. The sauce will be thick.
2. Toast the bread. Arrange 2 slices of toast on an ovenproof plate. Top with 2 turkey slices then cover the turkey with sauce. Sprinkle paprika over the sauce then top with a tomato. Arrange 2 halves of cooked bacon in an "x" on the tomato.
3. Bake for 10 minutes, or until sauce is bubbly. Garnish with grated Parmesan before serving, if desired.

# French Toasted-Ham Sandwiches
SERVES 6

*Ham sandwiches with a twist! The bread is dipped in an egg batter like French toast, giving this sandwich more flavor and character.*

12 slices firm white bread
Prepared mustard
12 thin slices cooked ham or smoked turkey
6 slices Swiss cheese
2 eggs, lightly beaten
½ cup milk
¼ teaspoon salt
Freshly ground black pepper
3 tablespoons butter

1. Spread a thin layer of mustard over each slice of bread. On each of 6 slices, place 2 slices of ham or turkey, and 1 slice of cheese. Top with remaining 6 slices of bread, mustard side down.
2. In a shallow bowl, whisk eggs with milk, salt, and pepper.
3. Melt butter in a large skillet over low heat.
4. Dip sandwiches in the egg mixture, turning to coat well. Depending on the size of the skillet, cook 2 or 3 at a time. Place sandwiches in the hot skillet, brown well on each side.

**WHAT'S HOT**

▶ I have couple of recipes similar to this one on my About.com site. One is French Toasted Tuna Sandwiches, made with a combination of tuna, mayonnaise, celery, and lemon juice on bread. The bread is dipped in an egg batter, then browned in butter. Check it out at http://about.com/southern food/toastedtuna. You'll also find a recipe for a Turkey and Ham Monte Cristo, made with sliced turkey and ham, along with Swiss or Gruyere cheese and a little mayonnaise and mustard. The bread is then dipped into an egg batter and browned. Check this recipe out at http://about.com/southernfood/montecristo.

## Pulled Pork Barbecue Sandwiches
SERVES 8

*Long, slow cooking in the oven is the way most people cook the pork.*

I large pork shoulder or butt roast, 7 to 9 pounds
3 cloves garlic, minced
I teaspoon Creole seasoning
½ teaspoon salt
½ teaspoon ground black pepper
I large onion, sliced
I large onion, chopped
2 teaspoons vegetable oil
I cup bottled barbecue sauce
½ cup cider vinegar

1. Heat oven to 350°F. Rinse pork and pat dry.
2. Spread a large sheet of heavy duty foil across a roasting pan. Place the pork roast on the foil. Rub pork with the minced garlic, Creole seasoning, salt, and pepper. Arrange onion over top of roast. Bring foil up around the roast, wrapping well. Bake pork for 4 to 5 hours, or until a meat thermometer registers about 185°F. The meat should be tender, almost falling apart.
3. Let the roast cool slightly. Shred with 2 forks or chop the meat, discarding excess fat and bone as you find it.
4. In a skillet, heat oil over medium heat; sauté chopped onion until tender. Put the onion and pork in a slow cooker or large saucepan or Dutch oven. Stir in barbecue sauce and vinegar.
5. Heat on LOW setting or over low heat on the stovetop for 20 to 30 minutes, or until thoroughly heated. Serve hot with split buns, coleslaw, and beans, if desired. A potato salad also goes well with this for a bigger meal or party.

ELSEWHERE ON THE WEB

▶ Here's a terrific site with great instructions for a real pig-pickin' done in a home-made pit or metal pit-style barbecue: www.ibiblio .org/lineback/bbq/smoke .htm. These instructions take you from the wood you should choose for the best coals and the size of the hog to the best pits and flavorings. Derrick Riches also has a delicious Pulled Pork with Spicy Chile Sauce recipe on his site at About.com. It's made with pork shoulder on the grill. Check it out at http://about.com/bbq/ pulledporkspicy.

## Chicken Sandwiches with Curried Mayonnaise and Golden Raisins

SERVES 4

*This makes a delicious sandwich, but you could also serve it on lettuce leaves for a lighter luncheon dish. I love this on toasted whole wheat or oatmeal bread.*

4 tablespoons mayonnaise
2 tablespoons fruit chutney
3 teaspoons curry powder, or to taste
¼ cup celery, chopped
1 tablespoon green onion, chopped
⅓ cup golden raisins, chopped
2 tablespoons pecans, chopped
1 ½ cups cooked chicken, diced
Heavy cream, as needed
Sliced bread
Fresh lettuce leaves, if desired

1. Combine mayonnaise and chutney in a small bowl. Add curry powder to taste.
2. In a medium bowl, combine the chopped celery, green onion, chopped raisins, pecans, and chicken. Stir in the mayonnaise mixture and add a little heavy cream to moisten, if desired.
3. Toast bread if desired; top one slice of bread with a lettuce leaf then spread 3 to 4 tablespoons of the chicken mixture on the lettuce. Top with another slice of bread. Repeat with remaining bread, making 4 to 6 sandwiches.
4. Cut sandwiches in half and serve with fresh sliced tomatoes, along with chips, if desired.

**ASK YOUR GUIDE**

*Are there other ways to make plain old chicken salad more interesting?*

▶ Absolutely! Jazz up a cup of chicken or turkey salad with a few tablespoons of chopped apple or tasty chopped dried cranberries, or a few chopped toasted pecans. Dark or golden raisins are also delicious, and do try some herbs, such as a little dried tarragon or basil. Roasted red peppers make a nice addition, too, as do sliced ripe or stuffed green olives, or try some chopped capers or a little pickle relish or chopped pickles. The possibilities are endless!

▶ Burgers and Sloppy Joes are popular and easy to make for game day, kids' parties, and other gatherings. Here are a few interesting versions. The first recipe is for Sloppy Joe Sandwiches cooked in the slow cooker. They're made with lean ground beef, onion, celery, chili sauce, and other ingredients. Check this recipe out at http://about.com/southern food/slowcooksloppyjoe. Another popular recipe is my Sloppy Saucy Joes, with ground chuck, tomato sauce, chopped vegetables, spices, and hot sauce. Check this one out at http://about .com/southernfood/sloppy saucyjoe.

## Chili Beef Burgers

SERVES 6

*These burgers pack a lot of flavor! You can make these with more beef and no beans, but I like the beans. These are super for parties.*

2 pounds extra-lean ground beef
1 large sweet onion, chopped
1 cup bell pepper, red and green, chopped
1 can (15 ounces) pinto beans, drained and rinsed
2 ½ cups water
2 cups ketchup
2 ½ tablespoons prepared mustard
4 teaspoons packed brown sugar, or to taste
2 ½ tablespoons chili powder
⅛ teaspoon garlic powder
½ teaspoon salt
⅛ teaspoon freshly ground black pepper
6 large hamburger buns or similar rolls, split

1. In a large skillet over medium heat, brown ground beef with onion and bell pepper. Drain off excess fat. Stir in beans.
2. Combine water, ketchup, mustard, brown sugar, chili powder, garlic powder, and salt and pepper in a bowl. Blend well then add to the beef and bean mixture. Simmer until thickened. Taste and adjust seasonings.
3. Toast split sandwich buns, if desired. Spoon beef and bean mixture over split buns.

## Out-of-the-Ordinary Burgers
SERVES 4

*Herbs help to flavor this lean ground-round mixture. You'll love these delicious grilled burgers. To top the burgers off, try sautéed mushrooms or onions, barbecue sauce, prepared chili, peppers, or cooked bacon.*

1 slice crusty bread
¼ cup milk
1 ½ pounds ground round or ground sirloin
2 tablespoons fresh parsley, chopped fine
½ teaspoon dried leaf oregano
½ teaspoon dried leaf tarragon
½ teaspoon dried leaf thyme, crumbled
½ teaspoon seasoned salt
1 teaspoon salt
¼ teaspoon ground black pepper
1 large egg, lightly beaten

1. In a medium bowl, soak bread in milk for a few minutes. Squeeze milk out. Put bread back in bowl; add ground beef, herbs, and salt and pepper. Use hands to combine. Mix in beaten egg.
2. Shape the beef mixture into 4 large patties, about 1-inch thick. Place burgers on a hot oiled grill about 4 inches above coals. Grill for about 10 to 15 minutes on each side, or until cooked through and juices run clear.
3. Toast split hamburger buns, if desired. Serve on buns with chips and a salad.

**WHAT'S HOT**

▶ Here are five great add-ins and tips for making the best burgers: (1) Mix the ground beef mixture lightly; (2) Add a little tomato juice or vegetable broth for flavor and moisture; (3) Add chopped leftover vegetables to mixture; (4) Add a little diced bacon for a smoky flavor; (5) Freeze shaped burgers, separated with plastic wrap.

## Get Linked

*Here are more delicious sandwich and burger recipes at my Southern Food site on **About.com**.*

**BURGER RECIPES**

Here's a big variety of burger recipes, including Mushroom Burgers with Cheese, Beef and Bacon Burgers, Swiss Burgers, Zesty Outdoor Burgers, and many more.

 http://about.com/southernfood/burgerrecipes

**MUFFULETTA SUBS**

Another New Orleans tradition, these are made with sub rolls, ham, cheese, salami, olives, artichokes, condiments, and seasonings.

 http://about.com/southernfood/muffulettasubs

## Chapter 6

# Beef, Veal, and Lamb

**About**

ASK YOUR GUIDE:

How could this recipe be adapted to the slow cooker?
▶ PAGE 84

What are the best beef cuts to use for pot roast?
▶ PAGE 88

What can I use to replace wine in a recipe?
▶ PAGE 100

What is the easiest way to make fluffy mashed potatoes?
▶ PAGE 101

Can I substitute dry herbs for fresh herbs in a recipe?
▶ PAGE 102

## Beef and Sweet Onions with Rice
SERVES 6

*This is an easy everyday skillet recipe your family will ask for again and again. Use sweet Vidalia onions if you can get them.*

2 pounds beef sirloin
2 large sweet onions, quartered and sliced
2 tablespoons vegetable oil
1 tablespoon butter
3 tablespoons flour
1 teaspoon salt
½ teaspoon ground black pepper
¼ teaspoon dried leaf thyme, crumbled
2 cups beef broth
2 tablespoons vinegar
1 tablespoon tomato ketchup
3 cups hot cooked rice

1. Trim sirloin steaks; cut into bite-size cubes. Set aside.
2. In a large skillet, heat the oil and butter over medium heat until hot. Add sliced onions. Cook the onions, stirring constantly, until tender and lightly browned. Add beef to the skillet with the onions. Increase heat to medium-high and sauté until beef is browned. Reduce heat to medium.
3. Combine the flour, salt, pepper, and thyme; add to the skillet, stirring to incorporate and blend well. If necessary to moisten flour, add a little more butter.
4. Add the beef broth, vinegar, and ketchup. Stir to blend. Reduce heat to low; cover and cook for about 1 hour, or until meat is very tender.
5. Serve with hot cooked rice.

▶ There are a number of varieties of sweet onions on the market these days, and you're likely to find them at almost any time of the year. Some of these include Vidalia, Maui, Walla Walla, Texas Sweets, Sweet Imperial, Mayan, Grand Canyon, and a few others. For best results, these onions should be stored in the refrigerator, individually wrapped in paper towels. Another effective way to store these onions is to put them in the legs of panty hose, making a knot between each onion. Hang in a cool, dry, well-ventilated place. To use, just cut an onion off just below the next knot.

# Beef and Biscuit Pie

SERVES 4

*This is an easy family recipe, a tasty meal in one dish.*

1 ½ pounds sirloin steak, about ¾-inch thick
1 tablespoon vegetable oil
8 ounces fresh sliced mushrooms
1 medium onion, quartered then sliced
1 medium clove garlic, minced
¼ cup broth or water
1 jar (12 ounces) beef gravy
1 ½ cups frozen peas and carrots, thawed
¼ teaspoon dried leaf thyme
1 tube (12 ounces) refrigerated buttermilk biscuits

1. Heat oven to 400°F.
2. Trim steak of excess fat. Cut into ½" x 3" strips.
3. Heat oil in a large skillet over medium-high heat. Add beef, working in batches, stirring to brown all sides. Remove beef strips from skillet with a slotted spoon and set aside.
4. To the same skillet add the mushrooms, sliced onion, garlic, and broth or water. Cook the mushroom and onion mixture, stirring constantly, for about 3 minutes, or until onion is tender. Stir the gravy into the skillet (use 1 ½ cups of thick leftover gravy, if you have it), along with the peas and carrots, and the thyme. Bring the mixture to a boil; simmer for 1 minute. Stir in browned beef.
5. Spoon beef and vegetable mixture into a 2-quart baking dish. Separate biscuits; cut in half. Arrange the biscuits, cut side down, on beef mixture. Bake for 12 to 14 minutes, or until biscuits are browned. Serve with a tossed salad.

**ELSEWHERE ON THE WEB**

▸ Here's a link to a recipe for Hachis Parmentier, a delicious-looking beef pie with potatoes and Gruyere cheese from French Cooking Guide Debra Weber: http://about .com/frenchfood/hachis parmentier. Debra says it is very simple yet delicious, and it is named for a famous French man who, in the mid-1700s, set up potato-soup kitchens for the poor and pushed potato-based dishes. It is said he served Ben Franklin many potato dishes, including a potato after-dinner liqueur.

**How could this recipe be adapted to the slow cooker?**

▶ Replace the 4 cups of beef broth with a can of condensed beef broth (10 ½ ounces). Combine all ingredients, except flour and water mixture and frozen vegetables, in the slow cooker. Cook on LOW for about 8 to 9 hours, until meat and vegetables are tender. Cook the frozen vegetables slightly before adding them to the stew. Stir in flour and water mixture and cook on HIGH for a few minutes, until thickened. Tip: If the slow cooking produces too much liquid and the broth lacks flavor, pour the liquids into a saucepan and simmer until the broth is reduced slightly. Stir in the flour and water mixture and return to the slow cooker.

## Vegetable Beef Stew
SERVES 8

*This stew is loaded with vegetables, and if you have some fresh from the garden, so much the better!*

| | |
|---|---|
| 2 pounds stewing beef, cut in small cubes | ½ cup lima beans or butter beans |
| 4 cups beef broth | ¼ cup red wine |
| 3 medium potatoes, cut in small cubes | ½ teaspoon salt |
| 1 small rutabaga or turnip, cut in small cubes | ¼ teaspoon ground black pepper |
| 2 medium carrots, sliced thin | ¼ teaspoon dried leaf thyme, crumbled |
| 1 small onion, chopped | ½ cup frozen mixed vegetables, optional |
| 2 ribs celery, sliced | 3 tablespoons flour |
| 1 cup sliced mushrooms, optional | ¼ cup cold water |

1. In a large stockpot or Dutch oven, combine the beef and beef broth; bring to a boil. Reduce heat; cover and simmer for about 1 ½ hours.
2. Add potatoes, rutabaga or turnip, carrots, onion, celery, mushrooms, lima beans, wine, salt, pepper, and thyme. Cover and simmer for about 25 to 35 minutes longer, or until vegetables are tender. If using frozen mixed vegetables, thaw and add to the stew about 10 minutes before it's done.
3. Combine 3 tablespoons of flour with the ¼ cup cold water; stir until smooth. Slowly stir the flour mixture into the simmering stew. Continue cooking for a few more minutes, stirring, until thickened. Serve with crusty bread.

## Beef and Chili Bean Stew

SERVES 8

*Serve this flavorful stew on game day, or for any hearty fall or winter meal. I like this stew with freshly baked hot cornbread.*

2 pounds lean stewing beef, cut in ½-inch cubes
2 tablespoons vegetable oil
1 large onion, chopped
1 green bell pepper, seeded and chopped
2 ribs celery, chopped
2 cloves garlic, minced
2 tablespoons chili powder
1 can (14.5 ounces) diced tomatoes

1 can (4 ounces) chopped mild green chile pepper
1 cup beef broth, warm
1 teaspoon salt
2 tablespoons flour
¼ cup cold water
2 cans (15 ounces each) red beans or kidney beans
1 can (11 to 15 ounces) whole kernel corn, drained

**TOOLS YOU NEED**

▶ I find that my Dutch oven is one of my most-used pots. It's big enough for hearty chili and stews. It can go from the stovetop to the oven, and the cast iron Dutch ovens can even be used over an open fire. When you buy a Dutch oven, make sure you get one that can withstand oven heat.

1. In a Dutch oven over medium-high heat, brown the beef in the vegetable oil, stirring frequently. With a slotted spoon, remove beef to a plate and set aside. Drain off all but 2 tablespoons of the drippings, or add oil to make 2 tablespoons.
2. Add to the pan chopped onion, green pepper, celery, and garlic; sauté until vegetables are just tender. Stir in chili powder and continue cooking, stirring, for about 1 minute. Add tomatoes and green chile. Stir in warm beef broth. Add the salt and return beef to the pot. Reduce heat to low; cover and simmer for about 1 ½ to 2 hours, until beef is tender.
3. In a cup, blend flour with ¼ cup cold water. Gradually stir into the stew. Cook the stew, stirring constantly, until thickened.
4. Drain and rinse beans and corn. Add to the stew mixture and heat through. Serve stew with cornbread.

## Grillades and Grits

SERVES 6

*This is a delicious Louisiana-style dish, traditionally served for brunch or breakfast, but it makes a delicious meal for any time of day.*

1 ½ pounds lean beef steaks
¼ cup all-purpose flour
½ teaspoon salt
¼ teaspoon freshly ground black pepper
2 tablespoons vegetable oil
1 large onion, quartered then sliced
3 ribs celery, chopped
1 cup bell pepper, red and green, chopped
2 medium cloves garlic, minced
2 tablespoons vegetable oil
2 tablespoons all-purpose flour
1 cup beef broth
1 can (14.5 ounces) diced tomatoes with juices
½ teaspoon dried leaf thyme, crumbled
½ teaspoon dried leaf basil, crumbled
¼ teaspoon crushed red pepper
2 tablespoons vinegar
Salt and pepper, to taste
2 tablespoons fresh flat-leaf parsley, chopped
3 to 4 cups hot cooked grits

*Grillades and Grits (continued)*

1. Flatten steaks to ½-inch thickness; cut into 2-inch pieces. Combine the ¼ cup flour, ½ teaspoon salt, and ¼ teaspoon pepper in a food storage bag. Add beef and toss gently to coat.
2. Heat 2 tablespoons of oil in a heavy skillet over medium-high heat. Cook the steak pieces, turning to brown both sides. Remove beef to a plate and set aside.
3. Add the sliced onion, chopped celery, and chopped bell pepper to the skillet and sauté until tender. Stir in the minced garlic. Transfer vegetables to a plate and set aside.
4. To the skillet add the remaining 2 tablespoons of oil. Stir 2 tablespoons of flour into the oil and cook, stirring constantly, until a light- to medium-brown color. Do not let the mixture burn. Add the cooked vegetables back to the pan, along with the beef broth. Stir until well blended and bubbly.
5. Add steak back to the pan along with tomatoes. Sprinkle with the herbs and crushed red pepper. Stir in vinegar. Reduce heat to a simmer and cook for about 45 minutes, or until beef is tender. Taste and add salt and pepper, as needed. Stir in the chopped parsley.
6. Serve beef over hot creamy cooked grits, or substitute cooked rice.

**ELSEWHERE ON THE WEB**

▶ Here's a link to another delicious grillades and grits recipe, this one with veal, tomatoes, Creole seasoning, roux, and chopped vegetables, along with cooked grits. This recipe is from New Orleans.com, written by New Orleans restaurant critic Tom Fitzmorris: http://foodfest.neworleans.com/rec_inv.php?RESID=187. You'll see more New Orleans food features and recipes in the right margin index of the page, along with other New Orleans news and happenings.

***What are the best beef cuts to use for pot roast?***

▶ There are a number of beef cuts which make great pot roasts, and when you shop for a pot roast, you'll find the best method of cooking is usually right there on the grocer's label. Some of my favorites are chuck arm, chuck fillet, and top round. Rump and blade roasts also make great pot roasts.

## Home-Style Pot Roast
SERVES 6 TO 8

*Dried herbs and condensed beef broth give this pot roast great flavor.*

1 beef pot roast, about 3 pounds (chuck, top round, rump, etc.)
2 tablespoons vegetable oil
1 medium onion, quartered and sliced
1 clove garlic, minced
1 teaspoon dried leaf thyme, crumbled
1 teaspoon dried leaf marjoram, crumbled
1 teaspoon salt
¼ teaspoon ground black pepper
1 can (10 ½ ounces) condensed beef broth
6 medium carrots
12 small white onions, peeled
1 small rutabaga, cut in 1-inch pieces
3 tablespoons all-purpose flour
¼ cup cold water

1. Heat oil in a large stockpot or Dutch oven over medium heat. Brown the beef roast well on all sides.
2. Add sliced onion, minced garlic, thyme, marjoram, salt, and pepper. Stir to combine.
3. Add beef broth and bring to a boil. Reduce heat to low; cover and simmer for 1 ½ to 2 hours, or until the pot roast is tender.
4. Slice the carrots in half crosswise then cut in half lengthwise. Add to the broth. Add the small white onions and rutabaga. Cover and simmer until vegetables are tender.
5. Move the roast to a warm platter. With a slotted spoon, arrange the vegetables around the roast. Cover and keep warm.
6. Combine flour with the cold water; whisk until smooth. Gradually stir the flour mixture into the simmering broth. Continue cooking, stirring constantly, until the broth is thickened. Serve the gravy with pot roast and vegetables.

## Country-Fried Steak

SERVES 4

*Serve with gravy and mashed potatoes, along with your favorite vegetable.*

1 ½ pounds round steak
Salt
1 cup plus 3 tablespoons all-purpose flour, divided
¾ teaspoon salt
¼ teaspoon freshly ground black pepper
1 large egg, beaten
Vegetable oil
2 tablespoons butter
1 cup milk
½ cup water or broth
Salt and pepper, to taste

1. Cut steak into 4 portions. Place between two pieces of plastic wrap. Using a meat mallet, flatten to about ½-inch thickness.
2. In a bowl, combine 1 cup of the flour with ¾ teaspoon salt and ¼ teaspoon pepper. Dredge steaks in the seasoned flour. Dip in beaten egg, then dredge again in flour mixture.
3. Heat 1 inch of vegetable oil in a heavy skillet. Using tongs, put steaks in the oil. Cook the steaks, turning once to brown both sides. Lower the heat to medium-low, cover, and continue to cook for about 3 to 4 minutes, until steaks are cooked through. Move steaks to paper towels on a warm platter; cover with foil.
4. Drain off all but 1 tablespoon of the oil and add butter. Add 3 tablespoons of flour, stirring and scraping the bottom of the skillet to get any browned bits. Cook the flour, stirring, for 1 minute. Stir in milk and water or broth; cook, stirring constantly, until thickened and bubbly. Season gravy with salt and pepper to taste.

WHAT'S HOT

▶ Here's a hot tip: When thinning pieces of beef, veal, chicken, and other cuts of meat, put the piece of meat in a large, heavy-duty food storage bag, then gently pound until flattened. The bag is strong enough to resist tearing, flips over easily so you can pound on the other side, and it should stand up through several pieces of meat, probably all of the meat in your recipe. You'll also have much less mess!

## Beef Tenderloin with Mushroom-Wine Sauce
SERVES 4

*Beef tenderloin is a perfect choice for a very special dinner. The mushroom-wine sauce is the perfect accompaniment.*

2 pounds beef tenderloin roast
1 large clove garlic, halved
Salt and pepper
2 tablespoons olive oil
1 cup mushrooms, sliced thin
2 green onions, white only
1 small clove garlic, minced
3 tablespoons all-purpose flour
1 ½ cups dry red wine
2 cups beef broth
¼ teaspoon dried leaf thyme
Salt and pepper, to taste

1. Heat oven to 400°F. Rub roast with cut side of garlic halves. Sprinkle with salt and pepper and place in a shallow roasting pan.
2. **Roast** for 1 hour for medium rare, 75 minutes for medium. Remove the beef to a warm platter when a meat thermometer registers 135°F (for medium rare) or 150°F (for medium). Let the roast stand for 15 minutes. The temperature will rise another 10°F or so.
3. Place the roasting pan over medium heat; add the vegetable oil, mushrooms, chopped green onion, and minced garlic. Sauté until mushrooms are tender. Stir in flour until well incorporated, and then stir in the red wine and beef broth. Simmer until reduced by about a third. Add thyme and the salt and pepper, to taste.
4. Slice tenderloin and serve with mushroom sauce.

## Standing Rib Roast

SERVES 8

*This is a terrific oven roast for a special family dinner, and it's relatively easy to fix. Serve this roast with baked or mashed potatoes and a wilted spinach salad, along with your favorite special vegetable side dish.*

1 standing rib roast, about 6 pounds
2 teaspoons salt
¾ teaspoon ground black pepper
¼ teaspoon garlic powder
½ cup beef broth, optional
Salt and pepper, to taste, optional

1. Heat oven to 450°F.
2. Rub the roast all over with the 2 teaspoons salt, ¾ teaspoon pepper, and garlic powder.
3. Place on a rack in a shallow pan and roast for 25 minutes. Reduce heat to 350°F and roast for about 15 minutes per pound, or to an internal temperature of about 135°F for medium-rare. Cover loosely with foil and let stand for 10 minutes before carving.
4. If desired, for beef **au jus**, add ½ cup beef broth to the drippings; bring to a boil. Season the **jus** with salt and pepper, to taste.

ELSEWHERE ON THE WEB

▶ Roasting isn't the only way to cook a great rib roast. Here's a link to an easy and delicious grilled standing rib roast from About.com Barbecues and Grilling Guide Derrick Riches: http://about.com/bbq/standingribroast. If you scroll down past the recipe, you'll see more prime rib and standing rib roast information from Derrick.

## Corned Beef and Cabbage
SERVES 4 TO 6

*This recipe will leave you with plenty of delicious leftover corned beef for sandwiches or a casserole.*

4 pounds corned beef brisket, with spice packet
1 medium bay leaf
¼ teaspoon freshly ground pepper
1 medium head cabbage, cut in wedges
2 small rutabagas, cut in large chunks
8 medium carrots, peeled and halved
12 small whole onions, peeled
6 medium potatoes, peeled and halved

1. Put corned beef in a deep stockpot or large kettle with spice packet, bay leaf, and pepper, and cover with water. Bring to a boil; skim off foam. Reduce heat to low; cover and simmer for about 50 minutes per pound.
2. Add the vegetables to the kettle. Cover and simmer for about 45 minutes, or until vegetables are tender.
3. Arrange corned beef on a platter and surround with the vegetables. Slice meat across the grain.

▶ Corned beef leftovers are great for sandwiches and casseroles. Or make an easy corned beef hash—sauté a little chopped onion and bell pepper in a skillet in a small amount of butter then add chopped leftover corned beef and leftover diced potatoes. Press in the skillet and cook, turning frequently with a spatula until cooked through and nicely browned. Season and serve!

# Beef and Barbecue Bean Stew

SERVES 6

*This is a quick and easy stew to make, and it's just the thing for fall or winter meals. Serve this easy stew with cornbread or corn muffins and a salad.*

1 pound lean ground beef
½ cup onion, chopped
½ cup green bell pepper, chopped
½ cup celery, chopped
1 large can (28 ounces) barbecue-flavored baked beans
1 small carrot, cut into small dice
1 can (8 ounces) tomato sauce
1 cup water
½ teaspoon garlic powder
1 can (14.5 ounces) diced tomatoes
6 tablespoons sour cream

1. In a Dutch oven or large saucepan over medium-low heat, brown the ground beef. Add onion, green pepper, and celery; continue to sauté, stirring, until vegetables are tender.
2. Add the beans, carrots, tomato sauce, water, garlic powder, and tomatoes. Reduce heat to low; cover and simmer for 45 minutes to 1 hour.
3. Add a dollop of sour cream to each serving. Serve with hot cornbread or corn muffins.

**ELSEWHERE ON THE WEB**

▶ Here's a tasty and light ground-beef-and-bean bake from Low Fat Cooking Guide Fiona Haynes. It's made with extra-lean ground beef, pinto beans, tomatoes, tortillas, and seasonings, along with reduced-fat cheese and chopped onions and other vegetables: http://about.com/lowfatcooking/beefbeanbake. As you scroll down past the recipe, you'll see links to more of Fiona's low-fat recipes using ground beef.

## Salisbury Steaks with Bacon

SERVES 6

*These hamburger steaks are delicious with mashed potatoes and a vegetable, along with leftover or purchased beef gravy.*

6 slices bacon, chopped fine
2 pounds ground round
2 tablespoons minced onion
1 tablespoon green bell pepper, chopped fine
1 tablespoon fresh parsley, chopped fine
1 teaspoon salt
¼ teaspoon freshly ground black pepper
1 ½ cups beef gravy, optional

1. In a large bowl, combine bacon with ground sirloin, chopped onion and bell pepper, parsley, salt, and pepper. Shape the mixture into 6 oval patties about ¾-inch thick.
2. Place patties on an oiled broiler pan. Broil about 4 inches from the heat source for about 18 minutes. Turn and broil the other side for 10 to 15 minutes, or until steaks are no longer pink inside.
3. Serve with hot beef gravy, if desired, along with mashed potatoes and a side vegetable or salad.

TOOLS YOU NEED

▶ I often use my hands when mixing ground meat mixtures, but a potato masher can be a great tool for combining meat and other ingredients for meat loaf, meatballs, burgers, and related ground-meat mixtures. Sturdy potato mashers made with heavy curved wire work best for this. You can also put the ground meat and other ingredients into a large, sturdy food storage bag, seal, and then squeeze the bag until the ingredients are combined.

## Country-Style Meatloaf
SERVES 6

*I usually serve meatloaf with mashed potatoes and peas and carrots.*

2 tablespoons butter
8 ounces sliced mushrooms
1 medium onion, chopped
3 ribs celery, chopped
2 medium carrots, shredded
2 tablespoons water or broth
2 pounds ground round
1 large egg, lightly beaten
½ cup fine dry bread crumbs
1 teaspoon salt
1 teaspoon seasoned salt
¼ teaspoon dried leaf thyme, crumbled
1 teaspoon dried parsley flakes
1 teaspoon Worcestershire sauce
⅓ cup ketchup or barbecue sauce, optional

1. Heat oven to 350°F. In a skillet, melt the butter over medium heat; add mushrooms, onion, celery, shredded carrots, and water or broth. Bring to a simmer and continue cooking for about 10 minutes, until vegetables are just tender.
2. In a bowl, combine the ground beef, egg, bread crumbs, salt and seasoned salt, thyme, parsley, and Worcestershire sauce. Gently mix to blend in vegetables. Pack into a meatloaf pan or shape into a loaf and place on a greased shallow baking pan.
3. Bake for 60 to 70 minutes, until browned and cooked through. If desired, spread ketchup or barbecue sauce over top of meatloaf about 5 minutes before done.

**WHAT'S HOT**

▶ Looking for a way to spice up the classic meatloaf? You're in luck! My French Onion Meatloaf is a very popular and tasty dish, and so easy to make, with condensed French onion soup, lean ground beef, an egg, crumbs, and seasonings. Check it out at http://about .com/southernfood/french onionmeatloaf.

## Spicy Beef Chili
SERVES 6

*This chili is made with ground beef and beans, along with a delicious combination of vegetables and spicy seasonings.*

1 tablespoon vegetable oil
1 large sweet onion, quartered then sliced
1 green bell pepper, seeded and chopped
1 pound ground round or sirloin
1 clove garlic, minced
1 can (14.5 ounces) diced tomatoes
1 can (8 ounces) tomato sauce
1 can (4 ounces) chopped mild green chile pepper
2 teaspoons jalapeño pepper, chopped fine
1 tablespoon chili powder
1 ½ teaspoons salt
Dash ground cayenne pepper
1 small bay leaf
2 cans (15 ounces each) red kidney beans

1. In a large skillet, heat oil over medium heat. Add onion, bell pepper, and ground beef. Sauté until beef is no longer pink and vegetables are tender.
2. Add minced garlic, tomatoes, tomato sauce, green chile, jalapeño, seasonings, and bay leaf. Cover and simmer for 1 ½ hours. Add water as needed to keep from sticking.
3. Drain beans and rinse; add to the chili and heat through.
4. Serve chili with crackers or freshly baked cornbread.

**ELSEWHERE ON THE WEB**

▶ If you're really serious about your chili, browse the Chili Appreciation Society International (CASI) site at www.chili.org. Find out all about how to participate in chili cook-offs, see what's coming up, get some delicious recipes from dozens of past winners, and learn some of the experts' secrets.

# Grace's Cabbage Rolls

SERVES 4 TO 6

*These are delicious with boiled potatoes.*

1 large head cabbage
1 pound lean ground beef
½ cup cooked rice
1 small onion, chopped fine
1 large egg, beaten
½ teaspoon salt

¼ teaspoon black pepper
½ teaspoon cinnamon, divided
1 can (10 ½ ounces) condensed
    tomato soup, undiluted
2 cans (14.5 ounces each)
    whole tomatoes

1. Cut the core out of the cabbage and carefully cut off the leaves, keeping them as large as possible. **Blanch** the leaves in a pot of boiling water for about 5 minutes, or until pliable. Drain and run cold water over the leaves. Cut out the large center veins of the largest leaves to make them easier to roll up.
2. Combine the ground beef, rice, chopped onion, beaten egg, and salt and pepper. **Blend** with hands or a wooden spoon. Stir in ¼ teaspoon of the cinnamon.
3. Shape a few tablespoons of the meat mixture into a round or cylindrical shape and place on a cabbage leaf. Roll the leaf up, keeping filling enclosed. Secure the roll with a toothpick and place in a Dutch oven or large kettle. Repeat with remaining meat mixture and cabbage leaves. I usually put the extra small or broken leaves in with the cabbage rolls, but you could save them for a soup or salad the next day.
4. Combine the tomato soup and tomatoes in a bowl with remaining ¼ teaspoon of cinnamon. Stir to blend ingredients, breaking up tomatoes. Pour the tomato mixture over the cabbage rolls. Bring to a boil over medium-high heat. Reduce heat to low; cover and simmer for about 1 ½ hours.

**WHAT'S HOT**

▶ Reminiscent of my mother's cabbage rolls, my beef and cabbage casserole is an easy and flavorful meal to make, with tomatoes, seasonings, and shredded Cheddar cheese. Check it out at http://about.com/southern food/beefcabbagecasserole.

## Barbecued Meatballs with Rice
SERVES 6 TO 8

*These tangy meatballs are just wonderful cooked with a flavorful home-made barbecue sauce and served over hot boiled rice.*

1 pound ground round or sirloin
1 pound mild bulk pork sausage
⅓ cup minced onion
2 eggs, lightly beaten
½ cup fine dry bread crumbs
1 teaspoon salt
¼ teaspoon freshly ground black pepper
½ teaspoon dried leaf sage, crumbled
¼ teaspoon garlic powder
1 ½ cups tomato ketchup
⅓ cup brown sugar, packed
3 tablespoons vinegar
3 tablespoons soy sauce
Hot cooked rice

1. Combine the ground beef, sausage, minced onion, egg, bread crumbs, salt, pepper, crumbled sage, and garlic powder.
2. Shape meat into 1 ½-inch meatballs. Put half of the meatballs in a large, nonstick skillet over medium-low heat. Cook the meatballs slowly, carefully turning to brown all sides. This will take about 12 to 18 minutes for each batch. Pour off excess fat.
3. In a bowl, combine the ketchup, brown sugar, vinegar, and soy sauce; mix until well blended. Transfer meatballs to a saucepan or Dutch oven. Pour sauce over the meatballs, mixing gently.
4. Cover and simmer for about 30 to 45 minutes, stirring occasionally to keep the meatballs coated.

## Beefy Macaroni Casserole
SERVES 6

*This is an easy and flavorful everyday family casserole.*

1 ½ pounds lean ground beef
1 cup celery, chopped
1 cup onion, chopped
1 clove garlic, minced
1 can (14.5 ounces) tomatoes
1 teaspoon Worcestershire sauce
1 scant teaspoon salt
¼ teaspoon freshly ground pepper
1 teaspoon ground chili powder
1 cup small shells or elbow macaroni
1 ½ cups shredded sharp Cheddar cheese
Shredded Cheddar cheese for topping, optional

1. Heat oven to 350°F. In a large skillet over medium heat, cook ground beef, celery, onion, and garlic. When onion is tender and ground beef is no longer pink, drain off excess fat and transfer meat mixture to a large bowl.
2. Meanwhile, cook the pasta in salted boiling water just until tender; drain and set aside.
3. To the meat mixture, add the tomatoes, Worcestershire sauce, salt, pepper, and chili powder. Stir in hot cooked pasta and the 1 ½ cups shredded Cheddar cheese.
4. Transfer mixture to a 2 to 2 ½-quart baking dish sprayed lightly with nonstick cooking spray. Bake for 30 minutes, until hot and bubbly. If desired, top with a little more shredded cheese and bake for about 5 minutes longer to melt cheese.
5. Serve with a tossed salad and crusty bread.

**WHAT'S HOT**

▶ Don't have chili powder? Here's an easy blend to use as a substitute: Combine 1 tablespoon paprika, 2 teaspoons ground cumin, 1 ½ teaspoons dried crumbled oregano, 1 teaspoon garlic powder, 1 teaspoon onion powder, ¼ teaspoon ground cayenne pepper, and a dash of ground allspice. Add a little more cayenne if you like more heat.

**What can I use to replace wine in a recipe?**

▶ Some dishes are more dependent on wine for flavor, but it can be replaced in many recipes. Nonalcoholic wine, though it's a bit sweeter, can be used, or you can use a broth that will go with the recipe—beef broth in a beef or lamb dish or chicken broth in a veal, pork, or poultry dish. Other possibilities include soaking liquid from dried tomatoes or mushrooms and vegetable broth. For marinades, use three parts grape or apple juice and one part vinegar or lemon juice to take the place of wine, using red or white juice, depending on the color of the wine you are replacing.

## Ground Beef and Noodle Skillet
SERVES 4

*Another one-dish family meal, this beef-and-noodle skillet is a favorite in my house—it's very quick and easy.*

1 pound lean ground beef
2 tablespoons butter
1 small onion, chopped
2 cloves garlic, minced
8 ounces mushrooms, sliced
¼ cup dry red wine
1 tablespoon lemon juice
1 can (10 ½ ounces) condensed beef broth
4 ounces uncooked wide noodles, about 2 cups
Salt and pepper
½ cup sour cream, or to taste
Paprika

1. In a skillet over medium-low heat, combine the ground beef, butter, onion, garlic, and sliced mushrooms. Cook, stirring and breaking up meat, until beef is no longer pink and vegetables are tender.
2. Add the wine, lemon juice, and beef broth to the beef mixture. Simmer for 10 minutes. Add noodles; cover and simmer for about 15 minutes, or until noodles are tender. Check occasionally and stir to make sure the mixture is not sticking to pan; add a little water as needed. Season the mixture with the salt and pepper and stir in sour cream, as desired. Heat through.
3. Sprinkle with paprika just before serving.

# Veal Chops Marsala

SERVES 4

*These veal chops make a wonderful choice for a special weekend meal. Serve with mashed potatoes and a vegetable side dish.*

1 tablespoon butter
3 tablespoons olive oil, divided
4 ounces mushrooms, sliced thin
4 green onions, sliced thin
1 clove garlic, minced
2 tablespoons all-purpose flour
¼ cup dry Marsala wine
1 ½ cups beef broth
Freshly ground black pepper
4 veal chops, each 1 inch thick
Salt and freshly ground black pepper

1. Heat oven to 375°F. In a heavy medium saucepan over medium-low heat, melt butter with 2 tablespoons of the olive oil. Add mushrooms and sauté until just tender. Add green onions and garlic; sauté for 1 minute. Add flour and cook, stirring, for about 30 seconds. Add the Marsala wine and beef broth. Continue cooking, stirring, until thickened and slightly reduced. Add a little fresh pepper; set aside.
2. Season both sides of the veal chops with salt and pepper.
3. Heat 1 tablespoon vegetable oil in a large ovenproof skillet over medium-high heat. Add the veal chops; sear for about 3 to 4 minutes on each side. Pour sauce over chops and move the skillet to the oven. Bake for about 15 to 20 minutes, until the chops are cooked to desired doneness. Arrange veal on a serving plate and spoon sauce over the chops.

**ASK YOUR GUIDE**

***What is the easiest way to make fluffy mashed potatoes?***

▶ For fluffy mashed potatoes, boil about 3 pounds of baking potatoes. When the potatoes are tender, drain well and put through a ricer. Mash the hot drained potatoes with about ⅓ cup of milk or half-and-half, 4 tablespoons of butter, and salt and pepper to taste.

**Can I substitute dry herbs for fresh herbs in a recipe?**

▶ Fresh herbs are often the best choice for flavor, but you'll still get great flavor with good dried herbs. Use about ⅓ the amount of herbs when substituting for fresh. Dried herbs do lose their strength over time, so it's a good idea to mark them with an expiration date when you first break the seal. As a general rule, herbs stored in an airtight container in a cool, dry place should retain their flavor for a year or longer, and ground spices should be good for about two years. It's always a good idea to check herbs and spices for fragrance and flavor; if you think they're lacking in either, replace them.

# Lemony Veal Cutlets with Mushrooms
SERVES 6

*This is a quick and easy dish to prepare, and it looks quite elegant. My family loves it with hot buttered noodles and a green vegetable, or you could serve the cutlets with hot cooked rice.*

1 ½ pounds thin veal cutlets
Salt and pepper
¼ cup flour
2 tablespoons olive oil
4 tablespoons butter, divided
8 ounces mushrooms, sliced
1 medium clove garlic, minced
Zest and juice of 1 lemon
1 teaspoon fresh rosemary, chopped
2 tablespoons fresh parsley, chopped
2 tablespoons dry white wine

1. Sprinkle cutlets with salt and pepper. Dredge veal in flour to coat lightly.
2. In a large skillet over medium heat, combine olive oil and 2 tablespoons of the butter. Add several veal pieces and sauté, turning once, until browned. Remove the browned veal from the skillet and repeat with remaining cutlets.
3. Add remaining 2 tablespoons of butter to the skillet. When butter has melted, add the sliced mushrooms and sauté until tender and golden brown. Return the veal cutlets to the skillet. Add the minced garlic, lemon zest and juice, rosemary and parsley, and the wine. Bring to a simmer. Cover and let simmer for about 3 minutes. Arrange veal cutlets on a serving plate and top with the mushrooms and lemon sauce.

## Savory Veal Stew with Vegetables
SERVES 4

*This mushroom-packed veal stew is delicious served over hot cooked rice.*

1 ½ pounds veal roast or stewing veal
2 tablespoons flour
1 ½ teaspoons salt
¼ teaspoon freshly ground black pepper
1 pound mushrooms, sliced
1 cup water
12 small white onions, peeled
1 pound baby carrots
1 ½ cups frozen peas
Hot cooked rice

1. Cut veal into bite-size cubes. Combine with the flour, salt, and pepper in a food storage bag; toss to coat well.
2. In a Dutch oven or large saucepan, heat oil over medium heat. Cook veal in 2 batches, turning frequently until browned on all sides. As the veal browns, transfer to a bowl.
3. Add mushrooms to the pan drippings and cook until browned and tender. Add more oil to the skillet if needed. Return the browned veal to the pan, and then add the water, onions, and carrots. Bring to a boil over high heat. Reduce heat to low; cover and simmer for about 1 hour, or until veal is tender. Stir in peas and cook for 10 to 15 minutes longer, or until peas are tender.
4. Arrange mounds of rice in individual shallow bowls or on plates. Spoon the veal stew over and around the mounds of rice.

**ELSEWHERE ON THE WEB**

▶ The About.com Italian Cuisine site offers a delicious recipe for veal stew with wine and peppers, also known as Spezzatino con i Peperoni. Visit http://about.com/italianfood/vealstew. On that same page, you'll also find links to several more veal recipes, along with recent additions and some of the most popular recipes on the site.

# Herb-Pecan Crusted Rack of Lamb

SERVES 2

*This is a delicious and elegant main dish for two, but you can also double the recipe to serve four people. I love rack of lamb with mashed potatoes and buttered green beans or wilted spinach.*

1 rack of lamb (about 8 chops)
2 teaspoons olive oil
Salt and pepper
1 ½ teaspoons dried rosemary leaves, crumbled fine
1 ½ teaspoons dried leaf oregano, crumbled
1 tablespoon fresh parsley, chopped
⅓ cup pecans, chopped fine
1 tablespoon Dijon mustard

1. Heat oven to 400°F.
2. Wash lamb; pat dry and cut between ribs into 2 equal portions. Rub the lamb with olive oil, salt, and pepper. Position the lamb, meaty side up, in a roasting pan. Roast for 12 minutes. Remove from the oven and let cool for 10 minutes.
3. Combine the herbs and the chopped pecans in a shallow bowl or plate. Rub mustard over the lamb, then coat with pecan and herb mixture. Return to the oven and bake for about 10 minutes longer, or to desired doneness.

## Spring Lamb Stew with Okra

SERVES 4

*The flavors of okra and tomatoes complement each other and enhance this lamb stew beautifully.*

1 pound frozen sliced okra
¼ cup white vinegar
3 tablespoons olive oil
1 ½ pounds lean lamb, cut in small cubes
1 medium onion, chopped
1 teaspoon salt
½ teaspoon freshly ground black pepper
¼ teaspoon ground cumin
Dash garlic powder
1 can (14.5 ounces) tomatoes with juice
1 can (8 ounces) tomato sauce
2 tablespoons fresh lemon juice

1. Thaw okra and place in a bowl; pour vinegar over and let stand for about 25 minutes. Drain and rinse okra under cold water.
2. Meanwhile, heat the olive oil in a large saucepan or Dutch oven over medium heat; add the cubed lamb and chopped onion. Sauté the lamb and onion, stirring frequently, until both are browned.
3. Sprinkle lamb and onion with the salt and pepper. Add cumin, garlic powder, tomatoes, tomato sauce, and lemon juice, and the prepared okra. Reduce heat to low; cover and simmer for about 1 hour or until lamb is tender.
4. Serve with hot cooked rice and a salad.

**TOOLS YOU NEED**

▶ A rice cooker is the easiest way to make perfect rice, but if you don't have one, you can cook rice using an old fashioned tool: the stovetop. Use 2 cups of water for each cup of long-grain rice. Bring water to a boil and add the rice, along with 2 to 3 teaspoons of butter, if desired, and about ½ teaspoon salt. Cover and simmer over low heat for about 15 minutes, or until water has been absorbed. Remove from heat and let stand, covered, for about 10 minutes. Fluff with a fork just before serving.

## Garlic-Roasted Leg of Lamb

SERVES 6

*This is a wonderful roasted leg of lamb with garlic and herbs, perfect for Sunday dinner or a family holiday meal.*

1 bone-in leg of lamb, about 6 pounds
2 tablespoons lemon juice
2 cloves garlic, minced
1 ½ teaspoons dried rosemary, crumbled
1 teaspoon dried leaf thyme, crumbled
1 teaspoon kosher salt
¼ teaspoon freshly ground black pepper
Lemon wedges

1. Heat oven to 325°F.
2. Rinse leg of lamb with cold water, and then pat dry. Rub lamb all over with the lemon juice.
3. Combine minced garlic, herbs, salt and pepper; rub all over the lamb.
4. Place the lamb, fat side up, on a rack in roasting pan. Insert a meat thermometer in thickest part of the roast without touching bone or fat. Roast for 20 to 25 minutes per pound. The lamb should register from 125°F to 145°F, depending on what degree of doneness you like. Remove lamb from the oven and let stand for 10 minutes before carving.
5. Arrange slices of lamb on a serving platter with lemon wedges.

**TOOLS YOU NEED**

▶ If you're going to be roasting meat on a regular basis, you'll probably want to have your own rack and roasting pan. If you don't have a rack, try this quick alternative. Cut a few carrots in half lengthwise, and cut a few ribs of celery in half crosswise. Place the halved carrots and celery pieces in the roasting pan, flat side down. Place the roast on top of the vegetables. When the cooking is done, just throw the vegetables away.

## Orange and Thyme Lamb Chops

SERVES 4

*Orange and thyme add great flavor to these lamb chops. Serve with mashed or baked sweet potatoes and leafy greens.*

4 shoulder lamb chops, about ¾-inch thick
½ teaspoon orange peel, grated fine
¼ cup fresh orange juice
½ teaspoon dried leaf thyme, crumbled
1 tablespoon olive oil
4 ounces sliced mushrooms

1. Trim the lamb chops. Combine orange peel, juice, and thyme. Pour over lamb chops and let stand for 4 hours in the refrigerator. Turn a few times to keep lamb chops coated with orange mixture. Drain lamb chops, reserving the orange marinade mixture.

2. In a large skillet over medium-high, heat 1 tablespoon olive oil; brown the lamb chops quickly on both sides. Reduce heat to medium-low; add the mushrooms and orange mixture. Cover and simmer for about 40 minutes, until lamb is tender. Uncover and simmer 5 minutes longer.

3. Arrange chops on a serving plate; spoon juices over them. Serve with baked or mashed sweet potatoes and a leafy green vegetable, if desired.

WHAT'S HOT

▶ I love sweet potatoes with lamb, and these baked sweet potatoes are easy and delicious. Brush each small to medium sweet potato with a little vegetable oil. Bake at 450°F, until tender. With a sharp knife, cut slits in the tops lengthwise and crosswise; open the sweet potatoes up a bit and top with butter and a sprinkling of salt and paprika or cinnamon sugar.

## Get Linked

*My Southern Food site on **About.com** has many more recipes using beef and lamb, including beef stews, oven and pot roasts, meatloaf recipes and burgers, casseroles, lamb roasts, and much more. Here are a few of the best links to related recipes.*

**THE POT ROAST**

There are a variety of ways to cook a pot roast, including braising and slow cooking, and the flavoring and seasoning possibilities are nearly endless. The pot roast is very adaptable, so don't hesitate to substitute with the ingredients and seasonings you have on hand. Here are several pot roast recipes:

 http://about.com/southernfood/potroastrecipes

**MEATLOAF RECIPES**

This is a list of dozens of meatloaf recipes, including some that are quick and easy, and many delicious flavor combinations. You'll also find several favorites from forum members:

 http://about.com/southernfood/meatloafrecipes

**TOP PICKS: GROUND BEEF**

Here are some of my favorite recipes using ground beef, along with some of the most popular on my site. Recipes include burgers, casseroles, meatballs, slow-cooker dishes, and more.

 http://about.com/southernfood/groundbeefrecipes

## Chapter 7

# Pork and Ham

**About.**

**ASK YOUR GUIDE:**

I've heard pork can harbor parasites, so it has to be cooked thoroughly. Should I cook pork a little longer just to be on the safe side?
▶ **PAGE 115**

Can I cook spareribs on the stovetop?
▶ **PAGE 118**

What kinds of apples are best for cooking, and which are best for eating raw?
▶ **PAGE 120**

What are grits?
▶ **PAGE 122**

How can I eliminate the floury taste from my sauces and gravies?
▶ **PAGE 123**

What is country ham?
▶ **PAGE 127**

## Herb and Garlic Roasted Pork Loin and Potatoes
SERVES 8

*This is a wonderful meal and so easy to prepare. I love the fact that the potatoes are roasted right along with the pork.*

1 boneless pork loin roast, about 4 pounds
1 medium clove garlic, minced
1 teaspoon onion powder
2 ½ teaspoons dried leaf thyme, crumbled
8 medium Yukon Gold potatoes, peeled and quartered
2 tablespoons olive oil
½ teaspoon garlic powder
2 teaspoons minced fresh or freeze-dried chives
Salt and freshly ground black pepper

1. Heat oven to 325°F.
2. Rub the pork roast all over with minced garlic, onion powder, and 1 ½ teaspoons of the dried thyme. Sprinkle with salt and pepper. Place in a shallow roasting pan and roast for 1 hour.
3. Meanwhile, peel and quarter the potatoes or cut in wedges. If desired, substitute 1 ½ to 2 pounds of small new potatoes or fingerlings. Cook the potatoes in boiling water for about 10 minutes. Drain and let cool slightly. In a large bowl, toss potatoes with the olive oil, the remaining 1 teaspoon of dried thyme, chives, and garlic powder; sprinkle with salt and pepper.
4. Arrange the potatoes around the pork loin roast and return to the oven. Roast for about 1 hour longer, or until pork registers 155°F to 160°F. Remove from oven and loosely cover with foil. Let rest for 15 minutes before slicing.
5. Slice pork and arrange on a serving platter with the potatoes.

**BEFORE YOU BEGIN**

▶ Here's another good herb blend that could replace the pork-rub mixture of rosemary and thyme. Combine 1 teaspoon each dried sage and parsley flakes and ½ teaspoon each rosemary and thyme. Fresh chopped parsley would also be very good tossed with the potatoes. If you're lucky enough to have fresh herbs, you can always use them in place of the dried herbs—just chop and double or triple amounts.

# Cajun-Seasoned Pork Tenderloin

SERVES 4

*This pork tenderloin is both easy and delicious, and it cooks up quickly. I love this with creamy butter beans or Creamy Lima Bean and Corn Succotash (page 180), along with mashed potatoes or sweet potatoes.*

2 pounds pork tenderloin
1 ¼ teaspoons salt
1 teaspoon garlic powder
½ teaspoon onion powder
½ teaspoon dried leaf thyme, crumbled
½ teaspoon dried leaf oregano, crumbled
½ teaspoon freshly ground black pepper
¼ teaspoon ground cayenne pepper, more or less

1. Cut pork tenderloins into 1-inch medallions (about sixteen). With the heel of your hand, gently flatten medallions slightly.
2. Combine remaining herbs and spices. Sprinkle over both sides of medallions, lightly rubbing the spices into both sides.
3. Using a stovetop grill pan or skillet, grill the medallions over medium-high heat for about 2 minutes on each side to sear or make nice grill marks. Lower heat to medium and cook for about 12 minutes longer, turning occasionally, until cooked through. Pork should register about 155°F on an instant-read thermometer.
4. Serve with sweet potatoes or mashed potatoes and a vegetable side dish.

**ELSEWHERE ON THE WEB**

▶ According to the National Pork Board, lean and delicious pork tenderloin is actually lower in calories than boneless skinless chicken breasts. Pork tenderloin makes a healthy alternative to beef and other cuts of pork, and judging by Internet searches, pork tenderloin has become a very popular meat. The National Pork Board Web site is a terrific resource where you'll find safety information, news, nutritional facts, and a great variety of recipes. Visit www.pork.org.

## Stuffed Crown Roast of Pork with Apples
SERVES 8

*A tasty stuffing of apple and dried cranberry complements this impressive roast. You might have to order this cut from your butcher or grocer ahead of time, so keep that in mind if you're planning a special dinner.*

2 tablespoons butter
½ cup minced onion
¼ cup celery, chopped
2 cups apple, diced
¼ cup dried cranberries or raisins, chopped
¼ cup brown sugar
¼ cup hot chicken broth or water
1 tablespoon fresh lemon juice
1 ½ teaspoons salt, or to taste
½ teaspoon dried leaf sage, crumbled
¼ teaspoon leaf thyme, crumbled
⅛ teaspoon freshly ground black pepper
Dash marjoram
4 cups bread cubes
1 crown roast of pork, 7 to 9 pounds

1. Heat oven to 325°F.
2. Spread bread cubes on a large baking sheet; put in the oven to dry and toast lightly.
3. Heat butter in a large skillet over medium-low heat. When butter is hot, add the chopped onion, celery, apple, and chopped cranberries or raisins. Cook the mixture, stirring frequently, for about 8 minutes, or until vegetables are tender.

*Stuffed Crown Roast of Pork with Apples (continued)*

4. Remove from heat and stir in the brown sugar, broth or water, lemon juice, salt, sage, thyme, and marjoram. Stir in the toasted bread cubes.

5. Place roast on a rack in a roasting pan. Scoop out any extra pork trimmings the butcher might have put in the center and carve out a little more so you'll have room for the stuffing. If desired, dice some of the leaner trimmings then brown and mix into the stuffing. (I cook the trimmings and freeze for stew or beans.)

6. Stuff the center of the roast, piling the stuffing in a mound. Cover stuffing with a piece of foil and wrap the ends of each bone with a small piece of foil.

7. Roast for 3 to 4 hours, or until the temperature registers about 175°F on a meat thermometer or instant-read thermometer. Insert the thermometer into a meaty section, trying not to touch bone or fat.

8. Remove foil and decorate tips of bones with white paper frills.

9. For a complete meal, serve with mashed potatoes or sweet potatoes, another vegetable side dish, and a tossed salad.

**TOOLS YOU NEED**

▶ Paper frills really dress up this roast for a special family dinner or holiday meal. You might find the frills at a kitchen or housewares store, or your butcher might be able to supply you with some. If these sources fail you, you could probably find them at an online kitchen resource. Here is a handy link with information on how you can make them at home: http://about.com/experts/cutletfrills.

# Roasted Pork Tenderloin with Rosemary
SERVES 4

*This is a delicious and light main dish made with only four ingredients, plus salt and pepper.*

2 pounds pork tenderloin
3 tablespoons fresh rosemary leaves
1 tablespoon olive oil
2 medium cloves garlic, halved
Salt and pepper, to taste

1. Heat oven to 400°F.
2. Line a large baking pan with foil; spray with nonstick cooking spray. Place the baking pan in the oven.
3. While pan is heating, trim pork, discarding excess fat. Using a sharp knife, **butterfly** the pork tenderloin. Cut tenderloin nearly in half lengthwise. Open, turn over, and cut each thick side nearly in half lengthwise. Pound the pork lightly with the palm of your hand to make the meat an even thickness.
4. Chop fresh rosemary. If using dried rosemary, use about 3 teaspoons and crumble. Rub the butterflied pork tenderloin all over with the garlic halves, then the olive oil. Sprinkle rosemary on both sides. Sprinkle with salt and pepper.
5. Place pork on the hot baking pan; return to the oven. Roast for about 20 minutes, or to about 155°F to 160°F on a meat thermometer or instant-read thermometer. Remove from the oven and let stand for about 5 minutes. Slice and serve with potatoes and a side vegetable or salad.

# Oven-Barbecued Pork Chops
SERVES 6

*Make the barbecue sauce in the morning and let these chops **marinate** while you're at work, then pop them in the oven when you get home.*

¾ cup tomato ketchup
¾ cup vinegar
1 ½ cups water
2 medium onions, 1 chopped fine and 1 sliced
1 clove garlic, minced
2 teaspoons salt
½ teaspoon pepper
2 teaspoons Worcestershire sauce
3 tablespoons light brown sugar
¼ teaspoon ground cayenne pepper
6 center-cut loin pork chops, about 1- to 1 ¼-inch thick

1. In a medium saucepan, combine the ketchup, vinegar, water, chopped onion, garlic, salt, pepper, Worcestershire sauce, brown sugar, and cayenne pepper. Bring to a boil. Reduce heat to low and simmer for about 15 minutes, stirring frequently. Let stand to cool slightly.
2. Rinse pork chops and pat dry. Place chops in a nonreactive bowl. Pour cooled sauce over the chops, turning to coat thoroughly. Cover and refrigerate for at least 3 hours, or all day.
3. Heat oven to 350°F. Arrange pork chops in a shallow baking dish. Top with sliced onion then pour sauce over all.
4. Bake for about 1 to 1 ½ hours, or until chops are tender, basting occasionally.
5. This would be delicious with boiled potatoes and Easy Fried Corn (page 183).

ASK YOUR GUIDE

*I've heard pork can harbor parasites, so it has to be cooked thoroughly. Should I cook pork a little longer just to be on the safe side?*

▶ There's really no need to overcook pork. Better pork production makes trichinosis quite rare these days, and an internal temperature of 155°F to 160°F will make pork perfectly safe. Use an instant-read thermometer to check pork chops, tenderloin, and other cuts, or a meat thermometer for pork roasts. Remember that the temperature will rise another 10 degrees or so over the 15 minutes you let it rest before carving.

## Cornbread Stuffed Pork Chops

SERVES 2

*This is great for a weekend meal or romantic dinner for two.*

2 bone-in loin pork chops, about 1- to 1 ¼-inch thick
Salt and pepper
3 tablespoons butter
¼ cup celery, chopped fine
¼ cup onion, chopped fine
1 tablespoon red bell pepper, chopped fine
¼ cup frozen corn kernels, thawed
1 cup cornbread crumbs, fresh or packaged
¼ cup pecans, chopped
¼ teaspoon dried leaf thyme, crumbled
Dash sage, crumbled
3 to 4 tablespoons chicken broth

1. Rinse pork chops; pat dry. Carefully cut a pocket into the meaty side of each pork chop, cutting to the bone. Sprinkle inside and out with salt and pepper; set chops aside.
2. In a saucepan, heat butter over medium-low heat; add the chopped celery, onion, and red bell pepper. Sauté the chopped vegetables until tender. Then add the corn, cornbread crumbs, pecans, thyme, sage, and enough chicken broth to moisten.
3. Heat oven to 350°F. Spoon stuffing into the pockets of chops. Set remaining stuffing aside. In a large skillet over medium heat, brown the pork chops, turning to brown both sides. If the skillet is not oven-safe, transfer to a baking dish. Push chops aside and spoon remaining stuffing in the middle of the skillet or baking dish. Position chops over the stuffing. Cover and bake for 25 to 35 minutes, or until pork chops are cooked through.

**WHAT'S HOT**

▶ Here's a recipe for spicy pork chops I really like, and they're packed with flavor. The ingredients include tomatoes, chile peppers, onions, herbs, and South-western seasonings. Check it out at http://about.com/southernfood/spicypork chops. Scroll down past the recipe to see links to many more pork chop recipes, including stuffed chops, oven pork chops, and some pork-chop casseroles and skillet combinations.

# Pork Chops with Orange Sauce

SERVES 6

*Pork and oranges or juice are very good together. I like the sweet orange flavor and the spices in this dish, and I usually serve it with rice and a vegetable side dish.*

6 pork chops, about 1 inch thick
Salt
2 tablespoons olive oil
½ cup all-purpose flour
2 navel oranges
3 tablespoons brown sugar
1 ½ tablespoons cornstarch
⅛ teaspoon allspice
1 ¾ cups water
3 tablespoons lemon juice
⅓ cup orange juice
¼ cup dried cranberries, chopped

1. Trim chops; sprinkle both sides with salt, then dredge in flour. Heat oil in a large skillet over medium heat; brown the pork chops on both sides. Section oranges and place a few sections on each chop.
2. In a medium saucepan, combine the brown sugar with cornstarch and allspice; stir in the water. Cook stirring, until thickened. Add the lemon juice, orange juice, and chopped dried cranberries. Pour sauce over the chops. Reduce heat to low; cover and simmer for 30 to 45 minutes, or until chops are tender.
3. Serve with hot cooked rice and green beans, if desired.

WHAT'S HOT

▶ You can use other cuts of pork in this recipe too! I like to use country-style ribs in this and other pork chop recipes. They're flavorful and meaty, and you can get them bone-in or boneless. You could also use pork steaks or lean tenderloin medallions in this recipe, and you could easily replace the dried cranberries with dried cherries, raisins, or other chopped dried fruit.

ASK YOUR GUIDE

**Can I cook spareribs on the stovetop?**

▶ Yes, after first broiling, you can simmer the spareribs on the stovetop over low heat, covered, for about 1 ½ hours. Or, cook them on the HIGH setting in the slow cooker for 3 to 4 hours. This recipe can easily be doubled for a crowd, and cooking instructions will remain the same.

## Slow-Cooker Spareribs
SERVES 4

*This main dish is designed to keep you out of the kitchen! Make these delicious ribs for visiting friends and relatives, parties, or potluck dinners.*

4 pounds pork spareribs, cut in serving-size pieces
Seasoned salt and freshly ground black pepper, to taste
1 large onion, quartered and sliced
1 bottle (16 ounces) barbecue sauce

1. Sprinkle ribs with seasoned salt and pepper; cut into smaller portions of about 3 to 4 ribs each, slicing between the ribs. Place on the oiled rack of a foil-lined broiler pan and broil about 4 inches from heat for 25 minutes. Turn ribs occasionally.
2. Transfer the spareribs to a 4- to 6-quart slow cooker along with the sliced onion and barbecue sauce. Cover and cook on LOW setting for 6 to 8 hours.
3. Serve with potato salad, beans, or other side dishes.

# Barbecued Ribs with Spicy Sauce

SERVES 6 TO 8

*These delicious ribs are oven-barbecued with a spicy homemade sauce.*

6 pounds pork spareribs, cut in serving-size portions
Salt and pepper
2 medium onions, sliced thin
1 tablespoon vinegar
1 tablespoon Worcestershire sauce
1 teaspoon salt
1 ½ teaspoons paprika
¼ to ½ teaspoon ground cayenne pepper
½ teaspoon freshly ground black pepper
1 ½ teaspoons chili powder
1 cup tomato ketchup
1 cup water

1. Heat oven to 350°F.
2. Cut racks of ribs into smaller portions of about 3 to 4 ribs each, slicing between the ribs. Sprinkle with salt and pepper. Place ribs in a roasting pan lined with heavy-duty foil. Cover with the sliced onions.
3. Combine remaining ingredients in a saucepan. Bring to a boil, stirring. Pour over ribs. Cover the roasting pan with foil and bake for about 1 ½ to 2 hours, or until very tender. **Baste** occasionally and turn spareribs a few times. Remove foil cover for the last 15 minutes to let the ribs brown.

**WHAT'S HOT**

▶ Here's a neat tip for the juiciest, most tender spareribs. Before cooking spareribs, remove the thin, cellophane-like skin from the back of the ribs. Put the ribs meaty side down, get your finger under the thin membrane then begin to pull it off. Repeat with remaining skin, loosening as much as possible with your finger before pulling. The ribs will be more tender and easier to cut.

**What kinds of apples
are best for cooking, and
which are best for eating
raw?**

▶ Some of the best baking or
cooking apples include Cortland, Gala, Golden Delicious,
Northern Spy, Rome Beauty,
Granny Smith, and Lady
Apple. The sweeter varieties include Golden Delicious
and Lady Apple, while the
rest tend to be on the tart
or tangy side. For eating,
some of the best apples are
Fuji, Red Delicious, Spartan,
Winesap, and McIntosh.

## Country-Style Pork Ribs with Apples
SERVES 4

*The sweet onions and apples are cooked slowly, but it's well worth it!*

| | |
|---|---|
| 1 large sweet onion | ½ cup all-purpose flour |
| 3 large apples | 1 teaspoon salt |
| 4 tablespoons butter | ¼ teaspoon freshly ground |
| 2 tablespoons honey | pepper |
| 2 tablespoons light brown sugar | ¼ teaspoon dried leaf thyme, |
| ½ teaspoon ground cinnamon | crumbled |
| 6 to 8 boneless country-style | 2 tablespoons olive oil |
| ribs | ¼ cup water or chicken broth |

1. Quarter the onion and slice it thin. Peel and core the apple, and slice it thin as well.
2. In a skillet or saucepan, melt about 2 tablespoons of the butter. Add the onion slices; sauté over medium-low heat until onion is yellow and tender. Add apple slices and remaining butter. Continue to cook, stirring frequently, until apples are yellowing and tender. Add the honey, brown sugar, and cinnamon. Continue cooking, stirring occasionally, until onions and apple are very tender and golden brown.
3. In a large food storage bag, combine the flour with 1 teaspoon salt, the pepper, and thyme. Add ribs a few at a time and shake well to coat with flour mixture.
4. Heat oil in a large, heavy skillet over medium heat. Add the country-style ribs and sear on all sides. Reduce heat, add ¼ cup water or chicken broth, and cover the skillet. Cook for about 25 minutes longer, until tender and cooked through.
5. Remove pork to a serving plate and serve with the apples and onions.

# Slow-Cooker Pork and Black Bean Stew

SERVES 8

*Serve with Southern Skillet Cornbread (page 24).*

1 ½ pounds lean pork
½ cup all-purpose flour
1 teaspoon chili powder
½ teaspoon salt
¼ teaspoon freshly ground
   black pepper
2 tablespoons olive oil
½ to 1 pound bulk pork sausage
1 large onion, chopped
1 can (10 ½ ounces) con-
   densed chicken broth
4 medium cloves garlic, minced

1 tablespoon parsley, chopped
¼ teaspoon dried leaf oregano
2 cans (15 ounces each) black
   beans, drained, rinsed
1 cup frozen corn kernels,
   thawed
1 red bell pepper, chopped
2 plum tomatoes, diced
1 teaspoon lemon juice
Salt and ground black pepper
Diced tomato and green onion,
   for garnish

1. Rinse pork; pat dry, then cut into small cubes. Set aside. In a food storage bag, combine the flour, chili powder, ½ teaspoon salt, and ¼ teaspoon pepper. Add the cubes and toss to coat.
2. In a large skillet, heat olive oil over medium heat. Add the coated pork to the skillet, along with any flour remaining in bag. Brown the pork cubes, stirring frequently. Transfer the browned pork to a 4- to 6-quart slow cooker.
3. Add pork sausage and onions to the same skillet and cook, stirring, until browned. Add to the slow cooker along with the condensed chicken broth and garlic. Cover and cook on LOW setting for 7 to 9 hours, or cook on HIGH setting for 3 ½ to 4 ½ hours. Add the parsley, oregano, black beans, corn, bell pepper, diced plum tomatoes, and lemon juice. Cover and cook on LOW for 1 ½ to 2 hours, or on HIGH setting for about 1 hour.

**TOOLS YOU NEED**

▶ Slow cookers come in several sizes and with many convenient features. The slow cooker is a wonderful way to cook tougher cuts of beef or pork for pot roasts or sandwiches, and slow-cooked stews are superb. Even if you don't use it often for family meals, you'll find that it comes in handy. You'll use it for keeping dips, meat-balls, and other appetizers warm at parties. You can also use a slow cooker to make a wonderful moist dressing for poultry, and it keeps your oven free for other holiday dishes. People also use them to caramelize onions over several hours and to cook spiced nuts—potatoes can even be wrapped in foil and "baked" in a slow cooker.

### What are grits?

▶ Hominy is made from corn, and the grits are ground from the hominy, using the same process used to make the finer masa harina flour. In fact, around Charleston, South Carolina, people call them "hominy grits." I often use quick grits, but whole-ground grits will have much better flavor if you can find them. Try the local natural foods store or an online source. If the grits are being used as a base for a main dish, such as Spicy Shrimp and Grits (page 160) or Grillades and Grits (page 86), you could substitute hot cooked rice in a pinch.

## Ham with Cheese Grits
SERVES 6

*I love this delicious ham-and-grits meal, and it's so easy to put together. Serve it with spinach or green beans for a complete dinner, or serve along with breads and other dishes as a brunch dish.*

1 ½ cups milk
1 ⅔ cups chicken broth
½ teaspoon salt
½ cup water
1 cup quick grits
3 tablespoons butter, divided
12 slices fully cooked ham (about 1 pound)
⅓ cup peach or apricot preserves
1 tablespoon cider vinegar
1 cup sharp Cheddar cheese

1. In a large saucepan, bring milk, chicken broth, salt, and water to a boil. Add 2 tablespoons butter and slowly whisk in grits. Reduce heat to low and cook, stirring frequently, for 15 to 20 minutes, until creamy. Cover and remove from heat; set aside.
2. Melt 1 tablespoon of butter in a skillet over medium high heat. Cook ham slices in batches, cooking for about 1 minute on each side. Remove to a warm platter and cover with foil. Set aside. To the skillet drippings, add the preserves and vinegar. Stir to blend well. Continue cooking, stirring, until reduced and slightly thickened. Pour over ham.
3. Add the shredded cheese to hot grits; stir until cheese is melted.
4. Serve grits with the sliced ham.

# Creamy Ham with Cornbread Wedges

SERVES 8

*This is a great combination of flavors, similar to an "a la king" type of dish. Bake fresh cornbread for this recipe, if you have the time.*

4 ounces mushrooms, sliced
4 tablespoons butter
4 tablespoons all-purpose flour
1 cup chicken broth, warmed
1 ½ cups half-and-half
Salt and pepper, to taste
1 cup cooked chicken, diced
2 cups cooked ham, diced
½ cup green bell pepper, chopped
¼ cup red bell pepper, chopped
Southern Skillet Cornbread (page 24)

1. Using a large skillet over medium-low heat, sauté the mushrooms in the butter until tender. Blend the flour into the mushroom mixture until well incorporated; cook for about 30 seconds.
2. Gradually add the chicken broth, half-and-half, and salt and pepper, stirring constantly. Continue cooking, stirring, until thickened and bubbly. Combine chicken, ham, and bell pepper; add to the sauce mixture. Taste and adjust seasonings. Heat thoroughly.
3. Serve over split wedges or squares of hot baked cornbread.

**ASK YOUR GUIDE**

*How can I eliminate the floury taste from my sauces and gravies?*

▶ One way to minimize the floury taste is to cook the flour and fat, stirring constantly, for 2 to 4 minutes before adding any liquid. Another solution is to toast the flour—you might want to toast a cup or so to keep on hand. Spread the flour on a baking sheet and cook in a 300°F oven for about 25 minutes. The flour will be lightly browned and makes a more flavorful addition to a basic sauce or gravy.

## Honey and Brown Sugar Glazed Ham
SERVES 10

*The honey and brown sugar make a flavorful **glaze** for this ham. You can also use maple syrup or sorghum in place of the honey.*

1 fully cooked ham, about 8 pounds
½ cup honey
½ cup light brown sugar
½ cup apple juice or apple cider
1 tablespoon plus 1 ½ teaspoons Dijon mustard
Dash cinnamon
Dash ginger
Whole cloves, optional

1. Heat oven to 325°F.
2. Line a roasting pan with foil. Place ham, fat-side up, on a rack in the foil-lined pan. **Score** fat in a diamond pattern and stud with several whole cloves, if desired. Bake for about 18 minutes per pound, or until the internal temperature reaches 148°F.
3. Meanwhile, in a saucepan, combine remaining ingredients; bring to a boil. Cook the glaze for about 2 minutes. Spoon half of the glaze over the ham about 20 minutes before the ham is done. Spoon the remaining glaze over the ham about 10 minutes before done.

## Glazed Cola Ham

SERVES 8

*This is a very popular way to cook ham, and I love to serve it with pine-apple slices, sweet potatoes, and green beans.*

1 fully cooked ham, about 7 pounds
2 teaspoons dry mustard
4 cups cola (not diet)
¾ cup light brown sugar, packed
1 ½ tablespoons Dijon mustard

1. Heat oven to 325°F.
2. Place ham, fat-side down, in a roasting pan. Pour the cola in the pan. Bake for about 18 minutes per pound, to an internal temperature of about 144°F, basting with the cola frequently.
3. Increase oven temperature to 350°F. Cut the rind from the ham. Combine brown sugar and mustards; spread the mixture over the ham. Place a rack in the roasting pan and lift ham onto it. Bake for 30 to 45 minutes longer, basting several times.
4. Remove ham from oven and let stand at room temperature for about 30 minutes before carving.

**ELSEWHERE ON THE WEB**

▶ This wonderful and unique baked ham recipe is from Home Cooking Guide Peggy Trowbridge. A large boneless ham is baked with dry champagne, honey, brown sugar, and spices. You can find the recipe at http://about.com/homecooking/bakedham. This extra-special ham would be perfect for a big family dinner or holiday meal.

## Ham and Rice Casserole

SERVES 6 TO 8

*This is a quick and easy dish to fix with leftover ham, and it's a delicious meal the whole family will enjoy.*

2 ½ cups hot cooked rice
2 ½ cups ham, diced
2 cups frozen mixed vegetables, cooked and drained
4 tablespoons butter
4 tablespoons flour
2 cups milk
1 cup shredded Cheddar cheese
Salt and pepper, to taste
1 cup soft bread crumbs
2 tablespoons melted butter
1 cup sliced mushrooms, optional

1. Heat oven to 325°F.
2. In a bowl, combine rice, ham, and cooked mixed vegetables.
3. In a medium saucepan, melt butter over medium-low heat. If you are using the sliced mushrooms, add and sauté until tender and golden brown. Blend in flour, stirring until hot and bubbly. Gradually stir in the milk. Cook the sauce, stirring constantly, until mixture is thickened. Stir in cheese until melted, and then add salt and pepper, to taste.
4. Stir the sauce into the rice, ham, and vegetable mixture. Transfer to a 2 ½-quart baking dish. Toss bread crumbs with the melted butter; sprinkle over the top of the casserole.
5. Bake for 30 minutes, or until hot and bubbly. If the bread crumbs aren't as brown as you like, turn on the broiler for about 2 minutes, just until browned.

**WHAT'S HOT**

▶ Like many casseroles, this one can be prepared in advance and frozen for up to two months. Just line your casserole dish with heavy duty foil. Prepare the casserole ingredients as directed, adding the mixture to the foil-lined baking dish. Once the casserole is frozen, grasp the overhanging foil, lift out of the casserole dish and then wrap completely with the foil. Label the casserole and include the current date. It will fit the same dish perfectly when you unwrap and get it ready to bake. You can thaw the casserole in the refrigerator, or if you don't thaw before cooking, double the baking time in a 350°F oven and check with a knife to make sure it's hot in the center.

# Ham with Red-Eye Gravy
SERVES 2

*This is a traditional Southern recipe, and the ham is delicious with grits and eggs. The name "red-eye" purportedly comes from what looks like a red eye in the center of the gravy.*

2 tablespoons butter
4 slices country ham, about ¼-inch thick
¾ cup coffee
¼ cup water

1. Melt butter in a skillet over medium-low to medium heat. Fry ham slices until browned on both sides. Remove ham to a platter; cut in serving-size pieces and keep warm.
2. To the same skillet, add the coffee and water. Bring to a boil and continue to boil for 2 to 3 minutes, until reduced slightly, stirring constantly.
3. Serve gravy with ham and hot cooked grits, along with eggs and other breakfast favorites.

ASK YOUR GUIDE

**What is country ham?**

▶ Country ham is a distinctly Southern product, and you might have trouble finding it outside of the South. Country ham is dry cured following federal guidelines that require at least 18 percent of the ham's weight to be lost during the curing and aging process, and the ham must contain at least 4 percent salt. It's easy to see why country ham is stronger in flavor and saltier than the conventional wet-cured ham. Country hams are time-consuming to soak then cook, but most producers offer ready-to-eat country hams and slices.

## Baked Ham and Pineapple Slices with Raisins
SERVES 4

*This is an easy and tasty dish to make with sliced leftover ham or packaged ham slices. I love ham with sweet potatoes, but mashed potatoes are good with this meal as well.*

**ELSEWHERE ON THE WEB**

▶ Debra Weber's French-style ham and noodles looks absolutely delicious, and I've tucked it away in my own recipe files. The creamy ham casserole is made with mushrooms, zucchini, thin-sliced ham, cream, noodles, Parmesan cheese, and garlic and seasonings. Check out the recipe at http://about.com/frenchfood/hamnoodles.

8 slices cooked ham, about ½-inch thick
1 can (8 ounces) sliced pineapple, drained
½ cup raisins
1 cup pineapple juice
½ cup water
1 ½ tablespoons cornstarch
1 tablespoon cold water

1. Heat oven to 350°F.
2. Arrange 4 slices of ham in a baking dish. Top with pineapple slices then remaining 4 slices of ham.
3. In a saucepan over medium-low heat, combine the raisins, pineapple juice, and water. Bring to a simmer; simmer for 10 minutes. Combine cornstarch with cold water; stir into the hot mixture. Continue cooking, stirring, until thickened.
4. Pour sauce over ham slices and bake for 20 minutes.
5. Serve the ham and pineapple slices with sweet potatoes or mashed potatoes and a green vegetable.

# Ham Loaf with Mustard Glaze

SERVES 6

*What a tasty way to prepare leftover ham! Serve this delicious loaf with baked sweet potatoes and a creamy succotash.*

1 ½ pounds ground cooked ham
1 large egg
¾ cup fine dry bread crumbs
¼ cup onion, chopped fine
1 tablespoon fresh parsley, chopped
¾ cup evaporated milk
1 tablespoon prepared mustard
¾ cup brown sugar, packed
1 teaspoon mustard powder
¼ cup vinegar
1 small tomato, sliced, optional

1. Heat oven to 350°F.
2. In a large bowl, combine the ground ham, egg, bread crumbs, chopped onion, parsley, evaporated milk and prepared mustard. Blend well and shape into a loaf. Place in a 9" x 5" x 3" loaf pan.
3. Bake the loaf for 1 hour.
4. Meanwhile, in a saucepan, combine the brown sugar, mustard powder, and vinegar. Heat over medium-low heat, stirring, until sugar is dissolved; set aside. Pour over the ham loaf and bake for about 20 minutes longer. Top with tomato slices before serving, if desired.
5. Serve this loaf sliced, with leftover potatoes and other vegetables or canned candied sweet potatoes (often labeled "candied yams").

**TOOLS YOU NEED**

▶ It's great to have a meat grinder, but a food processor will do quite a good job of grinding ham. To grind the ham, process in the bowl of a food processor fitted with a metal blade, using pulse action until it is the consistency you're looking for. You can also use the food processor to grind other cooked and raw meats, including pork, which is especially helpful when you only need a small amount for a meatloaf or meatballs.

## Get Linked

*I have a wide variety of pork and ham recipes on my **About.com** site, including recipes using sausage, bacon, leftover ham, and other cuts of pork. Most are broken down into sections based on the cut of meat or method of cooking. Here are some links to more recipes and resources.*

**SAUSAGE RECIPES**

This index includes recipes using breakfast sausage, link sausage, smoked sausage, and a few recipes for homemade sausage. Among the recipes you'll find Sausage-Noodle Casserole, Sausage Spinach Soup, Sausage Stew, Homemade Chorizo, Beans and Knockwurst, and many more.

 http://about.com/southernfood/sausagerecipes

**PORK RECIPES**

This is the main pork index, where you can browse by the cut of pork or type of dish. You'll find dozens of recipes for slow-cooker pork, pork roasts, pork chops, spareribs, country-style ribs, pork tenderloin, stews, chili recipes, and sweet-and-sour pork recipes.

 http://about.com/southernfood/porkrecipes

**HAM RECIPES**

I have a big variety of ham recipes on my site, including baked ham recipes, ham casseroles, ham salads, soups, and ham sandwiches.

 http://about.com/southernfood/hamrecipes

Chapter 8

# Chicken and Turkey

## About

**ASK YOUR GUIDE:**

How do I thaw frozen chicken safely?
▶ **PAGE 135**

Is there an easy Creole seasoning I can make at home?
▶ **PAGE 136**

Can the chicken and dumplings be made without rolling the dough?
▶ **PAGE 139**

Can I replace the sherry with another wine?
▶ **PAGE 142**

Is there a way I can make my own poultry seasoning?
▶ **PAGE 147**

## Southern Fried Chicken with Cream Gravy
SERVES 4 TO 6

*This is truly one of the rock stars of Southern cooking, and it's a dish that people around here like to talk about. This is a typical fried-chicken recipe, but there are many, many variations. You'll even find a few great cookbooks devoted to fried chicken from the South and other areas of the country.*

4 to 5 pounds chicken parts
2 eggs
2 cups milk
2 ½ cups all-purpose flour
1 tablespoon plus 1 ½ teaspoons salt, divided
2 teaspoons ground black pepper
½ teaspoon ground paprika
2 to 3 cups canola oil or shortening
2 tablespoons flour
1 cup chicken broth
1 cup half-and-half or whole milk
Salt and pepper

1. Rinse chicken with cold water and trim excess loose skin and fat; pat dry and set aside.
2. Heat oil or melt shortening in a large, deep skillet with a heavy bottom and a cover. Oil is ready when it registers 350°F. Watch carefully for overheating.
3. Meanwhile, in a large bowl, whisk together the eggs and milk.
4. Combine the flour, 2 tablespoons salt, and pepper in a large food storage bag.

*Southern Fried Chicken with Cream Gravy (continued)*

5. Dip a few chicken pieces in the milk mixture then drop in the bag and shake gently to coat thoroughly.

6. Working with about 4 pieces of chicken at a time, place in the hot oil. Cover and fry for 5 minutes. Uncover, fry for 5 more minutes on that side, then turn and fry the other side for about 10 minutes. Depending on thickness and whether the meat is white or dark, the time could vary a bit. White meat generally takes less time. Check a few pieces of chicken by cutting into the meat to see if juices run clear. Remove chicken to paper-towel–lined plate to drain; sprinkle with salt and keep warm. Repeat with remaining chicken pieces.

7. Carefully pour all but 2 tablespoons of the oil into a metal bowl or another pan; set it aside to cool before discarding. Place the skillet with 2 tablespoons of oil over medium heat; stir in flour, stirring up the browned bits in the bottom of the skillet. Cook the flour and oil, stirring, for about 30 seconds. Gradually stir in the chicken broth and half-and-half. Cook the gravy mixture, stirring constantly, until thickened and bubbly. Season the gravy with salt and pepper, to taste. If desired, strain before serving with the fried chicken.

**BEFORE YOU BEGIN**

▶ If you haven't done deep frying, think about safety. You should use long tongs or a long-handled slotted spoon to turn and move the chicken, and you might want to wear gloves and an apron while working near the skillet to save your skin and clothing from grease spatters. Always keep the handle of the skillet or pan to the side where it won't get bumped. A class ABC fire extinguisher is a good thing to have in the kitchen. In a pinch, slipping the lid on the skillet or dousing with baking soda will put a grease fire out, so keep a box handy. Never use water on a grease fire, as it will only make it spread. Let the fat cool thoroughly before moving to another container.

**ELSEWHERE ON THE WEB**

▶ I love to use lean chicken tenders or boneless chicken breasts wherever I can. This chicken quesadilla recipe is just the kind of dish you'd want to make for a party or friendly get-together. Chicken tenders are marinated then grilled with onion and eggplant. The grilled chicken and vegetables are assembled in warm tortillas with shredded cheese, and then the quesadillas are cut and served with sour cream. Here's the recipe, from Derrick Riches, the About.com Guide to Barbecues and Grilling: http://about.com/bbq/chickquesadilla

## Fried Chicken Strips
SERVES 4 TO 6

*These flavorful and spicy chicken strips are absolutely amazing with Come Back Sauce (page 205) or a sweet-and-sour sauce. Time these carefully so they'll be cooked through but still juicy.*

1 to 1 ½ pounds boneless chicken breast
1 ½ cups low-fat buttermilk
1 ½ teaspoons salt, divided
3 teaspoons Creole or Cajun seasoning, divided
2 cups all-purpose flour
½ teaspoon freshly ground pepper
2 cups canola oil
Salt

1. Rinse chicken and pat dry with paper towels. Cut into strips about 1 to 1 ½ inches in width.
2. In a large container or heavy-duty food storage bag, combine the buttermilk, 1 teaspoon of salt, and 2 teaspoons of the Creole seasoning. Add the chicken strips; seal the bag and refrigerate for 2 to 8 hours. When almost ready to cook, heat oil in a deep skillet over medium heat to about 350°F.
3. Meanwhile, combine the flour and remaining 1 teaspoon Creole seasoning, ½ teaspoon salt, and the freshly ground black pepper in a large food storage bag. Put the chicken strips in the bag, a few at a time, and shake the bag gently to coat thoroughly.
4. Fry several chicken strips at a time, turning a few times with tongs, until deep golden brown, or about 6 to 8 minutes for each batch. Serve with Come Back Sauce (page 205), fries, and a salad or slaw.

## Oven-Barbecued Chicken

SERVES 6

*I usually make this with chicken breasts, but you can use legs or leg quarters, thighs, or a combination of parts.*

5 pounds bone-in chicken parts
1 cup tomato ketchup
⅓ cup vinegar
Juice of 1 lemon
2 tablespoons onion, grated, optional
2 tablespoons Worcestershire sauce
⅓ cup light brown sugar
1 ½ teaspoons salt
½ teaspoon celery salt
2 teaspoons prepared mustard
Dash garlic
1 teaspoon paprika

1. Heat oven to 350°F.
2. Wash chicken pieces; pat dry with paper towels. Arrange in a baking dish. Bake the chicken for 45 minutes.
3. Meanwhile, in a medium saucepan, combine the remaining ingredients. Cook the sauce over low heat, stirring occasionally, for 10 minutes. Set aside.
4. Pour the sauce over the chicken, brushing and turning the pieces to coat thoroughly. Bake for about 45 to 60 minutes longer, or until juices run clear when chicken is pierced with a fork. Chicken breasts will generally take less time than smaller pieces and dark meat, and time will vary depending on the size of the pieces.

ASK YOUR GUIDE

***How do I thaw frozen chicken safely?***

▶ The best, safest way to thaw frozen chicken is on a plate in the refrigerator. The refrigerator temperature is usually about 40°F, and this helps minimize the chance of harmful bacteria developing and growing. The plate will help keep juices from dripping onto other foods. Be sure to keep raw poultry from touching foods that you will be eating raw, such as salad ingredients or fruit.

**Is there an easy Creole seasoning I can make at home?**

▶ Creole seasoning is easy to make at home, and you can control the heat level and adjust the other seasonings to suit your own tastes and needs. Combine 1 tablespoon each of onion and garlic powder, 1 tablespoon dried oregano, 2 teaspoons dried thyme, 2 teaspoons black pepper, 1 to 2 teaspoons ground cayenne, 2 tablespoons of paprika, and 1 ½ tablespoons of salt. Blend the seasonings well and store in an airtight container or jar. This will make about ½ cup.

# Chicken with Cajun Cream Sauce
SERVES 6

*Use a stovetop grill pan or skillet to make this tasty chicken recipe. I serve this delicious and rich spicy chicken over fresh fettuccine or linguine.*

6 boneless, skinless chicken breasts
2 teaspoons Creole seasoning
2 teaspoons olive oil
2 ½ cups whipping cream
3 teaspoons flour
3 teaspoons butter
Several drops hot sauce
Dash ground black pepper
½ teaspoon Worcestershire sauce
Salt, to taste
1 large tomato, seeded and diced
6 green onions, sliced thin
1 pound fettuccine or linguine

1. Trim the chicken, rinse, and pat dry. Put chicken between pieces of plastic wrap and flatten slightly to an even thickness.
2. Sprinkle chicken all over with the 2 teaspoons of Creole seasoning.
3. Heat 2 teaspoons of oil in a stovetop grill pan or skillet over medium-high heat. Sear chicken for about 2 minutes on each side. Reduce heat to medium and continue to cook, turning, for about 5 minutes longer.
4. In a medium saucepan over medium-high heat, bring the cream to a boil. Reduce heat to medium-low; simmer the cream for about 4 minutes. Blend the flour with butter until smooth. Whisk the flour mixture into the cream. Add the hot sauce, pepper, Worcestershire sauce, and salt, to taste. Taste and adjust seasoning.
5. Cook pasta and arrange on serving plates. Slice chicken and arrange on the pasta. Spoon a little sauce over each serving, then sprinkle with diced tomatoes and green onions.

# Skillet Chicken Breasts with Mushrooms
SERVES 6

*Serve this dish with Savory Rice Pilaf with Green Onions (page 169).*

6 boneless chicken breast
   halves, without skin
⅔ cup all-purpose flour
½ teaspoon salt
¼ teaspoon freshly ground
   black pepper
¼ teaspoon ground paprika
2 tablespoons olive oil
1 to 2 tablespoons butter

8 ounces sliced mushrooms
4 to 6 green onions, sliced
1 clove garlic, minced
Juice of 1 lemon (about 3
   tablespoons)
¼ cup chicken broth
1 tablespoon fresh parsley,
   chopped

1. Wash chicken and pat dry. Place a chicken breast half between 2 sheets of plastic wrap; pound gently until even in thickness. Repeat with remaining chicken pieces.
2. In a food storage bag, combine the flour, salt, pepper, and paprika. Add chicken pieces, a few at a time, and toss to coat thoroughly.
3. In a large skillet, heat the olive oil and 1 tablespoon of the butter over medium heat. Sauté chicken breasts for about 3 to 4 minutes on each side, or until cooked through. Remove to a warm platter; cover with foil and keep warm.
4. To the same skillet, add mushrooms. Sauté the mushrooms for 3 to 4 minutes, until tender and browned. Add green onions and minced garlic and sauté for about 1 minute longer. Add the lemon juice and chicken broth; simmer for about 2 minutes longer. Return the chicken to the skillet and bring back to a simmer. Simmer for about 1 minute longer.
5. Arrange chicken breasts on a serving plate then top with mushrooms and juices. Sprinkle with parsley.

**WHAT'S HOT**

▶ Parsley and basil, as well as other fresh herbs, can be bought in bulk and frozen to use in place of fresh herbs in cooked dishes. I often buy larger amounts of basil and chives to freeze. You can freeze a few sprigs in an airtight container or freezer wrap, or spread cleaned, dried, and chopped or sliced herbs on a cookie sheet and put the whole cookie sheet in the freezer. When the herbs are frozen, pack them in small, airtight containers with labels. Frozen herbs might not have the texture for a garnish, but they can be used in cooked dishes. When using frozen herbs, use the same proportion as fresh herbs.

## Chicken and Dumplings
SERVES 6 TO 8

*Every Southern cook has her own personal recipe for chicken and dumplings. Some prefer rolled dumplings, many pinch off pieces of dough, and some use a quick and easy biscuit mix dough. I like the rolled dough, and this is one of my favorite versions.*

1 chicken or chicken pieces, about 4 ½ to 5 ½ pounds
4 cups water
4 cups chicken broth
½ teaspoon salt
¼ teaspoon ground black pepper
½ teaspoon dried leaf thyme
2 carrots, cut in chunks
2 ribs celery, cut in chunks
1 medium onion, cut in chunks
2 cups flour
3 tablespoons shortening
½ teaspoon baking soda
½ teaspoon salt
¾ cup buttermilk
1 cup milk
2 to 4 tablespoons butter

*Chicken and Dumplings (continued)*

1. Wash chicken and pat dry. Place in a large stockpot; add water and chicken broth. Add the ½ teaspoon salt, ¼ teaspoon pepper, thyme, carrots, celery, and onion. Bring to a boil. Reduce heat to medium-low and simmer for about 60 to 75 minutes, or until chicken is very tender.
2. Remove chicken to a large bowl and set aside to cool. Strain broth into another bowl, then pour back into the stockpot, discarding the solids.
3. Combine the flour, baking soda, and ½ teaspoon salt. With a pastry blender or 2 knives, cut shortening into the dry ingredients until the mixture resembles a coarse meal. Stir in buttermilk just until dough clumps together. Turn out onto a floured surface and knead about 5 times. Roll the dough out to about ⅛-inch thickness and cut into 3- x 1-inch strips or squares. Use a sharp knife or a pizza cutter.
4. Meanwhile, bring the chicken broth to a boil. Stir in 1 cup milk and the butter. Taste and add more salt and pepper, if needed.
5. Drop the dumplings, a few at a time, into the boiling chicken broth. Reduce heat to medium low and continue to simmer for about 10 minutes, stirring occasionally.
6. Meanwhile, remove cooled chicken from bones and cut into pieces. Add the chicken pieces to the simmering broth and heat through.

**ASK YOUR GUIDE**

*Can the chicken and dumplings be made without rolling the dough?*

▶ My family likes the rolled dumplings, but you can use the same dough to make pinched and dropped dumplings. Instead of rolling the dough, pat it down to a ¼-inch thickness. Pinch off 1-inch pieces and drop into the boiling broth. If you're short on time, try using thawed frozen biscuits in place of the homemade dough. Just pat them to flatten slightly, pinch off 1-inch pieces, and drop into the boiling broth.

## Chicken-and-Rice Bake

SERVES 4 TO 6

*This dish is frequently made with cream of mushroom or cream of chicken soup, but I like to make a homemade sauce with the chicken broth.*

3 to 4 boneless chicken breast halves, rinsed and patted dry
1 ½ cups chicken broth
½ teaspoon seasoned salt
Dash ground black pepper
4 tablespoons butter
½ cup chopped celery
1 medium onion, chopped
4 tablespoons all-purpose flour
1 cup milk
Salt and pepper, to taste
2 ½ cups cooked rice
1 cup fresh bread crumbs
2 tablespoons melted butter

1. Place the chicken breasts in a saucepan with the chicken broth, seasoned salt, and a dash of pepper. Bring to a boil; reduce heat to medium-low, cover, and simmer for 20 to 30 minutes, until cooked through. With a slotted spoon, remove the chicken breasts to a plate. Cover loosely with foil and let cool.
2. Heat oven to 350°F.
3. Strain the broth into a large cup or small bowl; set aside. In the same saucepan, melt the butter. Over medium-low heat, sauté the chopped celery and onion until tender. Stir in the flour until well blended. Gradually stir in the reserved chicken broth and milk. Cook the sauce, stirring constantly, until thickened and bubbly. Taste and add salt and pepper, as needed.
4. Chop the cooled chicken into bite-size pieces. Add the chicken to the sauce mixture along with the cooked rice. Spoon the chicken and rice mixture into a 2-quart casserole dish.
5. Toss bread crumbs with melted butter; sprinkle over the casserole. Bake for 30 to 40 minutes, or until hot and bubbly, and bread crumbs are lightly browned.

**ELSEWHERE ON THE WEB**

▶ Chicken and rice go together beautifully, and the variations are endless. Here's a flavorful Chicken Fried Rice from Chinese Cuisine Guide Rhonda Parkinson: http://about.com/chinesefood/chickfriedrice. As you scroll down this page, you'll see fried-rice cooking tips, along with links to similar recipes.

## Chicken Noodle Casserole

SERVES 4

*This is another one of my favorites, and it makes a terrific family meal.*

4 ounces medium egg noodles
4 tablespoons butter
8 ounces mushrooms, sliced
2 ribs celery, sliced thin
1 medium onion, chopped
4 tablespoons flour
1 teaspoon salt
¼ teaspoon freshly ground
   black pepper

½ teaspoon dried leaf thyme
1 ½ cups milk
½ cup chicken broth
2 cups cooked chicken, diced
¼ cup dry white wine or
   chicken broth
¾ cup fine fresh bread crumbs
2 tablespoons melted butter
2 tablespoons parsley, chopped

1. Cook noodles in boiling salted water, following package directions, until just tender. Drain and set aside.
2. Heat oven to 400°F.
3. In a large saucepan over medium-low heat, melt butter. Add the sliced mushrooms, onion, and celery. Sauté for about 5 minutes or until the vegetables are tender. Stir flour into the mixture until well blended. Add salt, pepper, and thyme. Gradually stir in milk and chicken broth. Continue to cook, stirring constantly, until thickened and bubbly. Add the diced chicken, wine or broth, and the cooked noodles. Simmer for 1 minute.
4. Spoon the chicken and noodle mixture into a 2-quart baking dish. Combine the bread crumbs with melted butter and parsley; sprinkle over the casserole.
5. Bake for 20 to 25 minutes, until hot and bubbly.

**Can I replace the sherry with another wine?**

▶ Sherry is a fortified Spanish wine, and it can add nice flavor to creamy sauces and soups. For dry to medium-dry sherry, substitute dry vermouth, sake, or dry white wine with a pinch of sugar. If you would like to avoid alcohol altogether, feel free to add more chicken broth to replace the sherry.

## Southern Creamed Chicken with Biscuits
SERVES 6 TO 8

*This dish is perfect for a party or family get-together. I love this creamed chicken on biscuits, but it's wonderful over rice or baked puff pastry shells.*

3 tablespoons butter
8 ounces fresh mushrooms, sliced
3 tablespoons red bell pepper, minced
¼ cup green onion, sliced thin
4 tablespoons all-purpose flour
1 teaspoon salt
⅛ teaspoon freshly ground black pepper
1 ½ cups half-and-half
2 tablespoons sherry
2 cups chicken broth
3 cups cooked chicken, diced
Hot split and buttered biscuits

1. In a large saucepan, melt butter over medium-low heat. Add the mushrooms; sauté for about 3 minutes, or until tender. Add the red bell pepper and green onion and sauté for about 2 minutes longer. Blend in the flour, salt, and pepper.
2. Gradually stir in the chicken broth and sherry. Stir in half-and-half. Continue to cook over low heat, stirring constantly, until mixture is thickened and bubbly. Cook for about 1 minute longer. Add the chicken and heat through.
3. Serve the creamed chicken over hot Perfect Buttermilk Biscuits (page 26), allowing 1 or 2 biscuits for each serving.

# White Chicken Chili
SERVES 6

*I like to serve this dish with hot, fresh-baked cornbread or corn muffins.*

1 ½ pounds boneless chicken breasts
1 tablespoon vegetable oil
2 cups onion, chopped
4 cloves garlic, minced
1 jalapeño pepper, seeded and minced
2 teaspoons ground cumin
1 can (4 ounces) chopped mild green chile peppers
2 cans (14.5 ounces each) diced tomatoes with their juice
2 cans (15 ounces each) Great Northern beans
Juice of 1 small lime
2 cups fresh or frozen corn kernels, thawed if frozen
Salt and freshly ground black pepper, to taste
2 tablespoons fresh cilantro, chopped, optional
½ to ¾ cup sour cream
¼ cup green onion, chopped fine

1. Wash chicken and pat dry. Cut into 1-inch cubes. Set aside.
2. Heat vegetable oil in a saucepan over medium-high heat. Add onion and sauté until it begins to brown. Add garlic and sauté for about 30 seconds. Add the cubed chicken; cook, stirring, until chicken is browned on all sides. Add the minced jalapeño, cumin, chile peppers, and diced tomatoes. Drain and rinse beans; add to the mixture. Reduce heat and simmer for 5 minutes.
3. Add the lime juice and corn. Season the mixture with salt and pepper. Cook for 5 minutes longer. Stir in cilantro, if using.
4. Serve the chicken chili with a dollop of sour cream, a sprinkling of sliced green onion, and Southern Skillet Cornbread (page 24).

ELSEWHERE ON THE WEB

▶ Here's a fabulous recipe for White Chicken Chili from the Web site of Bon Appétit and Gourmet. This hearty version is made with mild green chile pepper, dried navy beans, and half-and-half, along with onions, shredded cheese, cumin, and other seasonings: www.epicurious.com/recipes/recipe_views/views/11452. Here's an easy five-ingredient slow-cooker chicken chili recipe from the About.com Busy Cooks site: http://about.com/busycooks/chickenchili.

## Savory Chicken Pot Pie

SERVES 6

*I like this with the pie crust topping, but it's great topped with biscuits, too. Feel free to substitute frozen mixed vegetables or baby lima beans for the frozen peas.*

4 pounds chicken parts
6 cups water
2 cups chicken broth
1 medium onion, cut in chunks
2 ribs celery, cut in large pieces
2 sprigs parsley
1 bay leaf
½ teaspoon dried leaf thyme
1 ½ teaspoons salt
⅛ teaspoon freshly ground black pepper
6 carrots, sliced
¼ cup flour
1 teaspoon salt
Dash freshly ground black pepper
½ cup milk
1 ½ cups frozen peas, thawed
Pastry for single-crust pie

*Savory Chicken Pot Pie (continued)*

1. Wash chicken and pat dry. In a large stockpot or Dutch oven, combine the chicken with the water, broth, onion, celery, parsley, bay leaf, thyme, 1 ½ teaspoons salt, and ⅛ teaspoon pepper. Bring to a boil over high heat; reduce heat to medium-low, cover, and simmer for about 1 ½ hours, or until chicken is very tender.
2. Remove chicken and strain the broth into a bowl. Return 2 cups of the strained broth to the pot. Refrigerate or freeze the remaining broth for another use. Add the carrots to the pot. Cover and simmer until carrots are tender.
3. Meanwhile, when chicken is cool enough to handle, remove meat from bones and chop. Place the chicken in a 2-quart baking dish.
4. In a cup or small bowl, combine the flour, 1 teaspoon salt, a dash of pepper, and the ½ cup milk. Whisk until smooth. Stir flour mixture into the stock with carrots, and then add the thawed peas. Bring to a boil, stirring constantly. Reduce heat to low and simmer until peas are tender.
5. Pour the sauce and vegetables over the chicken in the baking dish. Gently stir to combine ingredients.
6. Heat oven to 425°F.
7. Prepare crust; roll out to fit the baking dish with a ½-inch overhang. Turn edge under, seal, and crimp the edge. With a sharp knife, cut several vents in the top so steam can escape.
8. Bake the chicken pot pie for 20 minutes, or until crust is browned and filling is hot and bubbly.

**TOOLS YOU NEED**

▸ A food processor makes basic pie crust preparation a breeze. Put 1 cup of all-purpose flour and ¼ teaspoon of salt in the bowl of the food processor fitted with a metal blade. Cover and pulse a few times to combine. Add ¼ cup of cold shortening; pulse five times. With the processor running, slowly add ¼ cup of ice water to the mixture just until a ball of dough forms and begins to leave the sides of the processor. Chill for 30 minutes before rolling.

# Roast Turkey with Currant Jelly Glaze
SERVES 6 TO 8

*Serve with Giblet Gravy (page 201) and Home-Style Cornbread Dressing (page 171), if desired.*

(page 201)

| | |
|---|---|
| 1 turkey, 12 to 14 pounds | ½ cup red currant jelly |
| Vegetable oil | 2 tablespoons red wine or water |
| Salt and pepper | ¼ teaspoon ground black pepper |
| 2 tablespoons cold butter, optional | ½ teaspoon cinnamon |
| | ¼ teaspoon allspice |

1. Wash turkey inside and out. Remove the giblets to a bowl; reserve for Giblet Gravy (page 201). Rub vegetable oil all over the turkey. Sprinkle the turkey inside and out with salt and pepper. Cut the butter into pieces, if using. With fingers or the handle of a wooden spoon, loosen the skin over the breast of the turkey, and slide pieces of butter under the skin of the turkey.

2. Heat oven to 325°F. Place turkey, breast side up, on a lightly oiled rack in a shallow roasting pan. Fold the wings under the turkey and secure the drumsticks with twine if they are not already secured. Butter a piece of foil and place it, buttered-side down, over the breast of the turkey. Roast the turkey for 1 hour. Remove foil and roast until an instant-read thermometer registers 180°F when inserted deep in the thigh. The total roasting time will be about 3 to 3 ½ hours.

3. In a saucepan, combine the currant jelly, wine or water, coarsely ground black pepper, and spices. Bring to a boil, stirring constantly. Brush on the turkey about 20 minutes before done. If turkey begins to brown too much, cover again with lightly buttered foil. Turn oven off when turkey is done and cover with foil. Let rest for about 20 minutes. Remove from oven and carve.

## Turkey and Rice Casserole

SERVES 4

*This is a fantastic way to use leftover roast turkey, and it's easy to put together.*

¼ cup butter
1 cup mushrooms, sliced
¼ cup green onion, sliced thin, optional
¼ cup all-purpose flour
1 ¼ cups chicken broth
½ cup dry white wine or more broth

1 tablespoon parsley, chopped
¼ teaspoon poultry seasoning
1 cup sharp Cheddar cheese, shredded
2 cups cooked long-grain white rice
2 cups cooked turkey, diced
Salt and pepper
Ground paprika

1. Heat oven to 375°F. Spray a shallow 2- to 2 ½-quart baking dish with nonstick cooking spray.
2. In a large saucepan, melt butter over medium-low heat. Add sliced mushrooms and sauté until tender. Add green onion and sauté for about 30 seconds longer. Stir in flour until well blended. Gradually stir in chicken broth and the wine. Continue to cook, stirring constantly, until thickened and bubbly.
3. Stir in the parsley, poultry seasoning, and half of the cheese. Continue to cook, stirring, until cheese is melted. Add the rice and diced turkey. Season the mixture with salt and pepper, to taste.
4. Pour the turkey and rice mixture into the prepared baking dish. Sprinkle remaining shredded cheese over the top and sprinkle with paprika.
5. Bake for 25 to 30 minutes, until hot and bubbly.

ASK YOUR GUIDE

**Is there a way I can make my own poultry seasoning?**

▶ You probably already have all the ingredients you need to make your own home-made poultry seasoning. To make about 1 tablespoon of poultry seasoning, combine 1 ½ teaspoons dried crumbled sage, ½ teaspoon dried crumbled thyme, ½ teaspoon freshly ground black pepper, a dash of dried crumbled rosemary, and about ¼ teaspoon dried marjoram.

## Turkey Cutlets with Creamy Mushroom Sauce
SERVES 6

*Turkey cutlets are low in fat, and I often use them in a recipe in place of chicken or veal.*

6 turkey cutlets, about 1 ½ pounds
⅔ cup flour
1 teaspoon salt
¼ teaspoon freshly ground black pepper
½ teaspoon ground paprika
1 tablespoon olive oil
2 tablespoons butter, divided
8 ounces fresh mushrooms, sliced
1 ½ cups chicken broth
½ cup dry white wine
½ teaspoon dried rosemary, crumbled
1 tablespoon fresh parsley, chopped
Dash garlic powder
2 tablespoons flour
2 tablespoons cold water
½ to 1 cup heavy cream

*Turkey Cutlets with Creamy Mushroom Sauce (continued)*

1. Put a turkey cutlet between 2 sheets of plastic wrap and flatten gently with a rolling pin, the smooth side of a meat mallet, or similar tool. Replace with remaining cutlets. In a large food storage bag, combine ⅔ cup flour, 1 teaspoon salt, ¼ teaspoon pepper, and the paprika. Add cutlets, a few at a time, and coat well.
2. In a large skillet over medium heat, combine the oil and 1 tablespoon of butter. When the skillet is hot, add the cutlets, a few at a time. Sauté the cutlet, turning to brown both sides, until cooked through. Remove to a warm plate and cover loosely with foil. Keep warm.
3. Add mushrooms and remaining 1 tablespoon of butter to the skillet. Cook until tender. Gradually stir in the chicken broth and wine. Add the rosemary, parsley, and garlic powder. Simmer the mixture over medium-high heat for several minutes, until reduced by about one-third. Reduce heat to medium-low.
4. Combine the 2 tablespoons of flour with 2 tablespoons of cold water. Whisk until smooth. Stir into the sauce. Continue to cook, stirring, until thickened. Add about ½ cup of the cream. Taste and add more cream, if desired. Heat through.
5. To serve, spoon sauce over the turkey cutlets. These are delicious with hot buttered pasta.

**WHAT'S HOT**

▶ I love turkey cutlets, and one of my all-time favorites is a recipe for Turkey Cutlets Parmesan. These cutlets, with a tomato sauce and Mozzarella cheese, are really good with hot cooked spaghetti, and it's an easy meal to prepare. Check it out at http://about.com/southernfood/turkeycutletparm. Scroll down past the recipe, and you'll see more links to recipes using turkey cutlets.

## Get Linked

*I have hundreds of poultry recipes on my site on **About.com**, including chicken favorites and turkey recipes, as well as recipes using Cornish game hens, duck, and goose. Here are some of the best links to resources and recipes.*

**TOP CHICKEN CASEROLE RECIPES**

Here are fourteen delicious chicken casseroles, including my favorites and some of the most popular recipes. Recipes include Chicken Rice Divan Bake, Mexican Chicken Casserole, Chicken Tortilla Bake, Chicken Florentine, and more.

 http://about.com/southernfood/chickencasseroles

**CHICKEN BREAST RECIPES**

With lean and healthy boneless chicken breasts so readily available and economical these days, it's easy to see why this index is a popular one.

 http://about.com/southernfood/chickbreastrecipes

**POULTRY INDEX**

This is the main poultry index, with links to a huge variety of chicken recipes, Cornish game hen recipes, duck and goose recipes, and turkey recipes.

 http://about.com/southernfood/poultryrecipes

Chapter 9

# Fish and Shellfish

**ASK YOUR GUIDE:**

Is frozen fish going to taste as good as fresh fish?
▶ **PAGE 153**

Should the bones be removed from canned salmon?
▶ **PAGE 158**

What is the history of pilau?
▶ **PAGE 161**

Is it easy to make shrimp stock?
▶ **PAGE 162**

## Crispy Fried Catfish
SERVES 4

*Catfish is an absolutely delicious fish, especially when it's fried. Serve this wonderful Southern traditional favorite with plenty of lemon wedges.*

4 catfish fillets
½ cup evaporated milk or whole milk
¾ cup yellow cornmeal
½ cup all-purpose flour
2 ½ teaspoons seasoned salt
½ teaspoon ground cayenne pepper, optional
Canola oil, for frying
Lemon wedges

1. Rinse fish; dry with paper towels. Put in a bowl with the milk, turning to coat. Set aside.
2. In a large plate or wide, shallow bowl, combine the cornmeal, flour, seasoned salt, and cayenne pepper. Set aside.
3. Add oil to a deep, heavy skillet, to a depth of about ¾ to 1 inch. Heat the oil to about 350°F.
4. Using tongs, lift a fish fillet out of the milk, letting excess drip back into the bowl. Place the fillet in the cornmeal mixture, turning several times to coat thoroughly. Repeat with as many fillets as will fit easily in your pan. Place the fillets in the hot oil.
5. Fry the fish for about 5 to 7 minutes, depending on size. If the oil doesn't cover them, turn carefully with a wide spatula about halfway through cooking. Drain on paper towels. Repeat process until all fillets are fried.
6. Serve fried catfish with lemon wedges, Hush Puppies (page 28), Creamy Cabbage Slaw (page 62), and fries.

▶ A well-seasoned cast iron skillet is probably the most valued piece of cookware in a Southern cook's kitchen. Heat is evenly distributed in heavy cast iron cookware, making it a great choice for frying, searing, and even baking. Some cast iron cookware comes already seasoned, but if you need to season a pot or pan, it's easy. First, wash and dry the pot thoroughly. Coat the surface of the pot with oil, including the outside and handles. Place it in a 300°F oven with a baking sheet under it to catch dripping oil, and heat for 30 minutes. Let the cookware cool, then wipe with paper towels. After each use, wash with soapy water, dry thoroughly, then coat the inner surfaces with a little oil or melted shortening.

## Baked Dijon Catfish with Crumb Coating
SERVES 4 TO 6

*The Dijon mustard gives this catfish a nice flavor boost, and it's lower in fat than the more traditional fried catfish.*

> 4 to 6 catfish fillets
> 1 tablespoon shortening or vegetable oil
> 3 to 4 tablespoons Dijon mustard
> 1 cup plain bread crumbs
> ½ teaspoon salt
> ¼ teaspoon freshly ground black pepper
> ¼ teaspoon garlic powder
> ¼ teaspoon dried oregano
> 1 teaspoon dried parsley flakes

1. Rinse fish fillets; pat dry. Brush fish all over with the Dijon mustard to coat well.
2. Heat oven to 450°F. Add oil or shortening to a shallow baking dish; place in the oven.
3. In a wide, shallow bowl, combine the remaining ingredients. With tongs or hands, place fish in the bowl, turning to coat thoroughly.
4. Place coated fillets in the hot oiled baking dish in a single layer. Bake for 6 to 10 minutes, depending on size, until fish flakes easily with a fork.
5. Serve with lemon wedges, along with rice pilaf and fresh cooked broccoli.

ASK YOUR GUIDE

**Is frozen fish going to taste as good as fresh fish?**

▶ It can be very difficult to find fresh fish in many parts of the country, but farm-raised catfish is probably found frozen in most areas. To thaw the fish, place it in a plastic food storage bag then submerge the bag in cool water. To reduce any "frozen" taste, soak previously frozen fish fillets in milk before using them in a recipe.

## Broiled Red Snapper Fillets with Louisiana Seasonings
SERVES 4

*Red snapper is a big favorite of mine, and this is a super-easy way to cook it.*

4 red snapper fillets
¼ cup melted butter
1 teaspoon salt
½ teaspoon freshly ground black pepper
½ teaspoon garlic powder
½ teaspoon ground sweet paprika
Dash dried crumbled thyme
Dash ground cayenne pepper
Sherry Cream Sauce, seafood variation (page 207)
1 small tomato, seeded and diced
2 to 3 green onions, sliced thin

1. Preheat broiler. Lightly brush the rack of a broiler pan with a little vegetable oil.
2. Rinse snapper fillets; pat dry. Brush fillets all over with melted butter.
3. In a cup or small bowl, combine the salt, black pepper, garlic powder, paprika, thyme, and ground cayenne. Sprinkle over the fish fillets.
4. Place the fillets, skin-side down, on the oiled rack of the broiler pan. Place about 5 to 6 inches from the heat. Broil for 6 to 8 minutes, or until fish flakes easily with a fork.
5. Serve with the seafood variation of Sherry Cream Sauce (page 207) and top with diced fresh tomato and thin-sliced green onions.

**ELSEWHERE ON THE WEB**

▶ Did you know that when you purchase red snapper, you could be the victim of fish fraud? Red snapper is in such high demand that many fish labeled as red snapper are actually different types of snapper. Derrick Riches, the Barbecues and Grilling Guide, has some helpful tips on identifying and cooking the fish, along with links to some delicious recipes for the grill. Check out http://about.com/bbq/red snapper.

## Tuna Steaks with Peach Salsa

SERVES 4

*I make this delicious tuna in a stovetop grill pan, but you could just as easily broil the steaks. Feel free to use salmon in place of the tuna. Start this recipe early, since the tuna should marinate for at least 1 hour.*

> 4 tuna steaks, about 8 ounces each
> ¼ cup fresh lime juice
> 2 tablespoons olive oil, plus a little for the pan
> ½ teaspoon ground ginger
> ¼ teaspoon salt
> 1 tablespoon honey
> Dash hot sauce
> 1 clove garlic, minced
> Peach Salsa (page 206)

1. Place the tuna steaks in a large, heavy-duty food storage bag.
2. Combine the lime juice, 2 tablespoons of olive oil, ginger, salt, honey, hot sauce, and garlic. Pour the marinade mixture over the tuna steaks; seal the bag. Refrigerate for about 1 to 2 hours, turning frequently to keep tuna coated with marinade.
3. Brush a grill pan with a little olive oil and heat over medium-high heat. Grill tuna steaks for about 4 to 6 minutes on each side, or until the edges flake easily but the steaks are still somewhat pink in the center.
4. Serve with the Peach Salsa (page 206) and hot cooked rice, along with a tossed salad or steamed fresh vegetables.

**BEFORE YOU BEGIN**

▶ Fresh tuna steaks are delicious grilled or broiled, but you should buy the freshest tuna you can find. The tastiest tuna will be a deep pink to red, and it will be somewhat shiny and moist looking, but not wet. Dullness, browning, or flaking all mean the tuna is older, while fresh tuna will smell a little like the ocean but should not have a strong fishy odor. You might want to avoid the strong-flavored brown streak which runs through whole tuna steaks, or you could cut it out before cooking.

## Halibut with Creamy Crawfish Sherry Sauce
SERVES 6

*I buy halibut whenever I can find it, and that just isn't often enough. This is a delicious way to prepare halibut, and it's an especially nice dish to make for a dinner with friends or family.*

Vegetable oil
6 halibut fillets, about 6 ounces each
Salt and pepper
4 tablespoons melted butter
1 large clove garlic, minced
1 tablespoon fresh parsley, chopped
Sherry Cream Sauce, crawfish variation (page 207)

1. Heat broiler and brush the rack of a broiler pan with a little vegetable oil.
2. Rinse fish fillets and pat dry. Sprinkle halibut all over with salt and pepper. Combine melted butter with garlic in a small saucepan; cook over medium-low heat for about 1 minute to meld flavors. Stir in the chopped parsley and brush the mixture over the halibut. Place fish on the broiler rack.
3. Broil about 5 to 6 inches from heat for about 5 to 8 minutes per side, depending on thickness.
4. Serve with boiled new potatoes, fingerlings, or the Baby Dutch variety, along with spinach or other green vegetable. Top each serving with the crawfish variation of Sherry Cream Sauce (page 207).

**WHAT'S HOT**

▶ Here's a hot tip. Turning fish can result in frustration and broken fillets. To make the procedure easier, place each of the fish fillets on a piece of nonstick or oiled foil which is double the width of the fish and about 2 inches longer. Put the foil and fish on the broiler rack or baking dish. When you're ready to turn the fish, carefully grasp each edge of the foil and flip the fish over to the other side of the foil.

## Baked Tilapia with Pecan Topping
SERVES 4

*My husband and I love tilapia, and this is our favorite recipe for the fish. The pecans and Dijon topping are just amazing together.*

1 ½ pounds tilapia fillets
⅔ cup mayonnaise
⅓ cup Dijon mustard
½ cup pecans, chopped fine
2 tablespoons green onions, chopped fine

1. Heat oven to 350°F. Lightly butter a shallow baking pan.
2. Rinse tilapia fillets; pat dry. Arrange fillets in a single layer on the baking sheet.
3. In a bowl, combine the mayonnaise and Dijon mustard. Spread each fillet with the mixture. Sprinkle each with chopped pecans and chopped green onion.
4. Bake for 12 to 16 minutes, depending on size, or until fish flakes easily with a fork.
5. Serve the fish fillets with sliced tomatoes, hot cooked rice, and a green leafy vegetable, if desired.

**ELSEWHERE ON THE WEB**

▶ Peggy Trowbridge, the About.com Home Cooking Guide, has a wonderful recipe using tilapia. The tilapia fillets are brushed with mayonnaise and then coated with a delicious Parmesan cheese and spice mixture. The fillets are then quickly fried, and an easy wine sauce is made in the same pan, with lime juice and capers. Here's a link to Peggy's recipe: http://about .com/homecooking/ tilapiarecipe.

### Should the bones be removed from canned salmon?

▶ Whether you leave the bones in canned salmon or remove them is really a matter of preference, but everything in the can is edible and digestible. Salmon is pressure cooked when it is processed, so the bones become quite soft and easy to digest, and the bones are also a good source of calcium.

## Salmon Croquettes with Corn
SERVES 4

*Salmon* **croquettes**, *also known as salmon patties, make a delicious weeknight meal. My mother-in-law makes delicious salmon croquettes, and these are quite similar.*

1 can (14.75 ounces) salmon
1 cup corn kernels, cooked
2 eggs, slightly beaten
¼ cup ketchup
2 tablespoons green onion, chopped fine
2 tablespoons celery, chopped fine
¼ teaspoon salt
Dash freshly ground black pepper
¾ cup bread crumbs, plain
1 to 2 tablespoons vegetable oil

1. Drain the salmon; flake, removing any large pieces of bone or skin.
2. In a bowl combine the flaked salmon with the corn, beaten eggs, ketchup, onion, celery, and salt, pepper, and bread crumbs. Shape the salmon mixture into 12 patties.
3. Heat vegetable oil in a heavy skillet on medium heat. Fry the salmon croquettes for about 1 ½ to 2 minutes on each side, or until browned and cooked through.
4. Serve salmon croquettes with rice, fries, or your favorite vegetables, along with Come Back Sauce (page 205) or ketchup.

## Oven-Fried Fish Fillets

SERVES 4

*I love the fact that these are lower in fat than traditional fried fish. You can use catfish, orange roughy, haddock, tilapia, flounder, or your own favorite fish.*

Vegetable oil
4 fish fillets, about 4 to 6 ounces each
½ cup milk
1 teaspoon seasoned salt
½ teaspoon salt
½ cup corn flake crumbs or fine dry bread crumbs
4 teaspoons melted butter
Lemon wedges

1. Rinse fish and pat dry. If fillets are large, cut into serving-size portions.
2. Heat oven to 475°F. Lightly oil a shallow baking pan.
3. In a shallow bowl, combine milk, seasoned salt, and salt. Put corn flake crumbs or bread crumbs in another bowl.
4. Dip fish fillets in the milk, then put in the corn flake crumbs, turning to coat thoroughly. Arrange on the oiled baking sheet. Drizzle 1 teaspoon of melted butter over each fillet.
5. Bake for 12 to 15 minutes, or until fish flakes easily with a fork. The length of time depends on the thickness of the fish.

**ELSEWHERE ON THE WEB**

▶ If you're looking for low-fat fish ideas, Fiona Haynes, the About.com Low Fat Cooking Guide, has a nice index of links to delicious recipes for fish and seafood. You'll find recipes for fish kebabs, glazed salmon, flavorful baked tilapia, halibut cooked in foil, fish chowder, and shrimp with pasta. There are also recipes using sole, red snapper, cod, tuna, and others. Here's the link: http://about.com/lowfatcooking/fishseafoodrecipes.

## Spicy Shrimp and Grits
SERVES 4 TO 6

*I love shrimp and grits, and there are endless variations on this combination. This is one of my family's favorite versions.*

1 ½ to 2 pounds shrimp, large to colossal
6 slices bacon, diced
8 ounces fresh mushrooms, sliced
2 to 3 teaspoons butter
6 green onions, sliced thin
1 can (14.5 ounces) diced tomatoes
½ teaspoon Creole seasoning
Dash garlic powder
¼ teaspoon ground black pepper
Salt, to taste
Fresh parsley, chopped, for garnish

1. Remove shells from shrimp, leaving tails on. To remove visible sand veins, cut about ⅛-inch into the upper curve of the shrimp and rinse the vein out under cold water.
2. In a heavy skillet, cook the diced bacon until fat is rendered. Add the butter and the mushrooms and cook over medium heat, stirring constantly, until tender. Add the shrimp. Cook the shrimp and mushroom mixture, stirring, for 1 minute. Add the green onions and cook for 1 minute longer. Add the canned tomatoes, Creole seasoning, garlic powder, black pepper, and salt. Bring to a boil over high heat; reduce heat to low and simmer for 2 minutes, until slightly reduced. Add more salt or pepper, as needed.
3. To serve, spoon shrimp over hot Creamy Grits (page 172) and sprinkle with the fresh chopped parsley.

**WHAT'S HOT**

▶ Another deliciously different way to prepare shrimp and grits is with a coconut curry sauce. I had this wonderful dish at a restaurant while on vacation recently, and my own version is quite close in flavor. The sauce is made with cream of coconut, lime juice, and curry powder, and the shrimp and grits are served over a bed of fresh cooked spinach. Check it out at http://about.com/southern food/shrimpandgrits.

# Shrimp Pilau

SERVES 4

*This shrimp **pilau** is a wonderful rice main dish, similar to **jambalaya**.*

4 slices bacon, diced
2 tablespoons butter
½ cup celery, chopped
2 tablespoons green bell pepper, chopped
2 green onions, sliced thin
Dash dried leaf thyme, crumbled
1 pound medium shrimp, cleaned, peeled
1 tablespoon flour
1 teaspoon Worcestershire sauce
2 to 4 tablespoons chicken broth
1 large tomato, diced
2 cups hot cooked rice
Salt and pepper
¼ to ½ teaspoon curry powder, optional

1.  Fry bacon in a large heavy skillet or saucepan until crisp. Transfer to paper towels to drain.
2.  Add 2 tablespoons of butter to the bacon drippings left in the skillet. Add celery, green onion, and bell pepper. Continue to cook the chopped vegetables, stirring, until tender. Add thyme. Toss the shrimp with the flour and Worcestershire sauce; add to the vegetable mixture. Continue to cook, stirring, until shrimp is cooked through, adding chicken broth to keep the mixture from sticking. Stir in the diced tomato and the hot cooked rice and mix. Add salt and pepper to taste, along with curry powder and more butter, if desired. Heat through and toss with the bacon just before serving.

**ASK YOUR GUIDE**

### *What is the history of pilau?*

▶ Pilau, also known as pilaf, is a versatile rice dish with the addition of chopped vegetables, along with meat, poultry, or seafood. The Southern rice crop and spice trade contributed to the popularity of rice pilau, particularly in Louisiana, Florida, and South Carolina. Many of these flavorful rice dishes are made with the addition of curry powder and other spices, depending on the region and preferences.

**Is it easy to make shrimp stock?**

▸ Shrimp stock adds flavor to the recipe, and it is easy to make. Put shrimp shells from about 2 pounds of uncooked large to colossal shrimp into a large saucepan. Add 2 medium cut-up onions, ½ cup of chopped celery, 2 cut-up lemons, 2 bay leaves, and 1 teaspoon of dried leaf thyme. Add a few sprigs of parsley and about 8 peppercorns, along with a few halved cloves of garlic, if desired. Bring the broth to a boil; reduce heat to medium, and cook, uncovered, for about 25 to 30 minutes. Cool then strain through a fine sieve. Use what you need and freeze the remaining broth in small containers for up to one month.

# Shrimp Creole
SERVES 6

*This is a flavorful New Orleans–style shrimp Creole recipe with tomatoes, served over hot cooked rice and with crusty bread.*

2 pounds cleaned shrimp, shells removed
4 to 6 slices bacon
Vegetable oil
2 tablespoons flour
1 cup onion, chopped
1 cup celery, chopped
1 green bell pepper, sliced thin
2 teaspoons Creole seasoning
2 cans (14.5 ounces each) diced tomatoes
½ cup chicken broth or shrimp stock
Worcestershire sauce and Tabasco sauce to taste

1. Remove shells from shrimp, leaving tails on.
2. Cook bacon in a medium saucepan until crisp; remove to paper towels to drain. Crumble and set aside.
3. Pour bacon drippings into a cup; add enough oil to the bacon drippings to make 2 tablespoons. Pour oil and drippings back into the pan. Stir in the flour; continue to cook over medium heat, stirring constantly, until the roux is medium to deep brown.
4. Add the vegetables. Cook over medium heat, stirring, until tender. Add the Creole seasoning, tomatoes, chicken broth or shrimp stock, and Worcestershire sauce and Tabasco sauce to taste. Simmer the mixture for about 15 to 20 minutes, or until thickened, stirring occasionally. Add the shrimp and cook for 6 to 8 minutes. For each serving, mound about ½ cup of rice on a serving plate, then spoon shrimp and sauce over the rice.

## Spicy Crab Cakes

SERVES 4

*These delicious crab cakes can be served as a main dish or first course. I love them with a Remoulade Sauce (page 203) or Come Back Sauce (page 205).*

1 pound lump crabmeat
½ teaspoon lemon juice
¼ cup mayonnaise
1 egg, beaten
1 to 1 ¼ cups fine dry bread crumbs, divided
1 teaspoon Old Bay seasoning
Few drops Tabasco sauce
¼ teaspoon Worcestershire sauce
Oil for frying

1. Drain crabmeat and break up slightly, discarding any pieces of shell or cartilage. Sprinkle with lemon juice and set aside.
2. In a large bowl, whisk the egg; stir in mayonnaise, ¾ cup of the bread crumbs, Old Bay seasoning, Tabasco, and Worcestershire sauce. Gently fold crabmeat into the mixture until well combined.
3. With hands, shape the mixture into patties, flattening slightly. Cover with plastic wrap and refrigerate for at least 30 minutes.
4. Heat about ½-inch of oil in a large heavy skillet over medium heat. Gently roll or press the crab cakes into more bread crumbs. Fry the patties for about 3 minutes on each side, or until nicely browned. Drain on paper towels.
5. Serve with lemon wedges and your favorite sauce for seafood.

**BEFORE YOU BEGIN**

▶ Clarified butter is nice to have on hand because it will withstand a much higher heat than regular butter. To make clarified butter, put about 8 tablespoons of butter in a saucepan and melt over medium-low heat. Continue heating over medium-low heat until it begins to bubble and the solids become golden. The butter can easily burn, so watch carefully. Remove from heat and let the butter cool. With a spoon, skim foam off of the top. Carefully pour or spoon the clear liquids (that is, your clarified butter) off, and discard the solids left in the saucepan. Clarified butter will keep for several months in the refrigerator.

**WHAT'S HOT**

▶ Oysters have long been a favorite in some regions of the south, and there are many famous recipes. Oysters Rockefeller and Oysters Bienville were both made famous by New Orleans chefs, and oyster casseroles, dressings, and stews are popular throughout the Southern states. I have a delicious recipe for Oysters Rockefeller, made with butter, bread crumbs, chopped vegetables, oysters in their shells, and seasonings. Check it out at http://about.com/southern food/oystersrockefeller.

# Crispy Fried Oysters

SERVES 4

*These are classic Southern-style fried oysters with that delicious crispy cornmeal coating. These also make a great sandwich filling.*

24 raw oysters
3 large eggs
3 cups cornmeal
¼ cup flour
1 teaspoon salt
1 ½ teaspoons Cajun seasoning
1 ½ teaspoons freshly ground black pepper

1. Beat eggs in a medium mixing bowl. Add the oysters and stir to coat thoroughly. Set aside.
2. Combine cornmeal, flour, and seasonings in a large food storage bag. Working with a few at a time, let excess egg drip off of the oysters and put into the bag. Shake gently to coat the oysters thoroughly.
3. Heat oil in a deep fryer to 375°F.
4. Fry oysters in batches for about 3 minutes, or until golden brown. Remove to paper towels to drain. Serve hot with lemon wedges and tartar sauce or Come Back Sauce (page 205).

# Quick Seared Sea Scallops
SERVES 4

*These spicy seasoned scallops are flavorful and very easy to prepare! I have served them with grits, but they would also be delicious with rice or potatoes.*

1 pound sea scallops
Salt
1 tablespoon all-purpose flour
1 tablespoon Cajun seasoning
1 ½ teaspoons paprika
¼ teaspoon freshly ground black pepper
4 tablespoons melted butter
2 to 3 tablespoons vegetable oil
Fresh parsley, minced

1. Cut very large scallops in half, if desired. Pat scallops dry then sprinkle lightly with salt.
2. Heat vegetable oil in a heavy skillet over medium heat.
3. In a shallow bowl, combine the flour, **Cajun** seasoning, paprika, and pepper. Put melted butter in another bowl. Press the scallops into the mixture then turn to coat the other side. Quickly dip each side into the butter.
4. Cook scallops in hot oil for about 3 minutes on each side, or until browned and cooked through.
5. Sprinkle with fresh minced parsley and serve with hot cooked rice or Creamy Grits (page 172). These are also delicious drizzled with a little of the crab variation of Sherry Cream Sauce (page 207).

ELSEWHERE ON THE WEB

▶ Debra Weber, the About.com French Cuisine Guide, has a unique recipe using sea scallops. The scallops are sautéed quickly in clarified butter and served with a flavorful espresso-cream sauce. Here's a link to Debra's recipe: http://about.com/frenchfood/scallopsespresso. Also on Debra's French Cuisine site, you'll find a fabulous Coquilles St. Jacques with Saffron, a delicious dish of scallops with creamy saffron sauce: http://about.com/frenchfood/scallopssaffron.

## Get Linked

*I prepare fish and seafood dishes once or twice a week, and you'll find many more tasty recipes on my Southern Cuisine Web site. Seafood main dish recipes and appetizers, grilled, broiled, baked, and fried fish recipes, fish and shellfish soups, and many more. Here are some links to more of my favorite recipes.*

**FISH RECIPES**

This big list of fish recipes includes catfish, flounder and sole, cod, haddock, halibut, orange roughy, snapper, canned and fresh salmon, swordfish, and tilapia, and more, along with recipes using canned and fresh tuna.

 http://about.com/southernfood/fishrecipes

**SHELLFISH RECIPES**

This is my index of shellfish recipes, including clams and mussels, lobster recipes, shrimp, oysters, scallops, and crab, along with crawfish recipes and recipes using seafood combinations.

 http://about.com/southernfood/shellfishrecipes

**TUNA CASSEROLE RECIPES**

Here you'll find dozens of tuna casserole recipes, including a tuna and noodle casserole, a tuna pie with biscuit topping, scalloped tuna recipes, a macaroni and tuna casserole, and other tuna casserole combinations.

 http://about.com/southernfood/tunacasseroles

Chapter 10

# Rice, Pasta, Grains, and Beans

**ASK YOUR GUIDE:**

Where does the name "Hoppin' John" come from?
▶ **PAGE 174**

Why do some beans never seem to become tender?
▶ **PAGE 175**

## Creamy Macaroni and Cheese
SERVES 4 TO 6

*Who doesn't love macaroni and cheese? This is a wonderful creamy version, with a flavorful Cheddar sauce.*

8 ounces elbow macaroni, uncooked
4 tablespoons butter
4 tablespoons flour
¼ teaspoon salt
⅛ teaspoon freshly ground black pepper
2 cups milk
1 cup shredded sharp Cheddar cheese
½ cup soft bread crumbs
1 tablespoon butter, melted
Ground paprika

1. Cook macaroni as directed on the package; drain and rinse under hot water.
2. Heat oven to 375°F. Lightly butter a 2 ½-quart baking dish.
3. In a medium saucepan over medium-low heat, melt the butter. Add flour, stirring until smooth and bubbly.
4. Stir in salt and pepper. Gradually add milk, stirring constantly. Continue to cook, stirring constantly, until sauce is thickened and bubbly. Stir in cheese until melted. Combine the macaroni with cheese sauce; spoon into the prepared baking dish.
5. In a small bowl, drizzle melted butter over the bread crumbs; toss to blend. Sprinkle over the macaroni and cheese mixture, then sprinkle entire dish with paprika.
6. Bake for 20 to 25 minutes, or until the macaroni and cheese is hot and bubbly and topping is lightly browned.

▶ Here in the South, macaroni and cheese is a beloved side dish, one I like to call "food for the soul." Our family's holiday dinners often include a macaroni and cheese casserole, and it could be served in place of potatoes or rice at just about any family meal. Serve macaroni and cheese with meat or poultry, sliced tomatoes, and green beans for a very satisfying meal.

## Savory Rice Pilaf with Green Onions
SERVES 4

*I love the flavors in this rice dish. The pecans jazz it up a bit, but it's also delicious without them.*

2 tablespoons butter
1 tablespoon olive oil
1 cup mushrooms, sliced thin
½ cup green onions, sliced thin
1 cup long-grain white rice
2 cups chicken broth
⅛ teaspoon freshly ground black pepper
1 teaspoon lemon juice
½ cup pecans
2 tablespoons fresh parsley, chopped
Dash Tabasco, optional

1. Combine the butter and oil in a medium saucepan over medium heat. Add the mushrooms and cook, stirring, for 2 minutes. Add the green onions and cook for about 1 minute longer. Add the rice and cook for another 30 seconds. Add the chicken broth, pepper, and the lemon juice; bring to a boil over medium-high heat. Reduce heat to low; cover and cook for about 20 minutes, until the liquid has been absorbed and the rice is tender. If necessary, add more chicken broth. Remove from heat and leave the lid on for about 10 minutes.
2. Meanwhile, toast the nuts. Spread pecans out on a baking sheet and bake at 325°F for 8 to 10 minutes. Let cool, then chop.
3. Stir the pecans into the rice, along with chopped parsley and Tabasco, if using. Taste and adjust seasonings.

BEFORE YOU BEGIN

▶ Different types of rice and your own preferences make a difference in the rice-to-liquid ratio. Before you begin cooking, check the package directions to get the most accurate measurement, then adjust the amount of chicken broth accordingly. For the best results, use a heavy-bottomed pot with a tight-fitting lid for cooking rice. It's very important that the liquids stay in the pot where they can be absorbed by the rice.

## Cajun-Style Dirty Rice

SERVES 6

*This flavorful recipe gets its name from the "dirty" appearance of the rice.*

8 to 12 ounces chicken gizzards
3 ½ cups chicken broth, hot
6 tablespoons butter, divided
8 ounces lean ground pork
½ cup onion, chopped
½ cup green onions, including green tops, chopped
¾ cup celery, chopped
½ cup green bell pepper, chopped
3 cloves garlic, minced
2 teaspoons Creole seasoning
½ teaspoon salt
¼ teaspoon freshly ground black pepper
⅛ teaspoon ground cayenne pepper
1 ½ cups long-grain rice
8 ounces chicken livers, diced

1. Combine the chicken gizzards and broth in a large saucepan. Bring to a boil over high heat; reduce heat to low and simmer for about 30 minutes. With a slotted spoon, remove the gizzards and mince. Reserve the broth.
2. Combine the minced gizzards with pork in a heavy skillet over medium-high heat. Cook the mixture, stirring, until pork is no longer pink. Reduce heat to medium; add 4 tablespoons of butter, chopped onion, green onion, celery, and bell pepper. Cook vegetables for about 5 minutes, until tender. Add garlic and seasonings and cook for about 30 seconds longer. Add reserved broth and the rice. Increase heat to high and bring to a boil, stirring occasionally. Reduce heat to low; cover and simmer for 15 minutes, or until rice is tender.
3. In a skillet over medium heat; melt remaining 2 tablespoons of butter. Cook the diced chicken livers for about 3 to 4 minutes. Toss with the rice. Cover and let rice sit for 10 minutes. Remove the cover and fluff with a fork just before serving.

# Home-Style Cornbread Dressing
SERVES 8

*This delicious dressing is an essential holiday side dish. Use homemade cornbread and freshly-made chicken broth with chunks of chicken for the tastiest dressing.*

6 cups crumbled cornbread
3 cups soft bread crumbs
4 ounces butter
2 cups onion, chopped
2 ½ cups celery, chopped
3 to 4 cups chicken broth
2 cups chicken, diced, optional
1 heaping tablespoon dried sage, crumbled
1 ½ teaspoons dried leaf thyme, crumbled
1 teaspoon dried marjoram, crumbled
½ teaspoon dried rosemary, chopped
1 teaspoon salt
½ teaspoon freshly ground black pepper
2 eggs, beaten

1. Heat oven to 400°F. Grease a large shallow baking or roasting pan measuring about 10" x 15".
2. In a large mixing bowl, combine the cornbread and white bread crumbs. In a saucepan over medium heat, sauté the onion and celery in butter until tender. Do not brown. Combine the sautéed vegetables with the bread mixture. Stir in chicken broth until well moistened and then add diced chicken, if using. Stir in the seasonings and beaten eggs, blending well.
3. Spread the mixture in the greased baking dish.
4. Bake for 20 to 30 minutes.

**BEFORE YOU BEGIN**

▶ It's safer to bake dressing in a pan in the oven, but if you decide to stuff a turkey or chicken with the mixture, here are some safety tips. Stuff the bird just before roasting. If you stuff it in advance, bacteria might have an opportunity to move from the poultry to the stuffing. Make sure you stuff the bird loosely and that the stuffing is moist. The bird should register 180°F in the breast meat and 165°F in the center of the stuffing. Just before carving (about 20 minutes after the bird is removed from the oven), remove all of the stuffing to a separate bowl. Do not store the stuffing in the bird.

## Creamy Grits
SERVES 6

*These savory grits go perfectly with shrimp, pork medallions, chops, or just about anything you might serve over rice or polenta. I sometimes stir in a cup of shredded Cheddar or Havarti cheese, but these grits are just delicious as they are.*

2 cups chicken broth
⅔ cup heavy cream
1 cup water
¼ cup butter
¼ teaspoon salt, or to taste
¼ teaspoon freshly ground black pepper
1 cup quick grits

1. In a medium saucepan, bring chicken broth, cream, and water to a boil.
2. Stir in the butter, salt, and pepper. Whisk in the grits gradually so the mixture does not stop boiling. Lower heat to medium-low and simmer for 15 to 20 minutes, stirring frequently. Cover and remove from heat.
3. Serve grits with shrimp, pork medallions, tenderloin, or just about anything you might serve over hot cooked rice.

**ELSEWHERE ON THE WEB**

▶ If you don't have grits in your area, here are a few online sources. The Peas & Corn Co. offers stone ground flour, grits, and cornmeal, and they also have other hard-to-find Southern foods and utensils: www .peasandcornco.com. Hoppin' John's is the site of cookbook author John Martin Taylor. You'll find stone-ground grits and cornmeal, along with links to his cookbooks and other information: www .hoppinjohns.com. Bob's Red Mill has an online catalog with all of their grains, beans, nuts and seeds, flours and meals, seasonings, and baking aids: www.bobsredmill.com.

# Garlic Cheese Grits Casserole
SERVES 8

*This is my version of a very popular Southern grits casserole—a classic comfort food.*

2 cups milk
2 cups chicken broth
1 cup quick grits
4 tablespoons butter
3 cloves garlic, minced
1 teaspoon salt
½ teaspoon pepper
2 cups shredded sharp Cheddar cheese
3 large eggs, beaten

1. Heat oven to 350°F. Lightly butter a 2-quart casserole.
2. Bring milk and chicken broth to a rolling boil in a large saucepan over medium-high heat. Gradually whisk the grits into the boiling mixture. Continue boiling, stirring, for about 7 to 9 minutes, until thick and grits are done.
3. Meanwhile, melt butter with minced garlic in the microwave or in a small saucepan over low heat. Let stand for about 5 minutes. Strain butter into the boiling grits mixture. Discard garlic.
4. Stir in the salt, pepper, and shredded cheese. Stir in the beaten egg until well blended.
5. Spread the cheese grits mixture in the prepared casserole. Bake for 45 to 55 minutes, until puffed up and browned.

**WHAT'S HOT**

▶ On my site you'll find another tasty grits-and-cheese casserole from my sister-in-law, Sallye. Her version is made with a 6-ounce roll of garlic cheese and a 6-ounce roll of jalapeño cheese. It's also big enough for a potluck or big family dinner, and it's delicious. Take a look at Sallye's Cheese Grits Casserole at http://about.com/southernfood/cheesegrits.

**Where does the name "Hoppin' John" come from?**

▶ There are many theories on how the dish came by its name. According to one story, the ritual began on New Year's Day, when children would hop around the table before eating. Another claims guests were invited to eat with the phrase "Hop in, John." Whatever its origin, it was an important dish in the early South, and it's still an important dish. My family never misses a meal of black-eyed peas on New Year's Day!

## Spicy Hoppin' John
SERVES 6

*You just cannot bring in the New Year without a dish of black-eyed peas for good luck, and Hoppin' John is a tradition. To be extremely lucky in the New Year, serve this tasty dish with cooked greens or cabbage.*

I pound dried black-eyed peas
4 ounces **salt pork** or **hog jowl**, diced
I cup onion, chopped
½ cup celery, chopped
3 cloves garlic, minced
½ cup green bell pepper, diced
I ½ cups cooked ham, diced
I tablespoon Cajun seasoning
½ teaspoon salt
¼ teaspoon freshly ground black pepper
Dash ground cayenne pepper, or to taste

1. Soak peas in cold water overnight. Drain.
2. In a heavy skillet, sauté the salt pork or hog jowl and chopped onion until onion is browned.
3. In a large kettle or Dutch oven, combine the drained peas with the sautéed salt pork and onion; add chopped celery, garlic, bell pepper, and ham. Cover with water and bring to a boil. Reduce heat to low, cover, and simmer for I hour. Add seasonings and cook for about 30 to 60 minutes longer, until peas are tender. Check occasionally and add more water, if needed.
4. Taste and adjust seasonings. Serve with Southern Skillet Cornbread (page 24), rice, and cooked greens.

## Louisiana Red Beans and Rice
SERVES 8

*A classic Louisiana favorite, red beans and rice is pure comfort food to many. This recipe is simple, but it's one of my favorite versions of the dish.*

1 pound small red beans
1 cup onion, chopped
½ cup bell pepper, chopped
3 ribs celery, chopped
3 cloves garlic, minced
1 meaty ham bone or large smoked ham hock
1 pound smoked sausage, sliced
1 bay leaf
½ teaspoon dried leaf thyme
Few drops Tabasco
Few dashes Worcestershire sauce
1 teaspoon Creole seasoning
Salt, to taste
Hot cooked rice

1. Wash beans and discard any stones and shriveled or bad beans. Cover with water and let soak overnight. Drain well.
2. In a large stockpot or Dutch oven, cover the beans with fresh water and boil for about 45 to 60 minutes, until beans are tender. Add the chopped onion, bell pepper, celery, and garlic. Add ham bone or hock and sliced smoked sausage, along with the bay leaf, and thyme. Cover with cold water. Bring to a boil; reduce heat, cover, and simmer until beans are tender.
3. Add the Tabasco sauce, Worcestershire sauce, Creole seasoning, and salt. Continue cooking for about 20 minutes longer. Remove the ham bone or hock and chop the meat; return chopped meat to the beans. If desired, mash a few cups of the beans to make the mixture thicker.
4. Serve the red beans with hot cooked rice and crusty bread.

ASK YOUR GUIDE

***Why do some beans never seem to become tender?***

▶ There are many factors that might contribute to hard beans. Hard water is sometimes blamed, but most people agree that salt and acidic ingredients should always be added after the beans have become tender. I always add salt near the very end of cooking. Tomatoes, salsas, or related ingredients are acidic, and shouldn't be added until after the beans are completely cooked. If your recipe combines beans with acidic or salty ingredients, simmer the beans first until they become tender.

## Down-Home Pinto Beans
SERVES 6 TO 8

*I love these delicious Southern-style pinto beans with hot buttered cornbread.*

1 pound dried pinto beans
4 to 6 ounces thick-sliced bacon, **fatback**, or hog jowl
1 ½ cups sweet onion, chopped
2 medium cloves garlic, minced
1 teaspoon salt
½ teaspoon crushed red pepper
¼ teaspoon freshly ground black pepper

1. Sort beans and remove any small stones and damaged beans. Put in a large bowl and cover with about 1 ½ quarts of cold water. Soak overnight. Refrigerate after about 8 to 10 hours if not cooking until later in the day.
2. Drain and rinse beans; transfer to a large saucepan or Dutch oven. Add the diced bacon, fatback, salt pork, or hog jowl, onion, and garlic. Bring to a simmer. Reduce heat to low, cover, and cook for about 1 ½ to 2 hours, or until beans are tender.
3. Add seasonings to the beans. Continue to cook, uncovered, for about 20 minutes, or until beans are tender and juices are creamy.
4. Taste and adjust seasonings. Serve with Southern Skillet Cornbread (page 24) and rice, if desired.

**ELSEWHERE ON THE WEB**

▶ I usually cook beans on the stovetop or in a slow cooker, but they can also be cooked in the pressure cooker, microwave, or baked in the oven. The Whole Foods Market site (www .wholefoodsmarket.com) has a helpful guide to cooking beans using all methods, with useful information on several varieties of beans, dried peas, and lentils. You'll also find some tips for seasoning beans and a page about how to reduce the flatulence beans can produce.

# Barbecue Baked Beans

SERVES 8

*These easy and delicious beans make a wonderful side dish to take to a cookout or potluck dinner or to serve with any family meal.*

1 tablespoon vegetable oil
1 pound lean ground beef
½ cup chopped green bell pepper
1 cup chopped onion
1 cup chopped celery
1 large can (15 ounces) tomato sauce
¾ cup water
2 cloves garlic, minced
¼ cup cider vinegar
2 teaspoons dry mustard
1 teaspoon dried leaf thyme, crumbled
3 tablespoons brown sugar
Salt and pepper, to taste
2 large cans (about 28 ounces each) pork and beans

1. Heat oven to 375°F.
2. In a large skillet over medium heat, heat the vegetable oil. Add the ground beef, onions, green bell pepper, and celery; sauté until beef is no longer pink and vegetables are tender.
3. Add the tomato sauce, water, garlic, vinegar, mustard, thyme, and brown sugar to the skillet. Blend ingredients to combine. Bring to a boil; reduce heat and simmer for 5 minutes. Add salt and pepper to taste.
4. Add the beans to the beef and vegetable mixture. Transfer to a 2-quart baking dish. Bake for 30 minutes, until hot and bubbly.

**WHAT'S HOT**

▸ Baked beans with pineapple? It might sound like a strange mix, but it's quite a flavorful and popular combination. Canned baked beans are cooked with crumbled bacon, molasses, chili sauce, red bell pepper, onion, and crushed pineapple in this tasty, tangy recipe. And probably the best part of all, it's super easy! Check it out at http://about.com/southernfood/pineapple beans.

## Get Linked

*I have more bean recipes and recipes for rice, grits, and other grains on my Southern Cuisine site on* **About.com.** *Here are some of my favorite recipes and related resources.*

**BEANS AND RICE**

This article goes into some of the history surrounding red beans and rice, and you'll find recipes for red beans and rice along with some other popular bean dishes.

http://about.com/southernfood/beansandrice

**JAMBALAYA**

Here you'll find information, a little history, and a variety of recipes for one of the most versatile dishes from the South.

http://about.com/southernfood/jambalaya

## Chapter II

# Vegetables

**About**

**ASK YOUR GUIDE:**

What is the difference between butter beans and lima beans?
▸ PAGE 180

Can I use zucchini in this recipe?
▸ PAGE 182

How do I choose an eggplant at the market?
▸ PAGE 186

Why should sweet potatoes be cooked before peeling?
▸ PAGE 187

What's the easiest way to peel tomatoes?
▸ PAGE 192

I love cabbage, but I hate the odor. Is there a way to keep the smell down?
▸ PAGE 196

**What is the difference between butter beans and lima beans?**

▶ The varieties are very closely related, but the seeds and pods differ in size. Butter beans are generally smaller than the larger-seeded lima beans. Butter beans or baby lima beans are creamier and more delicate in flavor than the higher-starch, larger lima beans. Many Southern-ers will call them butter beans whether they are but-ter beans or lima beans, so the terms have essentially become interchangeable. If you haven't had the greatest experiences with lima beans, try seasoned baby lima beans. You'll be pleasantly surprised!

## Creamy Lima Bean and Corn Succotash
SERVES 6

*This is one of my favorite vegetable combinations. I usually use frozen baby lima beans, and the dish is perfect with just about anything.*

1 pound frozen baby lima beans
2 cups frozen corn kernels
½ teaspoon salt
4 tablespoons butter
¾ to 1 cup heavy cream
Salt and pepper, to taste

1. Put baby lima beans in a saucepan with ½ teaspoon salt. Cover with water and bring to a boil. Reduce heat; cover and simmer for 10 minutes. Add the corn and more water to cover. Bring to a boil, cover, and continue to simmer for 5 to 8 minutes longer, or until vegetables are tender.
2. Drain vegetables well. Add butter and heavy cream. Taste and add salt and pepper, to taste.

## Green Bean Casserole

SERVES 6

*This casserole is a standard on our family's holiday dinner table, and it's delicious.*

5 tablespoons butter
½ cup chopped onion
½ cup chopped mushrooms
6 tablespoons flour
2 ½ cups milk
Salt and pepper, to taste
3 cans (14.5 ounces each) French-style green beans
1 can (8 ounces) sliced water chestnuts, drained
1 cup shredded sharp Cheddar cheese, optional
1 container (2.8 ounces) fried onion rings, crumbled

1. Heat oven to 350°F. Lightly grease a 2 ½-quart baking dish.
2. In a large heavy saucepan, melt butter over medium-low heat. Add onion and mushrooms and sauté until tender. Stir in flour until blended. Gradually stir in the milk. Continue cooking, stirring, until thickened and bubbly. Add salt and pepper, to taste.
3. Combine the drained green beans and water chestnuts with the sauce. Stir in cheese, if using. Transfer the mixture to the prepared casserole. Top with crumbled French-fried onion rings.
4. Bake for 30 minutes, until hot and bubbly.

ELSEWHERE ON THE WEB

▶ Peggy Trowbridge, the About.com Guide to Home Cooking, has a simple recipe for Classic Green Bean Casserole: http://about.com/homecooking/greenbeancasserole. Busy Cooks Guide Linda Larsen has a Traditional Green Bean Casserole: http://about.com/busycooks/greenbeancasserole. Finally, here's a Quick Green Bean Casserole from Stay-at-Home Parents Guide Barbara Whiting: http://about.com/homeparents/greenbeancasserole.

**Can I use zucchini in this recipe?**

▶ Yes, zucchini is a summer squash, so it will be similar in texture and flavor. I sometimes like to add a combination of yellow squash and zucchini. Cracker crumbs or stuffing crumbs are often used as a topping for squash casserole, or you can top it with more shredded cheese. If you have lots of summer squash from the garden, freeze it. Just wash, cut off the ends, slice into ½- to 1-inch pieces, and blanch for 3 minutes. Freeze the squash in containers with about ½-inch headspace.

## Summer Squash Casserole
SERVES 4

*I use fresh yellow crookneck squash for this dish.*

2 pounds yellow summer squash (8 cups)
3 tablespoons butter
½ cup chopped onion
4 ounces mushrooms, chopped
3 ½ tablespoons flour
1 ½ cups milk
1 ½ cups shredded mild Cheddar cheese

2 tablespoons fresh parsley, chopped
½ teaspoon salt
¼ teaspoon seasoned salt
¼ teaspoon freshly ground black pepper
½ cup sour cream
¾ cup bread crumbs
1 tablespoon butter, melted

1. Slice squash about ¼-inch thick. Put in a saucepan and cover with water. Bring to a boil. Reduce heat; cover, and simmer for 10 to 15 minutes, until squash is tender. Drain and set aside.
2. Heat oven to 350°F. Lightly grease a 2-quart baking dish.
3. In a saucepan, melt butter over medium-low heat. Add onions and mushrooms; sauté until tender. Add flour and stir until well incorporated. Gradually stir in milk. Continue cooking, stirring, until thickened and bubbly. Stir in cheese, salts, parsley, and pepper. Remove from heat. Taste and adjust seasonings. Stir in the sour cream.
4. Combine squash and sauce. Pour mixture into the prepared dish. Toss bread crumbs with melted butter; sprinkle over squash mixture. Bake for 30 minutes, or until browned and bubbly.

# Easy Fried Corn

SERVES 4

*Fresh corn, also known as green corn, isn't really fried, but it is cooked in a skillet. It's a great Southern dish.*

6 ears of corn
2 tablespoons butter or bacon drippings
½ teaspoon salt, or to taste
¼ teaspoon freshly ground pepper, or to taste
Dash sugar, optional

1. Slice corn from the cob into a bowl. Scrape the cob downward to get any remaining corn and milky liquid.
2. Add butter or bacon drippings to a heavy skillet over medium-low heat. Add the corn; cook, stirring, for 15 to 20 minutes, taking care not to burn. Sprinkle with remaining ingredients and stir. Serve hot.

**TOOLS YOU NEED**

▶ If you plan to use fresh corn often, you might want to get a corn cutter. However, if you don't have a corn cutter, a sharp knife will do. First, place the cob over a shallow bowl, holding the top to keep it upright. With the sharp side of the knife, position it as close to the cob as you can to get about two-thirds of the kernel. Cut straight down to cut the kernels from the cob. Using the blunt side of the knife, scrape the juices left on the cob. If you're making cream-style corn, position the knife so you cut about halfway into the kernels, then scrape with the back of the knife. Add a little cream or milk to fried corn to make cream corn.

## Savory Collard Greens
SERVES 6

*Greens have long been a favorite in Southern kitchens, and collard greens are wonderful.*

3 pounds collard greens
2 to 3 meaty ham hocks
1 teaspoon seasoned salt
1 ½ teaspoons salt
Dash freshly ground pepper
Dash cayenne pepper
Dash garlic powder

1. Bring about 4 to 5 quarts of water to a boil with the ham hocks. Reduce heat to a simmer and continue cooking for about 1 to 1 ½ hours. Add more water as needed.
2. Strip the thick stalks out of the collard leaves or use a knife and cut them out. Smaller leaves should not need to be stripped. Wash leaves separately; rinse. I put them in the sink and swish them after first rinsing by hand. You can tell they're clean when you no longer feel any grit in the bottom of the sink. Stack several leaves together. Roll them, then cut into ½-inch slices.
3. Working with batches, add the sliced collard leaves to the pot of boiling water with ham hocks. You'll probably have to let some of the greens wilt down before adding more. Add the seasoned salt, salt, pepper, cayenne, and garlic powder. Bring to a boil. Reduce heat to medium and simmer for about 45 minutes, stirring occasionally.
4. Taste and adjust seasonings. Serve with plenty of hot sauce.

**ELSEWHERE ON THE WEB**

▶ Emeril's Southern Greens look deliciously different! His greens, from his *Real and Rustic Cookbook,* are flavored with chopped bacon and onions, cayenne, black pepper, garlic, and molasses, along with beer and vinegar. This is a big recipe for at least eight people, and you can use mustard greens, collards, turnip greens, kale, or spinach. Here's the link to Emeril's unique recipe online: www.emerils.com/recipes/by_name/Southern_greens.html.

# Spinach Casserole with Eggs and Cheese
SERVES 6

*Hard-cooked eggs are a popular addition to Southern casseroles.*

4 to 6 strips bacon
1 ½ pounds spinach, cleaned and chopped
½ teaspoon salt
⅛ teaspoon freshly ground black pepper
2 medium tomatoes, sliced
3 hard-cooked eggs, sliced
4 tablespoons butter
4 tablespoons flour
½ teaspoon salt
⅛ teaspoon freshly ground black pepper
Dash ground paprika
2 cups milk
1 ½ cups shredded mild Cheddar cheese

1. Cook bacon in a skillet over medium heat until crisp; drain on paper towels. Crumble and set aside.
2. Heat oven to 350°F. Lightly butter a 9" × 13" baking dish.
3. Place chopped spinach in the prepared dish; season with ½ teaspoon of salt and ⅛ teaspoon of pepper. Arrange sliced tomatoes and eggs over the spinach.
4. In a medium saucepan over medium-low heat, melt the 4 tablespoons of butter. Add flour and stir until smooth and bubbly. Add ½ teaspoon salt and ⅛ teaspoon pepper, and the paprika. Gradually stir in the milk. Cook, stirring constantly, until the sauce is thickened and bubbly. Add the cheese; stir until cheese is melted. Pour the sauce over the spinach and eggs. Top with crumbled bacon. Bake for 25 to 30 minutes.

**WHAT'S HOT**

▶ Spinach is nutritious and delicious! This leafy green vegetable is a rich source of vitamins A and C, as well as potassium and other nutrients. I like to serve spinach at least once a week, either as a side dish or in a salad. One of my favorite ways to cook spinach is in a teaspoon or two of bacon drippings with a little salt, pepper, and freshly cooked and crumbled bacon. More delicious flavors for spinach include hard-cooked eggs, freshly grated nutmeg, and, of course, butter.

### How do I choose an eggplant at the market?

▶ Eggplant is highly perishable, so you definitely want to choose the freshest possible eggplants. Fresh eggplants will have a thinner skin and will not taste as bitter. An eggplant should feel heavy for its size. Lift a few of similar size, and then choose the one that feels heaviest. The eggplant should spring back when gently pressed, and the skin should be smooth and free of blemishes or soft spots. If you can't use the eggplant the day you buy it, store it for up to two days in a cool dry place.

## Spicy Fried Eggplant Strips
SERVES 6

*I was surprised to see how popular eggplant was here in the South!*

1 medium eggplant
1 teaspoon salt
1 cup all-purpose flour
1 teaspoon baking powder
2 teaspoons Creole seasoning
½ teaspoon onion powder
¼ teaspoon garlic powder
Dash ground cayenne pepper
2 large eggs, beaten
⅔ cup milk
1 tablespoon canola oil
Vegetable oil for deep frying

1.  Peel the eggplant and cut into strips ½-inch in width and 3 inches in length. Place eggplant strips in a bowl; cover with water and sprinkle with 1 teaspoon of salt. Let the eggplant strips soak for 45 minutes to 1 hour. Drain; pat dry with paper towels.
2.  In a bowl, combine the flour, baking powder, Creole seasoning, onion powder, garlic powder, and cayenne pepper. Add beaten eggs, milk, and 1 tablespoon of Canola oil. Blend until smooth. Batter should be thin enough to drip a bit but thick enough to coat the eggplant. Add a little more milk if too thick, or more flour if too thin.
3.  Heat the oil to 375°F. Dip the eggplant strips in batter; let excess batter drip back into the bowl. Fry the eggplant strips in small batches in the hot oil for 3 minutes, turning to cook both sides, until golden brown.

## Easy Skillet-Glazed Sweet Potatoes
SERVES 6

*My family loves these skillet sweet potatoes, and the recipe is so simple. These make a great side dish with ham, pork, or lamb.*

> 4 to 5 medium sweet potatoes
> ¾ cup brown sugar, packed
> ½ cup water
> ¼ teaspoon salt
> 2 tablespoons butter

1. Boil sweet potatoes in their jackets until tender. Let cool slightly, then peel and slice into ½-inch thick rounds.
2. In a heavy skillet, combine the brown sugar, water, salt, and butter. Heat over medium heat until the mixture begins to simmer; reduce heat to low and simmer for 5 minutes. Add the sliced sweet potatoes and simmer for 10 minutes longer, turning often to keep them coated with the sugar mixture.
3. Spoon into a serving dish and serve hot, with pork, ham, or roast beef.

**ASK YOUR GUIDE**

*Why should sweet potatoes be cooked before peeling?*

▶ Sweet potatoes should be boiled in their jackets so they will retain their great nutrients. Boiled sweet potatoes are very easy to peel. Just pick them out of the water with a slotted spoon and dip in cold water. The skins will slip off easily. If you are working with peeled sweet potatoes to make a dish such as fries or a baked dish, keep them in cold water with lemon juice so they won't darken. You should use about 3 tablespoons of lemon juice to each quart of cold water.

## Sweet Potato Casserole
SERVES 8

*This casserole is similar to the one my mother-in-law serves for holiday dinners, and it is delicious.*

4 to 5 medium sweet potatoes, about 3 pounds
2 large eggs, slightly beaten
2 tablespoons melted butter
3 tablespoons packed light brown sugar
1 teaspoon salt
½ teaspoon ground cinnamon
¼ teaspoon ground ginger
⅛ teaspoon freshly grated nutmeg
Dash freshly ground black pepper
½ cup pecans, chopped

1. Scrub sweet potatoes and place in a large kettle or stockpot. Cover with water. Bring to a boil over high heat; reduce heat to medium-low and boil for about 30 minutes, until tender. Set aside to let the sweet potatoes cool slightly.
2. Slip sweet potatoes out of the skins into a medium bowl. If you have a ricer, cut them into smaller pieces and put them through a ricer, then mash until smooth. If you don't have a ricer, just mash with a potato masher. Add beaten eggs, butter, brown sugar, salt, cinnamon, ginger, nutmeg, and pepper. Whisk or beat until smooth.
3. Heat oven to 350°F. Lightly butter a 7" x 11" baking dish.
4. Turn the sweet potato mixture into the prepared baking dish. Sprinkle pecans over the top. Bake for 35 to 45 minutes, or until puffy and hot. Serve hot.

**ELSEWHERE ON THE WEB**

▶ The annual Vardaman, Mississippi, Sweet Potato Festival takes place during the first week of November. It's a great way to learn more about sweet potatoes from local farmers and towns-people of Vardaman, the third-largest sweet potato producer in the nation. Their Web site offers photos of recent festivities, a calendar of events, information on area sweet potato farmers, sweet potato facts, some merchandise, and several of their favorite recipes. Check it out at www.vardaman sweetpotatofestival.com.

## Creamy Potato Scallop

SERVES 6

*I grew up in a potato-producing area, and not only did I work on the farms in the fall, my family ate potatoes almost every night of the week. Here's one of my favorite potato casseroles, a nice departure from the everyday boiled or mashed potatoes.*

2 pounds red or round white potatoes
1 teaspoon salt
¼ teaspoon pepper
2 tablespoons flour
¼ cup chopped onion
2 cups shredded sharp Cheddar cheese
2 tablespoons butter, cut in small pieces
2 cups milk

1. Heat oven to 350°F. Lightly butter a 2-quart baking dish.
2. Peel potatoes, slice into about ¼-inch thick rounds. You should have about 4 cups. Arrange half of the potatoes in a greased 2-quart baking dish.
3. Sprinkle with half of the salt, pepper, flour, onion, and cheese. Dot the layer all over with half of the small pieces of butter. Repeat layer; dot with remaining butter and add milk to cover potatoes. Cover with foil.
4. Bake the casserole for about 30 to 40 minutes, or until potatoes are tender. Take the lid off near the end of cooking time or put under the broiler for a minute or two to brown the top.

**BEFORE YOU BEGIN**

▶ Before you choose potatoes for a recipe, be sure you know the difference between the various types. Waxy potatoes are low-starch potatoes, and they hold up better for dishes such as potato salads and scalloped potatoes. Starchy potatoes make great mashed potatoes, French fries, and baked potatoes. If you aren't sure what kind you have, test by slicing. If the knife is coated with a creamy white film or if the potato lightly clings to the knife, the potato is starchy. If it doesn't, it's a waxy potato. If it has only a little creamy film, it's probably a good all-purpose potato, and it should work well in most dishes.

## Judy's Hash Brown Casserole
SERVES 8

*This popular country-style hash-brown side dish recipe is similar to one shared on the Southern Cuisine forum. It's easy and it makes a great brunch dish, or you could serve the casserole as a dinner side dish.*

1 package (30 ounces) frozen country-style hash browns
1 can (10 ¾ ounces) cream of chicken or cream of celery soup
1 cup sour cream
½ cup melted butter
2 cups shredded sharp Cheddar cheese
1 cup fine-chopped onion
½ teaspoon salt, or to taste
¼ teaspoon freshly ground pepper
1 cup soft bread crumbs
2 tablespoons melted butter

1. Thaw the hash browns quickly in defrost cycle of the microwave or leave in refrigerator overnight.
2. Heat oven to 350°F. Lightly butter a 13" × 9" × 2" baking dish.
3. In a large bowl, combine the thawed hash browns with remaining ingredients. Stir to blend ingredients thoroughly.
4. Spread in the prepared baking dish. Bake for 45 minutes, or until lightly browned and bubbly.

**ELSEWHERE ON THE WEB**

▶ This recipe combines tasty new potatoes, Cheddar cheese, onion, mayonnaise, and a topping of crumbled bacon to make an easy family side-dish casserole. The hearty potato casserole is from Jean Brandau, the Huntsville, Alabama, Guide for About.com, and Cathey Carney, of *Old Huntsville Magazine*. It looks delicious! Check the recipe out at http://about.com/huntsville/ potatocasserole. Just below the recipe you'll see a link to more of Jean's Alabama recipes, and you can even submit your own favorites.

# Crispy Fried Okra
SERVES 6

*I prefer okra fried with a crispy cornmeal coating, and this is one of my family's favorites.*

1 pound fresh okra
2 eggs, beaten
Several drops hot pepper sauce
1 cup cornmeal
½ cup flour
½ teaspoon salt
¼ teaspoon freshly ground black pepper
Dash ground cayenne
Vegetable oil for deep frying

1. Wash okra; cut off tips and stem ends. Cut the okra pods crosswise into ½-inch slices.
2. Beat eggs in a shallow bowl with the hot pepper sauce.
3. Combine the cornmeal, flour, salt, pepper, and cayenne in a large food storage bag or shallow bowl.
4. Heat oil in deep fryer to 375°F.
5. Add okra to the beaten eggs; stir to coat well. Drop several pieces of okra into the cornmeal mixture and shake gently to coat well. Repeat with remaining okra.
6. Fry the okra in the hot oil in batches until browned, about 4 to 6 minutes for each batch. Turn as needed to brown all sides. Drain on paper towels and keep warm.

**WHAT'S HOT**

▶ Okra is a natural thickener in gumbo, and it goes well with tomatoes and corn. I have a couple of popular okra recipes on my site, including one using okra and tomatoes with bacon, onion, and spicy seasonings. For this recipe visit http://about .com/southernfood/okra withtomatoes.

**What's the easiest way to peel tomatoes?**

▶ You can peel tomatoes with a sharp knife and some practice, but if you're peeling many, here's an easier way. Cut an "X" into the bottom of each tomato. Drop them into boiling water and leave for about 7 to 10 seconds (less if the tomatoes are very ripe). With a slotted spoon, remove the tomatoes to a bowl of ice water and leave them for about 1 minute. Use a small, sharp knife to peel the tomatoes, starting at the cut at the bottom. The peel should come off easily, then you can core the tomatoes and remove seeds, if desired.

## Quick and Easy Broiled Tomatoes
SERVES 6

*This is a perfect side to a backyard barbecue or a quick summer meal. I love these with grilled chicken or shrimp.*

4 medium tomatoes
Dijon mustard
Salt
Freshly ground black pepper
6 tablespoons melted butter
½ cup seasoned fine dry bread crumbs
½ cup grated Parmesan cheese

1. Cut tomatoes in half and arrange on the lightly oiled rack of a broiler pan; spread cut side with Dijon mustard and sprinkle with salt and pepper. Combine the melted butter with bread crumbs and Parmesan cheese; spoon over the tomato halves.
2. Place tomatoes under the broiler, about 6 inches from the heat source, and broil until crumbs are browned and tomatoes are tender.

# Fried Green Tomatoes

SERVES 4

*There are many ways to make these, but a cornmeal mixture is the preferred method in our household.*

4 large firm green tomatoes
Salt and pepper
¼ cup flour
2 eggs, beaten
1 cup cornmeal
½ cup all-purpose flour
Dash ground cayenne
Vegetable oil

1. Slice the tomatoes into rounds about ¼- to ½-inch thick. Sprinkle the tomatoes with salt and pepper on both sides. Dip in the ¼ cup flour to lightly coat.
2. In a bowl, whisk eggs. In another bowl, combine the cornmeal, ½ cup flour, and cayenne pepper.
3. Heat about ⅓ cup of oil in a heavy skillet over medium heat. The bottom of the skillet should be completely covered with oil to a depth of about ⅛ to ¼ inch.
4. Dip flour-dusted green tomato slices in the beaten egg, then dredge in cornmeal mixture to coat thoroughly. Fry in batches until browned, then turn to brown the other side. They'll take about 3 minutes on each side.
5. Serve these as a side dish or combine with a sauce or sliced cheese and serve as a first course.

**WHAT'S HOT**

▶ Fried green tomatoes are not only a great side dish served plain or with a salsa or sauce, they make a flavorful and interesting first course or appetizer. Stack a few with a round or two of goat cheese and a remoulade sauce, or serve on a bed of spinach with the crawfish or crabmeat variations of Sherry Cream Sauce (page 207). They would also be fabulous topped with a couple of medium cooked shrimp, or with sliced mozzarella cheese or freshly grated Parmesan cheese with a little basil-seasoned tomato sauce.

## Baked Vidalia Onions
SERVES 6

*This is one of my mother-in-law's favorite recipes, a wonderful way to enjoy sweet onions. Feel free to substitute any large sweet onions in season.*

6 large Vidalia onions
Softened butter for greasing foil
6 tablespoons cold butter, cut into pieces
1 ½ teaspoons salt
¼ teaspoon freshly ground black pepper
1 to 1 ½ cups fresh shredded Parmesan cheese

1. Heat oven to 350°F. Lightly butter 6 large squares of foil (large enough to wrap each onion).
2. Peel the onions, leaving the roots intact. Cut each into eighths, cutting just to, but not through, the roots.
3. Place each onion on a piece of foil. Divide butter equally among the onions, pressing it into the centers. Sprinkle with salt and pepper, and sprinkle each with 3 to 4 tablespoons of shredded cheese.
4. Wrap each onion in the foil and arrange in a 13" x 9" baking dish. Bake the wrapped onions for about 45 to 60 minutes, or until onions are tender.

ELSEWHERE ON THE WEB

▶ Peggy Trowbridge, the About.com Guide to Home Cooking, has a very informative article on sweet onions, with selection and storage tips, health and nutrition facts, and more about the different varieties of sweet onions and their availability. Visit http://about.com/homecooking/sweetonions. She also has a nice list of recipes using onions, including Braised Onion Slices with Bourbon, Caramelized Onions, Caviar Cream Pie, Fried Onion Rings, Fajitas, Chunky Guacamole, and many main dish recipes, salads, and side dish recipes.

# Broccoli with Cheese Sauce

SERVES 8

*This broccoli dish is delicious and uncomplicated, and the cheese sauce is wonderful with cauliflower as well.*

1 ½ pounds fresh broccoli
3 tablespoons butter
1 tablespoon grated onion
3 tablespoons flour
Dash garlic powder
Dash paprika
⅛ teaspoon pepper
1 ½ cups milk
1 cup grated sharp Cheddar cheese

1. Trim broccoli, discarding large leaves and tough ends of lower stalks. Wash well, drain, then cut the stalks and florets into bite-size pieces.
2. In a large saucepan, combine broccoli with a small amount of water; bring to a boil over medium-high heat. Reduce heat to medium-low, cover, and simmer for 10 to 12 minutes, or until broccoli is tender. Or, steam the broccoli for about 10 minutes, or to desired doneness.
3. Meanwhile, in a saucepan over medium heat, melt the butter; add grated onion and sauté until onion is soft. Stir in flour until well blended; add seasonings. Gradually stir in the milk. Continue cooking, stirring constantly, until sauce is thickened and bubbly. Stir in the cheese until melted; remove from heat.
4. Drain the broccoli and serve hot with cheese sauce.

**TOOLS YOU NEED**

▸ While a saucier pan isn't an essential pan, you might want to put it on your wish list. One of my favorite pans is a saucier, and it's perfect for whisking or stirring sauces. The rounded bottom means more sauce is in touch with the bottom, and the whisk can reach the whole surface easily. I like stainless steel with an aluminum core on the bottom and up the sides, and a cover comes in handy.

**I love cabbage, but I hate the odor. Is there a way to keep the smell down?**

▶ I agree—the odor of cooking cabbage can make the whole house smell bad. One remedy is to add a few thick chunks of crusty bread to the cooking liquid. The bread will absorb some of the odors. The best solution is to cook it quickly, because the odor compounds are released as the sulfur-containing compounds are cooked.

## Savory Baked Cabbage
SERVES 6 TO 8

*I like to use a mixture of red and green bell pepper, and I sometimes add a little yellow if I have it.*

1 medium head cabbage
4 tablespoons butter
½ cup chopped sweet bell pepper
¼ cup fine-chopped onion
¼ cup fine-chopped celery
¼ cup all-purpose flour
2 cups milk
½ teaspoon salt
¼ teaspoon freshly ground black pepper
⅓ cup mayonnaise
1 cup shredded mild Cheddar cheese

1. Heat oven to 375°F. Lightly butter a 13" x 9" baking dish.
2. Cut cabbage into 8 wedges; place in a kettle or Dutch oven with a small amount of lightly salted water. Cover and bring to a boil; cook for 10 minutes. Drain well and place the wedges in the prepared baking dish.
3. Heat butter in a large saucepan or skillet over medium heat. Add bell pepper, onion, and celery; sauté for about 4 to 5 minutes, or until tender. Add flour; stir to blend. Continue cooking, stirring for about 30 seconds. Gradually stir in milk. Cook sauce mixture, stirring, over medium heat until thickened and bubbly. Stir in the salt and pepper. Pour over the cabbage in the baking dish.
4. Bake for 20 minutes. Combine mayonnaise and cheese; spoon over the cabbage wedges and bake until cheese is melted.

# Asparagus Cheddar Casserole
SERVES 8

*If your family likes asparagus the way mine does, this delicious casserole will become a holiday dinner tradition.*

6 tablespoons butter
2 tablespoons grated onion
¼ cup chopped red or green bell pepper
6 tablespoons all-purpose flour
2 cups milk
2 ½ teaspoons salt
½ teaspoon freshly ground black pepper
6 cups cooked asparagus
5 hard-cooked eggs, sliced
1 ½ cups shredded mild Cheddar cheese
¾ cup bread crumbs
3 tablespoons melted butter

1. Heat oven to 350°F. Butter a 9" x 13" baking dish.
2. Melt butter in a medium saucepan over medium-low heat. Add onion and bell pepper; sauté until tender. Stir in the flour until well blended. Gradually add milk, stirring constantly over medium-low heat until thickened and bubbly. Stir in salt and pepper.
3. Arrange about half of the asparagus in the prepared baking dish; top with half of the sliced hard-cooked eggs and half of the cheese. Repeat layers.
4. Pour the hot sauce over the casserole. Toss bread crumbs with the melted butter; sprinkle over the casserole.
5. Bake for 25 to 30 minutes, until hot and bubbly.

ELSEWHERE ON THE WEB

▶ Here are two elegant asparagus preparations from Kyle Phillips, the About.com Italian Cuisine Guide. The first is a dish of asparagus with a topping of soft-boiled or poached eggs and grated Pecorino Romano cheese, at http://about.com/italian food/asparaguseggs, and the second recipe is a wonderful spring flan with asparagus, milk, grated cheese, and eggs. Kyle says this would make a tasty antipasto or side dish, but you can also serve it as part of a light lunch. Check this recipe out at http://about.com/italianfood/asparagusflan.

## Get Linked

*There are so many wonderful side dishes I wanted to include in this chapter, but there is only so much space and time. My Southern Cuisine site on* **About.com** *has many more recipes for a variety of vegetables, along with more helpful vegetable cooking resources. Here are a few of my favorites.*

**VEGETABLE RECIPES**

Here's the main vegetable recipe index, and you'll find a huge variety, from asparagus and cauliflower to mushrooms and winter squash.

 http://about.com/southernfood/vegetablerecipes

**VEGETABLE FREEZING GUIDE**

This vegetable freezing guide will come in handy as you harvest your vegetables or buy in bulk. This guide includes some basic preparation tips and instructions for dozens of specific vegetables, along with advice on cooking frozen vegetables.

 http://about.com/southernfood/vegetablefreezing

**FESTIVE SIDE DISH CASSEROLES**

This is an article with links to dozens of recipes, and the focus is on the holiday table. Vegetable side dish recipes include preparations for butternut squash, mashed potatoes, carrot casserole, creamy spinach, corn casserole, macaroni and cheese, green bean recipes, sweet potato and banana casserole, and more.

http://about.com/southernfood/festivesides

Chapter 12

# Sauces, Pickles, and Preserves

ASK YOUR GUIDE:

What is the origin of remoulade sauce, and are there many variations?
▶ PAGE 203

What is a boiling water bath?
▶ PAGE 209

Can I use berries to make freezer jam?
▶ PAGE 213

## Creamy Sausage Gravy
SERVES 8

*Serve this delicious old-fashioned Southern gravy with biscuits or grits.*

1 pound breakfast sausage
2 tablespoons shortening, bacon drippings, or lard
6 tablespoons flour
3 to 3 ½ cups milk
Salt and freshly ground black pepper
Dash cayenne pepper, or to taste

1. In a heavy skillet, cook the sausage, breaking up with a spatula, until no longer pink. Remove to a plate with a slotted spoon.
2. Add 2 tablespoons of shortening, oil, or lard to the skillet drippings and heat over medium-low heat. Add flour, stirring until well blended and bubbly, about 30 seconds. Gradually stir in 3 cups of milk, stirring and cooking until thickened and bubbly. Add more milk, depending on how thick you like your gravy. Stir in the sausage and season to taste with salt, black pepper, and cayenne pepper.
3. Serve over hot buttered split Perfect Buttermilk Biscuits (page 26) or with hot cooked grits.

WHAT'S HOT

▶ I love this delicious, thick sausage gravy on biscuits or with grits, but if you have leftovers, serve the gravy with Country Fried Steak (page 89), Fried Chicken Strips (page 134), or Southern Fried Chicken (page 132). Some other add-ins or substitutions that would jazz up this recipe include Creole or Cajun-style seasoning, chopped fresh parsley, garlic powder, fine-chopped onion, or a little dried leaf basil or thyme.

## Giblet Gravy

SERVES 8

*This delicious gravy is absolutely essential with the holiday turkey dinner.*

Giblets from 1 whole turkey
Roast turkey drippings
3 tablespoons all-purpose flour
4 cups chicken broth
Salt and pepper, to taste

1. Put turkey giblets in a saucepan; cover with chicken broth and bring to a boil. Skim off foam. Reduce heat to low; cover and simmer for 1 ½ hours.
2. Remove giblets from the cooking liquid and add more broth to make 3 cups.
3. Remove meat from neck and mince along with the liver and heart. Discard gristle and excess fat.
4. Put the juices from the turkey in a medium saucepan over medium-low heat, or remove the turkey to a platter and put the roasting pan over medium-low heat. Stir 3 tablespoons of flour into the juices until well blended. Gradually add the chicken broth, stirring constantly, along with the minced giblets. Continue cooking, stirring, until thickened and bubbly. Add salt and pepper to taste.

**TOOLS YOU NEED**

▶ A wire whisk is a must-have for a good smooth sauce or gravy, and this tool comes in many shapes and sizes. If you use some non-stick pans, make sure you have one or two coated whisks; for whisking in a sauté pan or roasting pan, a flat whisk works well. For separated or lumpy sauces, an immersion blender can be a lifesaver, just be careful when you're working with hot sauce or gravy.

## Jezebel Sauce
MAKES ABOUT 3 CUPS

*This tasty Jezebel sauce is delicious served with ham, pork, beef, or corned beef, or pour it over a block of cream cheese for a flavorful holiday spread.*

    1 jar (10 ounces) pineapple preserves
    1 jar (10 ounces) apple jelly
    ¼ to ½ cup prepared horseradish
    2 tablespoons dry mustard
    1 teaspoon coarsely ground black pepper

1. Combine all ingredients in a bowl or food processor. Whisk or process until smooth and well blended.
2. Cover and refrigerate for at least 2 hours before serving. Serve Jezebel sauce over cream cheese with assorted crackers for a delicious appetizer spread.

▶ The hot and pungent flavor of horseradish adds zest to many dishes, including dressings and sauces. Prepared horseradish can be stored in the refrigerator for about 1 month, but after that it will begin to lose its heat and will turn bitter. If you need to keep it longer, use a tablespoon and spoon it onto a foil-lined baking sheet. Freeze until solid then put chunks in an airtight container or plastic food storage bag. The horseradish can be frozen for up to six months. Make a quick and easy sauce with about 1 teaspoon of horseradish, ½ cup of applesauce, and a dash of dry mustard. This is great with pork chops or sliced pork roast.

## Remoulade Sauce

MAKES 1 CUP

*This sauce is delicious with just about any fish or seafood, and I love it with cold beef or corned beef or as a dip for fried vegetables. Recipes for remoulade sauce can vary widely; this is one I like.*

1 cup mayonnaise
1 ½ teaspoons Dijon mustard
2 teaspoons chopped sweet pickle
1 teaspoon chopped capers
2 teaspoons fresh parsley, chopped fine
½ teaspoon dried chopped chervil, crumbled
½ teaspoon dried leaf tarragon, crumbled
Dash Tabasco sauce
½ teaspoon salt
Dash ground white pepper

1. In a bowl, combine all ingredients and blend well.
2. Cover and refrigerate to chill thoroughly before serving.

**ASK YOUR GUIDE**

***What is the origin of remoulade sauce, and are there many variations?***

▶ Remoulade sauce is a French sauce made with mayonnaise and mustard or Creole mustard, along with capers, sometimes anchovy paste, and a variety of other herbs and seasonings. New Orleans-style remoulade sauce is usually made spicier than the French version, and it frequently includes horseradish, hot sauce, fine-chopped onion or green onions, or chopped hard-cooked eggs. There are many, many variations, limited only by the cook's tastes and preferences.

▶ Mayonnaise sauces are quick and easy to prepare, and they can add a great deal of flavor to certain dishes. I like a good tartar sauce with fish or seafood, and to make it at home I usually combine about ½ cup of mayonnaise, 1 teaspoon of mustard, 1 tablespoon of chopped sweet pickle, and a little chopped fresh parsley or grated onion. Another easy sauce for chicken wings or fried chicken strips is a curried mayonnaise sauce. This is made with equal amounts of mayonnaise and apricot preserves, along with a little curry powder, to taste.

## Quick Mayonnaise Mustard Sauce
MAKES 1 CUP

*This is a simple sauce, and quick to prepare. I make this sauce to go with sausage balls, chicken wings, fried fish, or other dishes. Feel free to use another herb in place of the dill.*

1 cup mayonnaise
2 teaspoons prepared yellow mustard
1 ½ teaspoons Dijon mustard
¼ teaspoon dried dill

1. In a small bowl, combine all ingredients.
2. Cover and chill until serving time. Serve with Fried Chicken Strips (page 134), Cheddar Sausage Balls (page 22), or other similar appetizers.

## Come Back Sauce

MAKES 1 CUP

*I love this flavorful Southern sauce with fish and seafood, and it also makes a nice salad dressing.*

1 cup mayonnaise
¼ cup chili sauce
¼ cup ketchup
2 teaspoons prepared yellow mustard
½ cup olive oil
2 teaspoons Worcestershire sauce
1 teaspoon coarsely ground black pepper
1 tablespoon grated onion
2 cloves garlic, minced
2 tablespoons fresh lemon juice
Few drops hot sauce

1. Put all ingredients in a large jar; screw on the top and shake until well blended.
2. Refrigerate for at least 4 hours before using, to let flavors blend. Serve with fried fish or seafood, Salmon Croquettes (page 158), Fried Chicken Strips (page 134), appetizer wings, or use in place of mayonnaise on a sandwich or as a salad dressing.

ELSEWHERE ON THE WEB

▶ I also love a tasty, tangy sweet-and-sour sauce with appetizers and some fried foods, and there are several excellent ones on About.com. Here are two good versions from Rhonda Parkinson, the Chinese Cuisine Guide. First, you'll find an easy sweet-and-sour dipping sauce, made with ketchup, vinegar, a little sugar, cornstarch, bell pepper, and water at http://about.com/chinesefood/sweetandsour. Also from Rhonda, this simple sweet-and-sour sauce is made with even fewer ingredients, including vinegar, brown sugar, ketchup, and soy sauce: http://about.com/chinesefood/simplesweetandsour.

▶ Salsas are just wonderful with grilled or broiled meat, poultry, and fish and seafood, and fruit salsas can really spice things up. Plan to prepare salsa at least 30 minutes early to give it time to let the flavors blend, and store any leftover fresh salsa in a tightly covered container in the refrigerator for up to five days. Fresh salsa is easy to prepare and makes a great addition to a basic meal or party, and it can even be used as a flavorful low-fat dressing for salad greens.

## Peach Salsa
SERVES 6

*This delicious salsa is the perfect accompaniment for grilled chicken, pork, or fish. Feel free to replace the peaches with diced mango or pineapple, or use a combination of fruits. Feel free to substitute a milder chile pepper for the minced jalapeño.*

3 medium peaches
2 medium plum tomatoes
½ cup diced red onion
2 tablespoons diced red bell pepper
¼ cup seeded diced cucumber
2 teaspoons minced jalapeño chile pepper
Juice of 1 lime
1 tablespoon fresh chopped cilantro
Freshly ground black pepper, to taste

1. Peel peaches, remove pits, and dice. Wash tomatoes, remove seeds, and dice.
2. In a serving bowl, combine peaches, tomatoes, and remaining ingredients. Stir to blend ingredients. Taste and add pepper, if desired.
3. Cover and let the salsa sit at room temperature for about 30 minutes to let flavors blend.

## Sherry Cream Sauce
MAKES 1 ½ CUPS

*Try a little of this sauce on a fish fillet or broiled shrimp. I usually add a little crabmeat or chopped shrimp, but mushrooms are delicious, too.*

3 tablespoons butter
1 medium clove garlic, minced
2 tablespoons grated onion
2 cups heavy whipping cream
¼ cup dry sherry
Salt and pepper, to taste
Dash ground paprika, optional

1. Melt the butter in a saucier or medium saucepan over medium-low heat. Add the garlic and grated onion. Cook the onion mixture, stirring, for about 1 minute, until onion is tender.
2. Stir in cream and sherry. Simmer for about 10 minutes to reduce by about one-quarter. Taste and add salt, pepper, and paprika, to taste.
3. If desired, make variations as follows.
4. Crawfish or Crabmeat Sherry Sauce: Add about ½ cup flaked crawfish or crabmeat, along with 1 tablespoon of fresh chopped parsley. If desired, add a dash of Tabasco sauce.
5. Creamy Shrimp Sauce: Add ½ cup chopped cooked shrimp just before done and replace the grated onion with green onion chopped fine.
6. Mushroom Sauce: Add 1 cup of sliced mushrooms with the grated onion and garlic; sauté for about 1 minute longer or until mushrooms are tender.

**WHAT'S HOT**

▶ One of my favorite sauces, and probably the most adaptable, is the sauce we often call white sauce. Also known as béchamel, this sauce is wonderful as a basic sauce with seasonings, or add cheese for a basic cheese sauce or Mornay sauce. Other easy additions include sliced mushrooms, herbs, minced onions, Cajun-style seasonings, and your own favorite add-ins. Check it out at http://about.com/southernfood/whitesauce.

## Barbecue Sauce with Bourbon
MAKES ABOUT 3 CUPS

*Here's a delicious bourbon barbecue sauce to use on beef, chicken, or pork—you can also serve it on the side.*

3 tablespoons butter
4 tablespoons Canola oil
1 ½ cups chopped onion
1 clove garlic, minced
½ cup good-quality bourbon
¾ cup ketchup
½ cup orange juice
½ cup vinegar
½ cup brown sugar
¼ cup molasses
1 tablespoon Worcestershire sauce
¼ teaspoon coarsely ground black pepper
½ teaspoon salt

1. In a medium saucepan, combine the butter and oil over medium-low heat; add chopped onion and garlic. Cook, stirring occasionally, until onion is tender.
2. Add remaining ingredients, stirring to blend. Reduce heat to low; cook for about 30 to 45 minutes, stirring frequently, until reduced and thickened.
3. Cover tightly and store in the refrigerator for up to 10 days.

**BEFORE YOU BEGIN**

▶ Barbecue sauces might be simple or complicated, but they all add fabulous flavor to meat, poultry, and seafood. When you prepare to grill or broil, consider marinades, mops, sauces, and rubs. The Barbecues and Grilling site at About.com will answer all of your questions, and you'll find a great variety of recipes. This article on basting and mops, from Derrick Riches, explains how to baste, when to do it, and what to use. Check it out at http://about.com/bbq/mop. When you scroll down the page, you'll see a number of links to Derrick's delicious sauce recipes.

## Bread and Butter Pickles
MAKES ABOUT 4 PINTS

*I like all kinds of pickles, but these bread and butter pickles are a big favorite of mine.*

4 quarts unpeeled cucumber, sliced thin
6 cups onion, sliced thin
1 green bell pepper, cut in thin slices
1 red bell pepper, cut in thin slices
4 small cloves garlic, peeled
Ice
⅓ cup kosher salt
5 cups granulated sugar
1 ½ teaspoons turmeric
1 ½ teaspoons celery seed
2 tablespoons mustard seed
3 cups vinegar (5% acidity)

1. In a large nonreactive kettle, combine the thin-sliced cucumber and onions, sliced peppers, and whole garlic cloves. Sprinkle cucumber mixture with the salt and cover with ice; mix well to combine ingredients. Let stand for 3 to 4 hours.
2. Drain cucumber mixture well. Combine remaining ingredients; pour over the cucumber mixture. Bring to a boil; remove from heat.
3. Transfer to hot, sterilized 1-pint jars. Clean jar rims of any spills and then seal and process the pickles in a boiling water bath for 15 minutes, or 20 minutes for altitudes from 1,000 to 6,000 feet.
4. Adjust lids and let cool. Check for seals and then store the pickles in a cool dark place for a week or two before using.

**ASK YOUR GUIDE**

***What is a boiling water bath?***

▶ This is the process in which canned, high-acid foods are covered with water then boiled to kill harmful molds, yeasts, and some bacteria. A boiling-water-bath canner should be tall enough to allow at least 1 inch of water over the jars and 1 inch of headspace. Preheat the water to 180°F before putting jars of hot-packed food into the water (to 140°F for raw-packed foods). Cover and bring to a boil over high heat, and then adjust heat to maintain a gentle boil. Remove lid and remove from heat when the jars have boiled for the recommended length of time. Place jars on a protected surface, not touching, to cool.

## Green Tomato Chow-Chow

MAKES ABOUT 16 PINTS

*This is a wonderful way to use the last of your garden's green tomatoes.*

4 quarts green tomatoes

1 large head green cabbage

6 large onions

6 medium green bell peppers

6 medium red bell peppers

½ cup kosher salt

15 cups vinegar (5% acidity)

5 cups granulated sugar

3 tablespoons dry mustard

2 teaspoons powdered ginger

1 tablespoon ground turmeric

¼ cup mustard seeds

3 tablespoons celery seed

2 tablespoons pickling spices

1. Chop the green tomatoes, cabbage, onions, and peppers; combine in a large nonreactive kettle. Stir in salt and let stand for at least 8 hours at room temperature. Drain well.

2. In nonreactive kettle, combine the vinegar, sugar, dry mustard, ginger, and turmeric. Wrap the mustard and celery seed and pickling spices in a square of cheesecloth or put in a cheesecloth bag and tie securely. Bring the mixture to a boil over high heat. Reduce heat to medium-low and simmer for 30 minutes longer. Drain the salted vegetables and add to the liquid; return to a simmer and simmer for 30 minutes longer. Discard bag with spices.

3. Spoon chow-chow into hot sterilized jars, clean spills from rims with dampened paper towels and screw on lids. Process the jars for 15 minutes in a boiling water bath canner. For altitudes from 1,001 to 6,000 feet, process the jars for 20 minutes. For altitudes over 6,000 feet, process the jars for 25 minutes. For boiling water bath canning instructions, see Bread and Butter Pickles (page 209).

4. Let cool on a protected surface with jars at least 1 inch apart; adjust lids and seals and store in a cool, dry place.

ELSEWHERE ON THE WEB

▶ Extension services are some of the best resources on the Web for safety information and informational brochures for food preservation. Here's a great resource from the National Center for Home Food Preservation. You'll find answers to canning, freezing, drying, curing and smoking, and fermenting questions, and information on pickling and jam- and jelly-making, along with storage advice. They also have links to recipes and complete publications you can download and store on your computer or print. Check it out at www.uga.edu/nchfp.

## Cranberry Chutney
MAKES ABOUT 4 CUPS

*This chutney is delicious, and it will take you right through the holiday season if you freeze it in containers or jars.*

I large orange
¼ cup fresh orange juice
12 ounces fresh cranberries
1 ¾ cups granulated sugar
1 large Golden Delicious or Cortland apple
½ cup golden raisins
¼ cup chopped pecans
1 tablespoon apple cider vinegar
½ teaspoon ground ginger
½ teaspoon ground cinnamon

1. Remove peel and tough white membrane from the orange; cut into small pieces. Combine with orange juice, cranberries, and sugar in a large saucepan.
2. Peel apple, remove core, and chop. Add to the cranberry mixture along with remaining ingredients.
3. Bring mixture to a boil; reduce heat and simmer, stirring occasionally, for 6 to 8 minutes, until cranberries are popping. Chill until serving time.
4. I freeze this in small canning jars or plastic freezer containers and take it out when I need it for a meal of turkey, chicken, pork, or ham.

WHAT'S HOT

▶ This chutney and others have plenty of other uses. This cranberry chutney makes a nice addition for a turkey salad with mayonnaise and curry powder, or chop fine, add a little oil, and use as a glaze for poultry or pork. Chutney is a great addition to cream cheese or butter—just chop it fine and mash it into the butter or cream cheese for a flavorful spread for bread or quick breads. Combine 2 or 3 tablespoons of chutney with mayonnaise for a tasty spread or dressing, or puree chutney with a little heavy cream and drizzle a little in a bowl of cream of squash soup or other cream soups.

## Corn Relish

MAKES 6 PINTS

*This old-time recipe makes a delicious condiment for pork, ham, or grilled poultry.*

1 quart fresh corn kernels
3 cups chopped green bell pepper
1 cup chopped red bell pepper
2 cups seeded, chopped cucumber (unpeeled)
4 cups chopped tomato
4 cups vinegar (5% acidity)
2 cups granulated sugar
¼ cup salt
1 tablespoon ground turmeric
1 tablespoon mustard seed

1. Combine chopped vegetables in a large nonreactive kettle; add vinegar, sugar, salt, turmeric, and mustard seed.
2. Bring mixture to a boil over high heat. Reduce heat to medium-low and simmer for 25 minutes, or until vegetables are tender.
3. Spoon into hot, sterilized canning jars; wipe mouths of jars with a wet paper towel and screw on lids.
4. Process in a boiling water bath for 15 minutes, or 20 minutes at altitudes from 1,001 to 6,000. Add another 5 minutes for altitudes over 6,000 feet. See Bread and Butter Pickles (page 209) for boiling-water-bath canning instructions.

ELSEWHERE ON THE WEB

▶ Here's an excellent list of pickle and relish recipes from The University of Minnesota Extension Service, along with links to resources on how to make fermented pickles, sauerkraut, and fresh-pack pickles. Recipes include Pickled Green Tomato Relish, Marinated Mushrooms, Pickled Dilled Okra, Pickled Peppers, Pepper-Onion Relish, Pickle Relish, Pickled Beets, Three-Bean Salad, Piccalilli, Pickled Zucchini, Mixed Vegetables, and more. The recipes include some very good instructions for preparation and canning. Check it out at www.extension.umn.edu/distribution/nutrition/DJ3471.html.

## Freezer Peach Jam

MAKES 8 PINTS

*This is an easy and tasty peach jam made for the freezer.*

4 cups peeled, pitted, crushed fresh peaches
¼ cup fresh lemon juice
1 package (1 ¾ ounces) powdered fruit pectin
1 cup light corn syrup
5 ½ cups granulated sugar

1. Measure 4 cups of crushed peaches into a large kettle; with a wooden spoon, stir in the fresh lemon juice. Stir in the pectin. Let the mixture stand for 20 minutes.
2. Add the corn syrup and stir to blend; add sugar and blend well. Cook the mixture over low heat to about 100°F. It should be warm to the touch. Do not allow the mixture to get very hot. Pour the jam into jars, leaving ½-inch headspace. Cover immediately and let stand until the consistency is that of jelly. Freezer jams can be stored for up to 1 year in the freezer, and they will keep for several weeks in the refrigerator.

ASK YOUR GUIDE

**Can I use berries to make freezer jam?**

▶ Yes! In general, the formula for blackberry, raspberry, or strawberry freezer jam is 3 cups cleaned and crushed berries, 5 cups sugar, 1 package of powdered pectin, and 1 cup cold water. To make the jam, measure the fruit into a large bowl and combine with the sugar. Let stand for 20 minutes, stirring occasionally. Dissolve the pectin in a saucepan in 1 cup cold water, bring to a boil, and boil for 1 minute. Add to the fruit sugar mixture and stir for 2 minutes. Pour into freezer containers or canning jars with ½-inch headspace, cover, and let stand until jam has become firm. Freeze.

## Get Linked

*I have a good variety of sauces and help for making pickles and preserves, along with links to other food preservation resources. Here are some of the most useful or popular on* About.com.

**BARBECUE SAUCES AND MARINADES**

Here you'll find a variety of barbecue sauce recipes, and recipes for marinades, including several from forum members. Recipes include Memphis-Style Barbecue Sauce, Doc's Jack Daniel's Marinade, Ruth's Barbecue Sauce, Honey Barbecue Sauce for Chicken, and marinades for pork roast, venison, and other meats.

 http://about.com/southernfood/bbqsaucemarinade

**SALSA RECIPES**

Several salsa recipes, including a mango salsa, tomato salsa recipes, Fresh Tomatillo Salsa, Carol's Salsa, Bea's Salsa, Zesty Salsa, Fresh Salsa Cruda, Pico de Gallo, Corn Salsa, Colleen's Margarita Salsa, and others.

 http://about.com/southernfood/salsarecipes

**SEASONINGS**

This index includes spice blends, homemade herb mixtures, and more. Recipes include mustard recipes from our forum, homemade Creole seasoning, a blackened seasoning recipe, easy cinnamon sugar, basil butter for bread or vegetables, poultry seasoning recipes, all-purpose blends, and more.

 http://about.com/southernfood/seasoningrecipes

# Chapter 13

# Cakes and Pies

## About

**ASK YOUR GUIDE:**

What is the origin of red velvet cake?
▶ **PAGE 224**

How can I be sure I've formed a soft ball correctly?
▶ **PAGE 225**

Can a cheesecake be frozen with good results?
▶ **PAGE 228**

Can I use the extra egg whites and make a meringue for this pie?
▶ **PAGE 229**

What varieties of apples make the best pies?
▶ **PAGE 235**

Is there any way to spice up an ordinary pie crust?
▶ **PAGE 237**

▶ Did you know that ovens can vary greatly in temperature? It isn't unusual for an oven to be up to 50 degrees off, and possibly more. Cakes are particularly picky when it comes to temperature, and oven thermometers are relatively inexpensive. Check the oven regularly to make sure it's heating correctly. Remember to position racks in the center of the oven before you heat, and decrease the temperature by 25 degrees if you're using a glass baking pan.

# Pineapple Upside-Down Cake
SERVES 8

*Feel free to use a seasoned iron skillet instead of the cake pan.*

3 tablespoons butter
¾ cup light brown sugar, packed
6 slices pineapple
Maraschino cherries
Pecan halves
½ cup butter
½ cup granulated sugar
1 egg
1 teaspoon vanilla
1 ½ cups all-purpose flour
1 ½ teaspoons baking powder
½ teaspoon salt
½ cup milk

1. Heat oven to 375°F. Melt the butter in a 9-inch square cake pan or 10-inch iron skillet. Sprinkle evenly with the brown sugar. Arrange pineapple slices, maraschino cherries, and pecan halves decoratively over the sugar and butter. Set aside.
2. Cream ½ cup butter with the ½ cup sugar; beat until light. Beat in egg and vanilla. Sift the flour, baking powder, and salt into a bowl. Add the sifted dry ingredients to the batter, alternating with the milk and ending with the dry ingredients. Beat until smooth. Pour the batter over the arranged pineapple layer.
3. Bake for 35 minutes, or until cake springs back when lightly touched with a finger. Let the cake cool in the pan on a rack for about 5 minutes. Put a serving plate over the top of the pan and flip to invert the cake onto the plate. Serve warm.

## Lemon-Glazed Pound Cake
SERVES 10 TO 12

*Try this cake with fresh blueberries or strawberries and whipped cream.*

10 ounces butter, softened (2 ½ sticks)
3 ¾ cups granulated sugar, divided
5 large eggs
1 teaspoon lemon extract or vanilla
3 cups all-purpose flour
2 ½ teaspoons baking powder
¼ teaspoon salt
1 cup milk
½ cup water
1 tablespoon grated lemon zest
½ cup fresh lemon juice

1. Heat oven to 300°F. Butter and flour a 10-inch tube pan.
2. In a mixing bowl with electric mixer, beat butter until light. Beat in 3 cups of the sugar until fluffy. Add the eggs, one at a time, beating well after each addition. Beat in lemon or vanilla extract.
3. Combine flour, baking powder, and salt. With mixer on low speed, gradually beat in the dry ingredients, alternating with the milk, just until blended. Do not overmix.
4. Spoon batter into the prepared tube pan. Set on a rack in the center of the oven and bake for 1 hour and 30 minutes, or until a wooden pick or cake tester comes out clean.
5. Cool the cake in the pan on a wire rack. Remove from the pan and set on the rack. Combine remaining ¾ cup sugar with water, lemon zest, and lemon juice. Brush glaze over sides of the warm cake and gradually spoon glaze over the top. Let cake cool completely.

**BEFORE YOU BEGIN**

▶ Too much flour could make your cake too dry, and not enough flour can cause the cake to fall. Unless the flour must be sifted before measuring, stir it with a spoon before measuring so it isn't packed. Spoon the flour into a measuring cup until it is mounded, then use the back side of a knife or spreading spatula to level it off. If you've been scooping your flour right out of the bag or canister with the measuring cup, you should notice a nice improvement in the things you bake!

## Coca-Cola Cake and Frosting
SERVES 10 TO 12

*This is absolutely delicious! I'm not sure what the cola adds, but it certainly does make a flavorful cake and creamy frosting. Generic or other brands of cola can be used in this cake.*

2 cups all-purpose flour
1 ½ teaspoons baking powder
¼ teaspoon salt
2 cups granulated sugar
8 ounces butter
3 tablespoons unsweetened cocoa powder
1 cup cola
1 ½ cups miniature marshmallows
2 teaspoons vanilla
½ cup buttermilk
2 eggs, beaten
2 teaspoons baking soda
4 ounces butter, softened
3 tablespoons unsweetened cocoa powder
1 pound powdered sugar
5 to 7 tablespoons cola
1 cup chopped pecans, optional

*Coca-Cola Cake and Frosting (continued)*

1. Heat oven to 350°F. Grease and flour a 13" x 9" baking pan.
2. Measure the flour, baking powder, salt, and sugar into a large mixing bowl. In a large saucepan, combine 8 ounces butter, 3 tablespoons of cocoa powder, and 1 cup of cola.
3. Bring the mixture to a boil over high heat; remove from heat and add the marshmallows and vanilla. Stir until marshmallows are melted. Pour the chocolate mixture over the dry ingredients in the mixing bowl; blend well. Add the buttermilk, beaten eggs, and baking soda. Beat well.
4. Pour batter into the prepared pan. Bake for 30 to 35 minutes, or until the cake springs back when lightly touched with a finger. Cool in pan on a rack.
5. Make the frosting: Blend 4 ounces of softened butter with 3 tablespoons of cocoa powder, the powdered sugar, and 5 tablespoons of cola. Beat, adding more cola as needed to make a smooth and creamy frosting. Spread over the cooled cake and top with chopped pecans, if desired.

**WHAT'S HOT**

▶ Here's a trick to take the raw sugar taste out of a powdered sugar frosting. Make the frosting, then spoon it into a metal bowl or top pan of a double boiler and set the bowl or pan over simmering water. Let the frosting heat over simmering water for about 8 to 12 minutes, stirring occasionally. Remove from the heat and let cool before frosting the cake.

## Kentucky Jam Cake

SERVES 12

*This is a delicious spice cake made with the addition of blackberry jam and a wonderful date filling. A caramel frosting is traditional, but a cream cheese frosting is just as delicious!*

3 cups flour
1 teaspoon baking soda
½ teaspoon salt
1 teaspoon ground cinnamon
1 teaspoon ground allspice
½ teaspoon ground cloves
1 cup butter, softened
1 ½ cups granulated sugar
6 large eggs
1 cup blackberry jam, seedless
1 cup buttermilk
1 cup pecans, chopped fine, optional
1 pound chopped dates
1 ½ to 2 ½ cups water
2 tablespoons packed brown sugar
1 teaspoon vanilla

*Kentucky Jam Cake (continued)*

1. Heat oven to 325°F. Generously grease the bottoms and sides of three 9-inch layer cake pans. Dust pans with flour.
2. Stir flour before measuring. Combine the flour, soda, salt, and spices into a bowl.
3. In a mixing bowl, cream butter and sugar until light. Add the eggs, one at a time, beating well after each addition. Beat in the jam. Gradually add the sifted dry ingredients, alternating with buttermilk; beat until smooth. Stir in chopped pecans, if using. Using a small measuring cup or spoon, evenly distribute the batter among the three prepared pans. Bake for 30 to 35 minutes, or until cake springs back when lightly touched with a finger.
4. Cool cake in pans on racks for 15 minutes. Carefully invert onto the racks. Cool completely then fill with date filling (below) and frost with Cream Cheese Frosting (page 227) or Caramel Frosting (page 225).
5. Date filling: In a saucepan, combine the chopped dates, brown sugar, and 1 teaspoon vanilla. Add 1 ½ cups water and bring to a boil over high heat. Reduce heat to medium-low and simmer until dates are very soft and thick. Add more water as necessary. If desired, push the mixture through a sieve. Cover and let cool completely.

**WHAT'S HOT**

▶ One of the biggest problems I have with a thick cake batter is uneven baked cakes. Lopsided cakes are hard to deal with, but you can prevent them. When the batter is put in the pan, hold the pan on both sides then gently spin, or gently shake back and forth then side to side. The force of the spin or shaking should level the batter out.

## Texts Sheet Cake

### Texas Sheet Cake

SERVES 12

*This is my version of the classic Texas sheet cake, made with a mocha batter and a creamy chocolate frosting.*

2 cups all-purpose flour
1 teaspoon baking soda
⅛ teaspoon salt
1 cup plus 6 tablespoons butter, divided
1 cup brewed black coffee
½ cup unsweetened cocoa powder, divided
2 cups sugar
2 eggs
½ cup buttermilk
2 teaspoons vanilla, divided
⅓ cup milk
1 pound (3 ¾ cups) powdered sugar
Pecans, chopped fine

1. Into a large mixing bowl, sift together the flour, soda, and salt, and sugar; set aside.
2. Heat oven to 350°F. Grease and flour a 15" x 10" x 1" jelly roll pan.
3. In a saucepan over medium heat, combine the 1 cup butter, coffee, and ¼ cup cocoa. Heat the mixture, stirring constantly, until butter is melted and mixture just begins to bubble. Pour over the dry ingredients in the mixing bowl and blend well.

*Texas Sheet Cake (continued)*

4. In another bowl combine the buttermilk, eggs, and 1 teaspoon of vanilla. Stir the buttermilk mixture into the chocolate batter. Pour into the prepared pan and bake for about 25 minutes. The cake should spring back when lightly touched with a finger.

5. Meanwhile, make the chocolate pecan frosting. Combine the 6 tablespoons butter, remaining ¼ cup cocoa, and ⅓ cup of milk in a medium saucepan and bring to a boil, stirring constantly. Sift the powdered sugar, then gradually stir into the saucepan mixture. Add the remaining 1 teaspoon vanilla and chopped pecans. Mix to blend thoroughly, then spread on the hot cake in the pan.

**ELSEWHERE ON THE WEB**

▶ If you love Texas and Southwestern recipes, check out www.texascooking .com. This site has a great collection of recipes, including traditional Texas fare, recipes from Grandma's Cookbook, Texas seafood favorites, a variety of food articles, dessert recipes, and more. Here's a link to their article, Texas Sheet Cake, Hospitality in a Cake: www .texascooking.com/features/ jun99texassheetcake.htm. Their Texas Sheet Cake is made with the addition of cinnamon, and they use part butter and part canola oil in the cake.

**What is the origin of red velvet cake?**

▶ The legend I see the most often is from the 1940s, though details are somewhat sketchy. The story claimed that the elegant Waldorf-Astoria restaurant granted a woman's request for a recipe for the delicious cake, and then sent her a bill for $100. With revenge in mind, the angry woman purportedly began circulating the tale along with the recipe. The delicious moist red chocolate cake is also known as the Waldorf-Astoria Cake.

# Red Velvet Cake
SERVES 10

*This beautiful red cake is one of the most popular cakes on my site.*

¾ cup butter
1 ½ cups granulated sugar
2 large eggs
1 ½ teaspoons vanilla
2 tablespoons unsweetened cocoa
2 tablespoons red gel food coloring
2 tablespoons water
1 teaspoon salt
2 ½ cups all-purpose flour
1 cup buttermilk
1 tablespoon vinegar
1 teaspoon baking soda

1. Preheat oven to 350°F. Generously grease and flour three 8" layer cake pans or two 9" layer cake pans.
2. Cream butter and sugar until light and fluffy; beat in eggs one at a time, beating well after each addition. Beat in vanilla.
3. Combine cocoa, food coloring, and water; blend well. Beat the cocoa mixture into the creamed mixture.
4. Combine the flour and salt; gradually beat into the creamed mixture, alternating with the buttermilk. Combine vinegar and soda in a cup and beat into the batter.
5. Spoon batter evenly into 2 or 3 prepared layer cake pans; bake for 22 to 30 minutes, until cake bounces back when lightly touched with a finger. Cool on racks.
6. Remove from pans; frost layers and sides with Cooked Vanilla Frosting (page 226) or Cream Cheese Frosting (page 227).

# Caramel Frosting

FROSTS 2 TO 3 LAYERS

*This is a delicious cooked frosting for a spice or caramel cake.*

3 cups packed light brown sugar
2 tablespoons light corn syrup
3 tablespoons butter
Dash salt
½ cup heavy cream or evaporated milk
1 teaspoon vanilla

1. Combine all ingredients in a large saucepan; bring to a boil over medium-high heat. Reduce heat to medium-low; cover and cook for 3 minutes. Uncover and position a candy thermometer into the mixture. Continue to cook until thermometer registers 236°F, or until a small amount of the mixture forms a soft ball when dropped in cold water.
2. Remove from heat and let cool for 5 minutes. Beat until thick. If frosting is too thick or becomes too thick while spreading, add a little very hot water to it. If necessary, dip the spatula in hot water to smooth the frosting.

ASK YOUR GUIDE

**How can I be sure I've formed a soft ball correctly?**

▶ This is really much easier than it sounds! Fill a wide cup about halfway with cold water, then drop about ½ teaspoon of the boiling mixture into it. Take your fingers and push the pieces of frosting together. If they adhere and form a ball of sorts, then lift it carefully out of the water. A soft ball will be soft enough to flatten a bit when held up on the finger. The temperature can be anywhere from about 234°F to 240°F. Though it's really more reliable to use the candy thermometer, I always double-check its accuracy with the soft ball test.

## Cooked Vanilla Frosting
FROSTS 2 TO 3 LAYERS

*This is an old-fashioned frosting, thickened with flour. The flour actually makes this frosting taste less sweet, but it's just as delicious.*

1 cup milk
⅓ cup all-purpose flour
1 cup butter
1 cup granulated sugar
1 ½ teaspoons vanilla
Milk or cream

1. In a large saucepan, whisk together the 1 cup milk and the flour. Cook over medium heat, stirring constantly, until thickened. Transfer to the refrigerator to cool quickly.
2. In a mixing bowl, combine the butter, sugar, and vanilla. Beat until light. Add the flour and milk mixture a little at a time. Beat well, adding a little more milk or cream if needed for spreading consistency.

**WHAT'S HOT**

▶ I have several delicious frosting recipes on my Southern Cuisine site to go with all kinds of cakes. Here's a delicious and easy chocolate cream cheese frosting: http://about.com/southernfood/chocccfrosting. Here's a fluffy white frosting I love with angel food cake: http://about.com/southernfood/whitefrosting. This is a flavorful mint-flavored cream cheese frosting with peppermint extract: http://about.com/southernfood/pepmintccfrosting. Finally, I love this rich chocolate sour cream frosting for a chocolate layer cake: http://about.com/southernfood/chocscfrosting.

## Cream Cheese Frosting

FROSTS 2 LAYERS

*This delicious cream cheese frosting is one of my favorites, and it is absolutely delicious on a spice cake, carrot cake, or a chocolate cake, along with many others.*

4 ounces butter, room temperature
8 ounces cream cheese, room temperature
Dash salt
1 pound powdered sugar, about 4 cups
2 teaspoons vanilla extract
Cream, as needed

1. In a large mixing bowl, combine all ingredients. Beat well with an electric mixer until smooth and fluffy. Frost a cooled cake.
2. Chocolate Cream Cheese Frosting: Add 3 ounces unsweetened melted chocolate and beat, adding 1 teaspoon vanilla and cream, as needed for consistency.

**BEFORE YOU BEGIN**

▶ Some basic rules apply when frosting a cake. Your cake should be completely cooled before frosting, unless the recipe states otherwise. If your cake has loose crumbs, take a pastry brush and brush it as free of the crumbs as possible. If your cake filling is different from the frosting, as in the Kentucky Jam Cake with Date Filling, don't spread the filling all the way to the edge. When you frost the sides, you don't want the filling to smear into the frosting. If your cake layers are a bit uneven, you can easily frost to hide the imperfections! It's best to frost the cake on the serving plate because transferring the frosted cake might be difficult.

## Praline Cheesecake with Pecan Crust

SERVES 12

*This wonderful cheesecake got a standing ovation at one event!*

| | |
|---|---|
| 1 ¼ cups graham cracker crumbs | 3 packages (8 ounces each) cream cheese, softened |
| 5 tablespoons melted butter | 3 eggs |
| 1 cup plus 5 tablespoons light brown sugar, packed and divided | 1 ½ teaspoons vanilla extract |
| | 1 cup heavy whipping cream |
| ¼ cup pecans, chopped fine | ½ cup dark corn syrup |
| | 2 tablespoons cornstarch |
| | 1 teaspoon vanilla extract |

1. Heat oven to 450°F. Combine graham cracker crumbs, melted butter, 3 tablespoons of the brown sugar, and the chopped pecans. Press into the bottom of a 9-inch **springform pan**.
2. In a mixing bowl, beat cream cheese until light. Beat in the remaining 1 cup brown sugar and blend well. Beat in the eggs and vanilla until blended. Blend in the heavy whipping cream. Pour the batter into the prepared crust.
3. Bake at 450°F for 10 minutes. Reduce heat to 250°F; continue to bake for 65 to 75 minutes, or until center is set. The edges will be firm and center will remain somewhat jiggly.
4. Cool for 12 minutes, then carefully remove the sides of the pan. Cool completely.
5. In a small saucepan, combine the dark corn syrup, cornstarch, and 2 tablespoons of light brown sugar. Cook, stirring, over low heat until thickened; stir in vanilla and remove from heat. Pour over the cooled cheesecake. Refrigerate leftovers.

ASK YOUR GUIDE

### Can a cheesecake be frozen with good results?

▶ Cheesecakes with a high fat content can be frozen with good results. A dense cheesecake with least 1 ½ pounds of cream cheese will freeze well, so the Praline Cheesecake can be frozen whole or in portions. If you're freezing a whole cheesecake, you might want to add the topping just before serving. Make sure the cheesecake is thoroughly cooled, and then make it as airtight as possible in plastic wrap, then in foil. Freeze for up to one month. Store it on a freezer shelf where it won't be bumped or damaged, and freeze serving portions; don't defrost and refreeze.

## Key Lime Pie
SERVES 8

*This version is my family's favorite. Feel free to use a purchased graham cracker crust for this recipe.*

2 cups graham cracker crumbs
½ cup melted butter
⅓ cup sugar
5 large egg yolks
1 can (14 ounces) sweetened condensed milk
½ cup **key lime** juice
½ cup heavy whipping cream
1 teaspoon lime or key lime zest
Whipped cream or whipped topping
Lime zest for topping, if desired

1. Heat oven to 325°F. Combine 2 cups graham cracker crumbs, ½ cup melted butter, and ⅓ cup granulated sugar. Press over the bottom and up the sides of a 9-inch pie plate.
2. Using a mixer on low speed, beat egg yolks with sweetened condensed milk. Blend in the whipping cream, key lime juice, and 1 teaspoon zest. Pour into the pie crust and bake for about 20 minutes. Let the pie cool for 15 minutes. Refrigerate for about 2 hours before serving.
3. Before serving, top the whole pie with whipped cream, or top individual servings with a dollop of whipped cream.

ASK YOUR GUIDE

***Can I use the extra egg whites and make a meringue for this pie?***

▶ Yes. Just beat 3 or 4 egg whites until soft peaks begin to form. Combine 6 tablespoons of sugar and about 1 teaspoon cornstarch, and then gradually beat the sugar mixture into the egg whites, along with a dash of salt. Continue beating until stiff peaks form, and test by rubbing a little of the meringue between your fingers. The sugar should be completely dissolved so that you don't feel any grittiness. Spread the meringue over the hot pie filling, spreading to the crust edge to seal and prevent the meringue from shrinking, then bake for about 12 to 15 minutes at 350°F.

## Peanut Butter Silk Pie

SERVES 8 TO 10

*This peanut butter pie recipe was inspired by a restaurant pie.*

1 ¼ cups graham cracker crumbs
1 ¼ cup granulated sugar
5 tablespoons melted butter
2 ounces bittersweet chocolate
⅓ cup evaporated milk
1 tablespoon corn syrup
½ cup plus 1 heaping tablespoon smooth peanut butter, divided
8 ounces cream cheese
1 cup powdered sugar
1 teaspoon vanilla
½ cup milk
3 cups whipped topping
Shaved chocolate for garnish, optional
Peanuts for garnish, chopped fine, optional

1. Combine the graham cracker crumbs, ¼ cup of the sugar, and the melted butter. Pat into a 9-inch pie plate. Chill for 25 minutes.

2. In a saucepan, combine the remaining 1 cup granulated sugar, bittersweet chocolate, evaporated milk, and corn syrup. Cook the fudge mixture over medium heat, stirring occasionally, to about 236°F on a candy thermometer, or soft ball stage. Remove from heat and stir in 1 heaping tablespoon of peanut butter. Beat for a few minutes; pour into the pie crust. Chill thoroughly.

3. In a mixing bowl, beat cream cheese with remaining ½ cup peanut butter, powdered sugar, vanilla, and milk. Fold in whipped topping. Spoon over the chilled fudge layer. Garnish with shaved chocolate or chopped peanuts, if desired. Chill before cutting.

**ELSEWHERE ON THE WEB**

▶ Here are a few peanut butter pies from other About sites. The first one is an ice cream pie, from Jean Brandau (About.com Huntsville, Alabama Guide) and Nancy Holliman, at http://about.com/huntsville/peanutbutterpie. From Baking Guide Carroll Pellegrinnelli, you'll find a Chocolate Peanut Butter Pie, at http://about.com/baking/chocpeanutbutterpie. If you're looking for a vegetarian offering, Vegetarian Guide Jolinda Hackett has a great peanut butter tofu pie, at http://about.com/vegetarian/veganpie.

# Mississippi Mud Pie
SERVES 8

*This easy chocolate pie is supposed to resemble the muddy bottom of the Mississippi river. It is delicious!*

4 ounces butter
2 squares unsweetened chocolate
3 large eggs
3 tablespoons white corn syrup
1 ⅓ cup granulated sugar
1 teaspoon vanilla
1 9-inch graham cracker pie shell

1. Heat oven to 350°F.
2. In a medium saucepan, combine the butter and chocolate over low heat, stirring frequently until melted and well blended.
3. In a mixing bowl, beat the eggs; stir in the corn syrup, sugar, and vanilla. Add the melted chocolate mixture to the beaten mixture, stirring well.
4. Pour the mixture into a prepared graham cracker pie shell. Bake for 35 to 40 minutes, or until the top is slightly crunchy and filling is set.
5. Serve warm with ice cream or whipped topping.

**WHAT'S HOT**

▶ Some of the most popular pies on my site are the easiest. My Cocoa Cream Pie, at http://about.com/southernfood/cocoa creampie, is a dark chocolate pie with whipped cream topping. Another popular pie is the pudding-like Banana Cream Pie with cream, eggs, cinnamon, butter, vanilla, and sliced bananas, in a baked pie shell at http://about.com/southernfood/banana creampie. The Coconut Cream Pie, at http://about.com/southernfood/coconut creampie, combines milk, eggs, butter, and shredded fresh coconut in a baked pie shell with a whipped cream topping.

## Chocolate Chip Pie with Bourbon Whipped Cream

SERVES 8 TO 10

*This is a wonderful Kentucky-style pie, and I have several versions on my site, including a chocolate chip pie in a jar for gift-giving.*

1 9-inch pie shell, unbaked
1 cup semisweet chocolate chips
1 cup chopped pecans, or walnuts
2 large eggs
½ cup brown sugar
½ cup granulated sugar
4 ounces butter
½ cup all-purpose flour
Dash salt
1 ½ teaspoon vanilla extract
1 cup heavy whipping cream, chilled
2 tablespoons powdered sugar
1 tablespoon good-quality Kentucky bourbon

1. Heat oven to 325°F. Sprinkle the chocolate chips and chopped nuts over the bottom of the unbaked pastry shell; set aside.
2. In a small mixing bowl, whisk eggs. Whisk in the granulated and brown sugar, ½ cup melted butter, flour, salt, and 1 teaspoon of the vanilla. Pour batter over the chocolate chips and nuts. Bake for 35 to 40 minutes, or until set. Remove to a rack and let cool.
3. Beat chilled whipping cream until thickened; add powdered sugar and remaining ½ teaspoon vanilla and beat until soft peaks form. Beat in bourbon. Cover and refrigerate until serving time.

▶ Here are some secrets to whipped cream. First of all, use real heavy cream. It takes just a few minutes to beat and it is far better than whipped topping. Have everything chilled, including the beaters and bowl. Beat just until the cream holds soft peaks when the beaters are lifted. Adding sugar or flavorings just when the cream begins to form soft peaks. If you've made the whipped cream a few hours in advance, put it in a sieve and position the sieve over a bowl; cover with plastic wrap and refrigerate. Any liquid that might have separated will run into the bowl. Whisk the separated liquids back in just before using.

## Sweet Potato Pie

SERVES 8

*This is a delicious sweet potato pie, made with just the right combination of spices and sugar.*

2 cups mashed sweet potatoes
4 ounces butter, softened
¾ cup granulated sugar
¼ cup packed light brown sugar
½ cup milk or half-and-half
2 large eggs
½ teaspoon ground cinnamon
½ teaspoon ground nutmeg
1 teaspoon vanilla extract
1 unbaked 9-inch pastry shell

1. Heat oven to 350°F.
2. Beat mashed sweet potato with the butter, sugars, milk, eggs, spices, and vanilla. Beat until smooth and well blended. Pour the filling into the unbaked pie shell.
3. Bake for 55 to 60 minutes, or until a knife inserted near the center comes out clean. Cool on wire rack. The pie will settle as it cools.

**BEFORE YOU BEGIN**

▶ Wondering how many sweet potatoes you'll need for this recipe? Sweet potatoes do vary in size, but 1 large or 2 medium sweet potatoes will probably make about 1 ½ to 2 cups of mashed. Cook the sweet potatoes in their skins in boiling water until tender, then run cold water over them and slip the skins off. You can also bake sweet potatoes for mashing, and the microwave oven will cook them even faster. Prick sweet potatoes in a few places with a fork. Place them on paper towels and microwave, turning, on HIGH power for about 12 to 15 minutes, until tender.

## Brown Sugar Pecan Pie
SERVES 8

*This is a delicious pecan pie, one I make for the holiday season.*

1 recipe Flaky Butter Pie Crust (page 237)
3 large eggs, beaten
1 cup light corn syrup
⅛ teaspoon salt
1 teaspoon vanilla extract
1 cup light brown sugar, firmly packed
2 tablespoons melted butter
1 ¼ cups pecan halves

1. Prepare pastry and fit into a 9-inch pie pan. Heat oven to 400°F.
2. In a mixing bowl, beat the eggs. Whisk in the corn syrup, salt, vanilla, brown sugar, and melted butter, blending well. Stir in pecan halves or pieces.
3. Pour the pecan mixture into the unbaked pie shell.
4. Bake pie at 400°F for 10 minutes. Reduce heat to 350°F and continue baking for 25 to 30 minutes longer. If the crust becomes too dark, cover the edge with a protective pie shield or fashion a ring of foil to lightly cover the pastry edge. When the pie is finished, the edge of the filling should be slightly puffed and firm, and the center should move only slightly.
5. Serve with whipped cream or vanilla ice cream.

**WHAT'S HOT**

▶ Here's a great tip for this type of pie with its unbaked crust. Set a cookie sheet in the oven while it's heating, and then set the filled pie right on the hot metal of the cookie sheet. The bottom of the crust will bake more quickly on the metal, and it will be flakier. If you save disposable pie pans, cut the bottom out and put the ring on the browned edge of the pie crust to keep it from getting too dark.

## Spiced Apple Crumb Pie
SERVES 8

*This is a cross between an apple pie and a spiced apple crisp.*

5 to 6 cups apples, peeled, cored and sliced thin
2 tablespoons fresh lemon juice
¾ cup granulated sugar, divided
½ cup light brown sugar, packed, divided
¼ cup melted butter
½ cup plus 3 tablespoons all-purpose flour, divided
2 teaspoons ground cinnamon
⅛ teaspoon nutmeg
1 9-inch deep-dish pie shell, baked
6 tablespoons cold butter, cut in pieces
¼ cup quick rolled oats
¼ cup chopped pecans

1. Heat oven to 375°F. Prepare the pie pastry shell.
2. Toss the sliced apples with lemon juice in a bowl. Add ½ cup of the granulated sugar and ¼ cup of the brown sugar, along with melted butter, 3 tablespoons of the flour, cinnamon, and nutmeg. Stir to blend ingredients; set aside.
3. Combine the remaining ½ cup flour, ¼ cup granulated sugar, and ¼ cup brown sugar, along with 6 tablespoons butter, rolled oats, and pecans. Mix with a pastry blender or fork.
4. Pour apple mixture into the prepared pie pastry. Sprinkle evenly with the crumb mixture. Bake at 375°F for 30 to 35 minutes, then check for browning. Make a foil ring to set on the crust edge to keep it from browning further or use a pie shield ring. Continue baking for about 15 to 25 minutes longer, until apples are tender. Cool before cutting.

ASK YOUR GUIDE

***What varieties of apples make the best pies?***

▶ Apple flavors and textures vary, and some become mushy and break down when baked in a pie. I like a combination of apples, some for flavor, and some because they hold up very well over the baking time. Some varieties I like to combine in pies and crisps include Golden Delicious, Granny Smith, Cortland, Gala, Winesap, Jonathan, Northern Spy, and Rome.

## Old-Fashioned Chess Pie
SERVES 8

*This is a old-time Southern pie. I like the meringue topping on this one.*

1 cup plus 6 tablespoons granulated sugar, divided
1 cup light brown sugar, packed
½ cup milk
¼ cup sifted all-purpose flour
½ cup butter
4 eggs, divided
2 teaspoons vanilla extract, divided
½ teaspoon salt
1 unbaked pie pastry shell, 9-inch

1. In a medium saucepan, combine 1 cup of the granulated sugar, the brown sugar, milk, flour, and butter. Cook over medium-low heat, stirring, until sugar is dissolved. Set aside and let cool.
2. Heat oven to 350°F.
3. Beat 3 egg yolks and 1 whole egg; add 1 teaspoon vanilla and salt. Combine the egg mixture with the cooled mixture and blend well. Pour the filling into the unbaked pie shell. Bake for 30 to 35 minutes, until crust is browned. Lower temperature to 250°F and continue baking until the pie is firm around edges and set in center but slightly jiggly, about 10 to 15 minutes longer. Remove the pie from the oven.
4. Increase oven temperature to 375°F.
5. Beat the 3 remaining egg whites until they begin to form soft peaks. Gradually beat in the sugar and dash of salt. Beat in 1 teaspoon vanilla. Spread meringue over top of hot pie, making sure to spread all the way to crust to seal in filling with the meringue. Put the pie back in the oven and cook for 10 to 12 minutes longer, until meringue is nicely browned.

# Flaky Butter Pie Crust

MAKES I CRUST

*This makes enough pastry to line a 9-inch pie pan for a single-crust pie.*

I cup all-purpose flour
⅔ cup cake flour
I tablespoon powdered sugar
½ teaspoon salt
4 tablespoons cold butter, cut in small pieces
5 tablespoons cold shortening, cut in small pieces
¼ cup ice-cold water

1. In the bowl of a food processor fitted with a metal blade, combine the all-purpose and cake flours, sugar, and salt. Pulse a few times to combine ingredients.
2. Sprinkle pieces of butter over the flour mixture; stir into the flour mixture lightly, then pulse about six times. Sprinkle shortening pieces over the mixture, stir in lightly, and then pulse six to eight more times. Sprinkle with half of the ice water. Pulse five times. Sprinkle with remaining water. Pulse about 6 times, or until the pastry dough begins to form large clumps. Empty into a bowl and knead two or three times, just until a ball holds together. Chill for about 20 minutes.
3. Roll out on a floured surface then fit into the pie plate. Crimp edge all around and cut away excess dough.
4. Fill the pie and bake according to recipe instructions. If pie shell must be baked first, prick it all over with a fork and bake at 450°F for about 10 minutes, or until lightly browned.

**ASK YOUR GUIDE**

*Is there any way to spice up an ordinary pie crust?*

▶ Sure! You can make some easy additions to jazz your pies up a bit. Spices can be added, such as ground allspice, cinnamon, a little nutmeg, ginger, or your own favorites. Try lemon oil or chili oil, depending on whether the pie is sweet or savory. Fennel seeds, celery seeds, coarse black pepper, and caraway seeds make nice additions to savory crusts, as does a little crumbled bacon. If you're making a crumb crust, try cereal or granola in place of cookie crumbs or graham crackers, or use a combination of cookie crumbs and cereal for a different flavor and texture, along with cinnamon or other spices, if they fit in with the filling.

## Get Linked

*You'll find hundreds of cake recipes, pies, and cheesecakes on my Southern Cuisine site on About.com, along with frosting recipes and other resources. Here are some of my favorite pages.*

**CAKE RECIPES**

This page contains hundreds of cake recipes, broken down into the type of cake or major ingredients. The recipes include angel food cakes, banana cakes, chocolate cakes, cupcakes, peach cakes, gingerbread, pound cakes, coconut cakes, fruitcakes, frostings, and more.

http://about.com/southernfood/cakerecipes

**CHEESECAKE RECIPES**

If you're a cheesecake lover, take a look at this page. Among the recipe titles you'll find are Easy Mini Cheesecakes, Maple Pumpkin Cheesecake, Sweet Potato Cheesecake, Lila's Individual Cheesecakes, Mocha Cheesecake, Almond Cheesecake with Peach Topping, Brownie Swirl Cheesecake, and many more.

http://about.com/southernfood/cheesecakerecipes

**CAKE MIX RECIPES**

Here you'll find cakes, bars, squares, and other desserts, all made with cake mix. Many of these recipes were contributed by forum members, and recipe titles include Cookies 'n Cream Chess Bars, Chocolate Nut Bundt Cake, Chess Squares, Elegant Citrus Cake, Easy Cherry Cake, German Chocolate Upside-Down Cake, Peanut Butter Cupcakes, and other delicious goodies.

http://about.com/southernfood/cakemixrecipes

## Chapter 14

# Cookies and Candy

**ASK YOUR GUIDE:**

Do you have any tips to make brownies and bar cookies easier to prepare and bake?
▶ **PAGE 245**

Can I make these with other nuts or butterscotch chips?
▶ **PAGE 246**

Is paraffin wax safe to eat?
▶ **PAGE 251**

## Pecan Sandies
MAKES 4 DOZEN

*This is a delicious little Southern cookie, loaded with chopped pecans and coated with powdered sugar. These are beautiful cookies to pack in small tins and give to friends and relatives.*

8 ounces butter, softened
⅓ cup plus ½ cup powdered sugar, divided
1 ½ teaspoons vanilla
¼ teaspoon salt
2 cups all-purpose flour
1 cup chopped pecans

1. In a mixing bowl combine the butter and the ⅓ cup powdered sugar; beat until light. Beat in vanilla. Gradually add the salt and flour; blend well. Blend in the chopped pecans. Chill dough for about 30 minutes.
2. Heat oven to 325°F.
3. Shape cookie dough into small balls and place about 1 inch apart on an ungreased cookie sheet. Bake for 18 to 20 minutes, or until just browned on bottoms. Cool completely.
4. Sift remaining ½ cup of powdered sugar into a large food storage bag. Add a few cookies at a time and gently turn the bag to coat cookies.

**BEFORE YOU BEGIN**

▶ For a nuttier pecan flavor, toast the chopped pecans before you start the cookies. Spread the chopped pecans out on a baking sheet and toast in a 325°F oven for about 8 minutes, or until the pecans are lightly browned and aromatic. I like to have a cup or two of toasted pecans in the freezer for recipes like this one or to use as an ice cream topping or garnish for desserts.

# Old-Fashioned Peanut Butter Cookies
MAKES 5 DOZEN

*These are delicious peanut butter cookies, just like Mom made, with the little criss-cross fork marks. Add fine-chopped roasted peanuts to the dough if you'd like a crunchier cookie, or dip them in a little melted chocolate for a special occasion.*

1 cup butter, softened
1 cup granulated sugar
1 cup light brown sugar, packed
1 cup smooth peanut butter
2 large eggs
1 teaspoon vanilla
1 teaspoons baking soda
1 teaspoon baking powder
2 ½ cups all-purpose flour
½ teaspoon salt

1. Cream granulated sugar and brown sugar with the butter and peanut butter until light. Beat in eggs and vanilla extract. Sift dry ingredients into a bowl; blend into the creamed mixture until well blended. Cover and chill the dough for about 30 to 45 minutes.
2. Heat oven to 350°F. Lightly grease cookie sheets.
3. Shape the dough into small balls and place about 1 ½ inches apart on the prepared baking sheet. Dip tines of a fork into flour then press each cookie, dipping again and pressing again to flatten slightly and form criss-cross marks.
4. Bake the cookies for about 10 to 12 minutes.

**WHAT'S HOT**

▶ Cookie dough can be frozen, so make some extra and freeze half of the dough. Freeze this peanut butter cookie dough into a disk or cylinder shape, then wrap well, first in plastic wrap then in foil. Freeze for up to one year, and make sure you label the package. When you're ready to bake the cookies, let thaw until the dough can be shaped into balls, and then shape as instructed. If you have time and the freezer space, go ahead and bake the cookies and then freeze them in airtight containers for up to one year.

## Pecan Praline Cookies
MAKES 5 TO 6 DOZEN

*These yummy, buttery, brown-sugar pecan cookies are one of my favorites for holiday baking. I like to make half of them with the powdered sugar coating and then roll the other half in cinnamon sugar.*

12 ounces butter, softened
¾ cup light brown sugar, packed
2 teaspoons vanilla extract
3 cups sifted all-purpose flour
2 cups pecans, chopped fine
Sifted powdered sugar, optional
Cinnamon sugar, optional

1. Heat oven to 325°F. Lightly grease baking sheets. Alternately, spray them with nonstick cooking spray or line with silicone baking mats.
2. In a mixing bowl, cream butter and brown sugar until light. Stir in the vanilla, then work in flour. Using hands, work in chopped pecans. The dough will be crumbly.
3. Shape the dough into small balls about 1 inch in diameter. Place on the greased baking sheets. Bake for 15 to 20 minutes, until the cookies are firm and lightly browned on bottoms.
4. Cool cookies slightly, then gently roll in powdered sugar or cinnamon sugar, if desired.

**ELSEWHERE ON THE WEB**

▶ Linda Stradley, author of *What's Cooking America,* has a great page of cookie baking tips. She talks about tools and utensils, pans, and ingredients, and gives advice for measuring and temperature of pans and ingredients, along with instructions on how to package and mail cookies. She also has tips for making bar cookies, drop cookies, rolled cookies, and more, and she answers some frequently asked questions. Check out Linda's excellent tips at http://whats cookingamerica.net.

# The Best Chocolate Chip Cookies
MAKES 4 DOZEN

*This is my delicious buttery version of the classic favorite.*

    1 cup butter, softened
    ¾ cup granulated sugar
    1 cup light brown sugar, packed
    2 large eggs
    1 ½ teaspoons vanilla extract
    1 teaspoon baking soda
    1 tablespoon very warm water
    3 cups all-purpose flour
    1 teaspoon salt
    2 cups semisweet chocolate chips
    1 cup chopped pecans, optional

1. Heat oven to 350°F.
2. In a large mixing bowl, cream butter with sugars. Beat in eggs and vanilla.
3. Combine baking soda and the water; blend into the batter. Gradually blend in the flour and salt. Stir in chocolate chips and chopped pecans, if using.
4. Drop by teaspoonfuls onto ungreased cookie sheets. Bake for about 12 minutes or until cookies are set and edges are browned. Watch carefully and don't overbake.

**WHAT'S HOT**

▶ Drop cookies can be frozen either baked or unbaked. Mix the cookie dough and drop on baking sheets. Set the baking sheet in the freezer so the cookies will freeze quickly. Layer the cookies in a freezer container with waxed paper between layers. Take as many as you want at a time and bake as directed. I like freezing cookies individually this way because I can bake a couple of cookies at a time and resist the temptation of eating more than I really want. And it's nice to know there's something I can bake fresh and quickly for company. Freeze these unbaked cookies for up to twelve months.

## Chocolate-Dipped Shortbread Cookies
MAKES 5 DOZEN

*These cookies are easy, and they look like you bought them at a bakery.*

1 cup butter, softened
2 cups all-purpose flour
⅔ cup cornstarch
½ cup light brown sugar, packed
⅔ cup ground almonds
2 teaspoons vanilla extract
½ teaspoon almond extract
8 ounces semisweet chocolate
4 tablespoons butter
1 cup chopped blanched almonds

1. Heat oven to 350°F. In a food processor fitted with a metal blade, combine the 1 cup softened butter, flour, cornstarch, sugar, ground almonds, and vanilla and almond extracts. Pulse until dough begins to clump.
2. Take dough out and shape into two cylinders. Divide one cylinder into four equal portions. Pinch and press each portion into a 14-inch rope about ¾ inch in diameter. Gently roll on a smooth surface to smooth out wrinkles and cracks. Cut each rope into 2-inch lengths and place on ungreased baking sheets. Bake for 18 to 20 minutes, or until golden brown on bottoms. Cool cookies on wire racks.
3. In a double boiler over hot water, combine the semisweet chocolate with 4 tablespoons of butter. Heat over low heat, stirring, until chocolate is melted. Dip about ⅓ of each cookie into the chocolate, then press into chopped almonds. Place on a wire rack over waxed paper to catch the drips. Let cool.

**BEFORE YOU BEGIN**

▶ Melting chocolate is usually easy and uneventful, but there are a few caveats. A few drops of water, if not part of the recipe, can cause chocolate to seize, or become a clump of chocolate you can't do a thing with. Keep any bowls or utensils thoroughly dry when working with melted chocolate. Milk chocolate is more delicate than dark chocolate, and it should be chopped finer so it will melt quicker with less heat. Dark chocolate can stand a little more heat, so it can be chopped a bit coarser.

## Mom's Blonde Brownies
MAKES 16 TO 24

*These were my favorite treats when I was growing up, and I have made them through the years for my own kids.*

1 cup all-purpose flour
½ teaspoon baking powder
¼ teaspoon baking soda
⅛ teaspoon salt
4 ounces butter, softened
1 cup light brown sugar, packed
1 large egg
1 teaspoon vanilla
1 cup semisweet chocolate chips
½ to 1 cup chopped walnuts or pecans

1. Heat oven to 350°F, or 325°F if using a glass baking pan. Grease and flour an 11" x 7" inch baking pan.
2. In a bowl, combine the flour, baking powder, baking soda, and salt; set aside.
3. In a mixing bowl, cream butter and brown sugar until light. Beat in egg and vanilla. Stir in the dry ingredients until well blended. Fold in chocolate chips and chopped nuts.
4. Bake for about 25 minutes, or until brownies are set and edges are browned. Be careful not to overbake.

ASK YOUR GUIDE

***Do you have any tips to make brownies and bar cookies easier to prepare and bake?***

▶ One way to make brownies or bars easier is to line the baking pan with foil. Just grease and flour the foil, then spread the batter in it. When the brownies or bars have baked and cooled, lift them out of the pan, foil and all. You save on cleanup and you don't have to cut them in the pan (which will mark your pans and dull your knives).

**Can I make these with other nuts or butterscotch chips?**

▶ These bars can have many variations. I like pecans, but walnuts work well in these bars. Also, I've seen them with 1 cup of chocolate chips and 1 cup of butterscotch chips, and peanut butter chips would add some nice flavor, too! Another variation you might try is cinnamon or chocolate graham cracker crumbs, or you could try using your favorite cookie crumbs or cereal crumbs as the base. You could also mix a teaspoon of vanilla extract or your favorite flavoring into the sweetened condensed milk before drizzling it over the top.

## Hello Dolly Bars
MAKES 16 TO 24

*These are very popular bars in the South, and they're truly delicious. I love to make these for the holidays.*

½ cup butter
1 ½ cups graham cracker crumbs
1 cup semisweet chocolate chips
1 cup sweetened flaked coconut
1 cup broken pecans
1 can (14 ounces) sweetened condensed milk

1. Heat oven to 350°F.
2. Melt the butter and pour into a 9" x 13" baking pan. Sprinkle evenly with graham cracker crumbs, stir lightly to blend, and then layer the chocolate chips, coconut, then pecans. Drizzle evenly with the sweetened condensed milk.
3. Bake for 25 to 30 minutes. Let cool and cut into squares to serve.

## Never-Fail No-Bake Chocolate Cookies

MAKES 4 DOZEN

*These have always been a favorite of mine, so easy to make up at a moment's notice. It's a quick chocolate fix, too!*

4 ounces butter
½ cup milk or evaporated milk
2 cups granulated sugar
1 cup semisweet chocolate chips
1 to 4 tablespoons peanut butter, optional
3 cups quick cooking rolled oats
1 teaspoon vanilla extract

1. In a medium saucepan over medium heat, combine butter, evaporated milk, and sugar. Cook, stirring occasionally, until mixture comes to a rolling boil. Boil for 1 minute.
2. Meanwhile put chocolate chips, peanut butter, oats, and vanilla in a large bowl. Pour hot mixture over the oat and chocolate chip mixture. Stir until chocolate is melted and all ingredients are well blended.
3. Drop by teaspoonfuls onto waxed paper. When cooled and firm, store the cookies in layers in airtight containers with waxed paper between the layers.

ELSEWHERE ON THE WEB

▶ There are several no-bake cookie recipes from other About Guides. No Bake Cookies from Stay-at-Home Parents Guide Barbara Whiting are similar to my recipe, but they're made with cocoa, margarine, peanut butter, and oats. Check this recipe out at http://about.com/home parents/nobakecookies. Another delicious no-bake cookie I love is an old Southern recipe. From Jean Brandau and Cathey Carney, these Old Southern Orange Balls are easy cookies you'll make again and again. Take them to a party, and take a copy of the recipe.

## Kentucky Bourbon Balls
MAKES ABOUT 48

*These delicious and easy little bourbon balls are a holiday tradition around here. Serve them around the Christmas and New Year's holidays.*

1 ½ cups vanilla wafer crumbs, crushed fine
1 cup pecans, chopped fine
1 ½ cups powdered sugar
3 tablespoons unsweetened cocoa powder
5 tablespoons bourbon
2 tablespoons corn syrup
Powdered sugar, sifted

1. In a large bowl, thoroughly blend the crushed vanilla wafer crumbs, chopped pecans, 1 ½ cups powdered sugar, and the cocoa powder.
2. In a small bowl, combine the bourbon and corn syrup; stir into the first mixture, blending well. Cover and chill for 2 hours.
3. Sift about 1 cup of powdered sugar onto waxed paper or a large plate. Shape the chilled mixture into small balls and roll in the powdered sugar.
4. Store the bourbon balls in the refrigerator, in tightly covered containers. Refrigerate for a day or two, and then roll in powdered sugar again just before serving, if desired.

**BEFORE YOU BEGIN**

▸ Because the flavors ripen with storage, plan to make these a few days before you'll be using them, and store in the refrigerator until serving. The bourbon balls may also be frozen for several months. A food processor makes quick work of blending the dry ingredients, and will make the crumbs finer, a real plus. Feel free to use rum in place of the bourbon, or use juice and a little rum flavoring or vanilla if you need to make them alcohol-free.

## Southern Pecan Pralines
MAKES ABOUT 36

*These delicious pecan praline candies are similar to the wonderful pralines I've bought in New Orleans, and they're quite easy to make.*

1 cup granulated sugar
1 cup light brown sugar, firmly packed
¾ cup evaporated milk
¼ teaspoon salt
2 tablespoons butter
1 teaspoon vanilla extract
1 cup chopped pecans

1. Butter the sides of a heavy, 2-quart saucepan. Add the granulated sugar, brown sugar, evaporated milk, and salt. Stir to blend well. Put the mixture over low heat and cook, stirring constantly, until sugar is dissolved.
2. Increase heat to medium and continue cooking, stirring, until the mixture begins to boil. Reduce heat to medium-low and continue cooking until the temperature reaches 234°F (soft ball stage) on a candy thermometer. Remove from heat, add the 2 tablespoons of butter and the vanilla, and let stand for 5 minutes.
3. Stir in nuts, then beat until the mixture is no longer glossy and has thickened, about 2 to 3 minutes. Quickly spoon the mixture onto sheets of waxed paper or lightly buttered baking sheets. If mixture becomes too stiff before you can finish, stir in very small amounts of hot water to make it workable.

ELSEWHERE ON THE WEB

▶ I love pralines and just about any cooked fudge, and there are some terrific recipes on the Web. It's always best to use a candy thermometer whenever making cooked fudge, but you can also test it using the soft ball test (described in the recipe for Caramel Frosting, on page 225). I use both methods when I make fudge. Here's a great recipe for cooked chocolate fudge from Linda Larsen at http://about.com/busycooks/cooked chocfudge.

## Rocky Road Fudge
MAKES ABOUT 2 POUNDS

*This is such a delicious treat, and it makes a great food gift.*

3 cups granulated sugar
1 cup evaporated milk
3 ounces unsweetened
   chocolate
1 tablespoon light corn syrup

Dash salt
3 tablespoons butter
2 teaspoons vanilla extract
1 cup miniature marshmallows
1 cup chopped pecans

1. Line an 8-inch square pan with foil, extending the foil over the edges of the pan. Butter the foil, and then sprinkle marshmallows evenly over the bottom. Place the pan in the freezer.
2. Butter the sides of a large saucepan; combine sugar, milk, chocolate, corn syrup, and salt. Stir to blend well. Cook over medium heat, stirring with a wooden spoon, until the mixture begins to boil. During this time, dip a pastry brush into hot water and brush the sides of the pan down to reduce the risk of sugar remaining undissolved. Reduce heat to medium-low and continue gently boiling, without stirring, until mixture registers about 236°F to 238°F on a candy thermometer.
3. Remove from heat; add butter and vanilla and let stand without stirring until it reaches about 110°F. Beat with a wooden spoon until the mixture just begins to thicken. Add chopped nuts and beat until it begins to lose its gloss but can be poured. Pour the mixture over the marshmallows. When partially set, score into squares. Cool completely.
4. When fudge is firm, use the ends of the foil to lift it out of the pan. Cut into pieces. Layer the fudge pieces in a tightly covered container with squares of waxed paper separating the layers. Store the fudge in the refrigerator.

**TOOLS YOU NEED**

▶ Some important tools for this recipe include a candy thermometer to monitor an accurate temperature while boiling and cooling, a wooden spoon for stirring and beating, and a pastry brush. Before the first boil, while sugar is dissolving, use the pastry brush dipped in a little hot water to wash down the sides. This will help remove any sugar crystals from the sides of the pan. One single crystal of sugar clinging to the side of the pan could encourage more crystallization in the fudge.

## Martha Washington Candy

MAKES ABOUT 48

*This is a popular candy I see again and again, and it's delicious! If you can't find paraffin, melt purchased dipping chocolate or almond bark and dip the chilled candies in that.*

2 pounds powdered sugar, sifted
1 can (14 ounces) sweetened condensed milk
1 teaspoon vanilla extract
2 cups flaked coconut
4 ounces butter, softened
3 cups chopped pecans
4 ounces paraffin wax
3 cups semisweet chocolate chips

1. Combine the powdered sugar, sweetened condensed milk, vanilla, coconut, softened butter, and pecans. Blend well and shape into small balls. Chill thoroughly, until hardened.
2. In the top of a double boiler over simmering water, melt the chocolate chips with the wax. Using a fork or toothpicks, dip candy in the chocolate mixture, coating thoroughly; let cool.
3. Store candy in airtight containers in the refrigerator.

ASK YOUR GUIDE

***Is paraffin wax safe to eat?***

▶ Food-grade paraffin wax is widely used in chocolates and other foods. Although it is edible, it is not digestible; the wax passes through the digestive system. Paraffin is often used as a coating for fruits and vegetables, protecting them and making them shinier and more attractive. Paraffin is added to the chocolate to help it stay firm at room temperature and to give the chocolate a glossy finish. Though paraffin is rarely used in canning these days, it's usually found in the canning section of the food market.

## Get Linked

*On my Southern Cuisine site on **About.com**, you'll find many more cookie and candy recipes, plus tips and advice of all kinds. Here are some of the best recipes and resources.*

**BROWNIES AND BARS**

Dozens of recipes for bars, including an index devoted to chocolate brownies. Recipe titles include Layered Pecan Bars, Fudge Swirl Bars, Chocolate Spice Bars, S'Mores Bars, Chocolate Mud Squares, Oat Bars, Butterscotch Brownies, Chess Squares, and many more.

 http://about.com/southernfood/browniesbars

**HOLIDAY COOKIE RECIPES AND TIPS**

This article features a long list of holiday cookie recipes, along with decorating ideas and tips on baking, freezing, and mailing cookies. Recipes include Candy Cane Cookies, Cream Cheese Christmas Cookies, Mocha Butterballs, Lemon Snowballs, Chocolate Thumbprints, Jam Crescents, and many more holiday favorites. You'll also see links to holiday candy recipes and some delicious gifts from the kitchen.

 http://about.com/southernfood/holidaycookierecipes

**BUTTER COOKIES**

Here you'll find a huge variety of delicious butter cookies for the holidays or any occasion. The recipes include cookie press favorites, shortbread cookies, refrigerator cookies, rolled cookies, crescents, tea cakes, drop cookies, and many more.

 http://about.com/southernfood/buttercookierecipes

Chapter 15

# Desserts and Sweet Sauces

**ASK YOUR GUIDE:**

What is the purpose of the larger pan of water?
▶ **PAGE 255**

How did this dessert come to be named cobbler?
▶ **PAGE 258**

Is a particular kind of apple best for this recipe?
▶ **PAGE 261**

How can I be sure the mixture is coating a spoon properly?
▶ **PAGE 264**

## Spiced Bread Pudding
SERVES 6 TO 8

*I have to admit, my biggest dessert weakness is bread pudding. I just can't resist a chef's special bread pudding when we go out to eat. This is a delicious classic version with spices and raisins.*

3 cups milk
5 cups torn French bread pieces
1 tablespoon butter, softened
¾ cup granulated sugar
½ teaspoon salt
1 ½ teaspoons ground cinnamon
1 teaspoon vanilla
3 large eggs, lightly beaten
½ cup raisins

1. Heat oven to 350°F. Butter an 8-inch square baking dish.
2. Heat milk until just hot. Pour over bread pieces; stir in butter. Let stand for 2 minutes.
3. In a bowl, beat eggs lightly; whisk in the sugar, salt, cinnamon, and vanilla. Stir into the bread mixture along with raisins.
4. Pour mixture into the prepared baking dish. Place in a larger baking pan and place in the oven. Pour very hot water in the larger pan to a depth of about ½ inch.
5. Bake for 20 to 30 minutes, until set.
6. Serve warm with Vanilla Sauce (page 265) or Bourbon Sauce (page 264).

**WHAT'S HOT**

▶ Bread pudding is the perfect way to end a special meal, and I have some very popular recipes on my site. One of my personal favorites is the individual bread pudding, baked in custard cups or ramekins. The great thing about baking bread pudding in individual cups is that you can customize them. Sprinkle with your favorite spices or stir them into the mixture, or spoon a little jam into the bottom of the custard cups before adding the pudding mixture. Serve with your favorite dessert sauce. Check it out at http://about.com/southernfood/breadpudding.

# Peach Custard Bread Pudding
SERVES 6

*This wonderful bread pudding has it all! The diced peaches shine like jewels in this delicious dessert.*

> 2 ½ cups diced fresh peaches
> ¼ cup peach nectar
> 4 cups soft bread pieces
> 2 tablespoons melted butter
> 4 large eggs
> ½ cup granulated sugar
> 1 ¾ cups milk
> 1 teaspoon vanilla extract

1. In a saucepan over medium heat, combine the diced peaches and peach nectar; simmer for 5 minutes, or until peaches are tender.
2. Heat oven to 325°F. Butter a 2- to 2 ½-quart baking dish.
3. Arrange the torn bread pieces in the baking dish. Drizzle melted butter over the bread. Add the peach mixture and toss to combine ingredients.
4. In a mixing bowl, whisk together the eggs, sugar, milk, and vanilla; pour the mixture over the bread and peach mixture and stir gently to combine ingredients.
5. Set the pan in a larger pan; pour very hot water into the larger pan to a depth of about ½ to 1 inch. Bake for 60 to 75 minutes, or until pudding is set. A knife should come out clean when inserted near the center.
6. Serve with Butterscotch Sauce (page 263) or your favorite dessert sauce.

ASK YOUR GUIDE

**What is the purpose of the larger pan of water?**

▶ A bain-marie is a large pan containing hot water into which smaller pans are set to cook the food or keep it warm. Cheesecakes and custards are often cooked in a bain-marie. The bain-marie will help prevent the top of a cheesecake from cracking and helps keep the custard or bread pudding from forming a top crust. On the stovetop, a bain-marie can simply be a saucepan set in a bowl of hot water, a very good way to melt chocolate.

## Sweet Potato Crème Brûlée
SERVES 6

*This is a delicious way to enjoy sweet potatoes, and it makes a beautiful dessert for a special occasion.*

1 ½ cups heavy whipping cream
2 teaspoons vanilla
5 large egg yolks
⅓ cup granulated sugar
1 teaspoon ground cinnamon
¼ teaspoon ground allspice
¼ teaspoon ground nutmeg
¾ cup cooked puréed sweet potatoes
Hot to boiling water
2 tablespoons granulated sugar
Pecans, for garnish, optional

1. Heat oven to 350°F. Place six 4- to 6-ounce baking dishes in a large baking pan with sides.
2. Bring the heavy whipping cream to a boil. Remove from heat and stir in vanilla.
3. In a medium bowl, beat the egg yolks with sugar, spices, and sweet potato. Whisk the hot cream into the egg yolk mixture. Ladle evenly into the small baking dishes.

*Sweet Potato Crème Brûlée (continued)*

4. Place the pan with baking dishes on oven rack, then fill with very hot to boiling water about halfway up sides of the dishes. Carefully slide the oven rack in, then bake for about 20 to 25 minutes. The centers will still be a little soft and will move just slightly. Use great care when filling and moving this pan of very hot water around. You might want to first take the custards out of the water and then remove the pan of water from the oven. Use a spatula and potholder or oven mitt to lift each custard out to a wire rack to cool. Let the water cool, then empty the pan and dry thoroughly.

5. Once ramekins are cooled, put them back in the baking pan, cover with wrap or foil, then refrigerate for at least 4 hours.

6. Just before serving, sprinkle about 1 ½ teaspoons of granulated sugar over each crème brûlée. Slide under broiler and broil for about 30 seconds. When sugar begins to melt and brown a bit, remove from the oven. If you have a torch, it's easier to control browning of the sugar. Place a few pecan halves on each, if desired.

**TOOLS YOU NEED**

▶ A culinary torch is a handy tool to have, and I use it for more than just browning the sugar topping of a crème brûlée or fruit desserts. If you don't have gas burners, this torch makes quick work of roasting sweet bell peppers and chile peppers. It also melts cheese and makes it easy to brown baked meringues in a controlled way. The culinary torch can be used for just about anything you bake that you'd like browned a bit more for cosmetic reasons or flavor.

### How did this dessert come to be named cobbler?

▶ The origin of the name of this American dessert is not known, but there is some speculation that it comes from the term "to cobble up," or to put something together quickly. The peach cobbler has become one of the stars of Southern cooking, whether it's made with fresh, frozen, or canned peaches, or a pastry crust, soft cake-like crust, or a delicious biscuit or dumpling topping.

## Old-Fashioned Peach Cobbler
SERVES 6

*Cobblers can be topped with batter crusts, pastry, or even dumplings. I like cobbler just about any way it's made, and this is one of my favorites.*

4 cups fresh sliced peaches
1 cup granulated sugar, divided
1 scant teaspoon ground cinnamon
1 large egg
⅓ cup half-and-half or whole milk
3 tablespoons melted butter
½ cup flour
2 teaspoons baking powder
½ teaspoon salt

1. Heat oven to 350°F. Lightly grease an 11" × 7" baking dish with butter.
2. Arrange peach slices in the baking dish; sprinkle with ½ cup of the granulated sugar and the ground cinnamon.
3. In a bowl, whisk egg with half-and-half. Whisk in the remaining ½ cup of sugar and the melted butter. Stir flour before measuring; add to the egg mixture along with baking powder and salt.
4. Spoon the soft batter over the peaches, spreading to cover as much as possible.
5. Bake for 30 to 40 minutes, until crust is nicely browned.
6. Serve peach cobbler warm, with heavy cream or vanilla ice cream.

## Fresh Fruit Ambrosia
SERVES 6

*Here's a heavenly fruit ambrosia recipe, an old Southern tradition. I love this with whipped cream or a thick custard sauce.*

3 oranges
1 cup orange juice
1 can (8 to 9 ounces) pineapple chunks, undrained
½ cup seedless red grapes, halved
¼ cup seedless green grapes, halved
½ cup flaked coconut
½ cup chopped pecans

1. Peel the oranges; section. Combine the orange sections with the orange juice, pineapple chunks, and grape halves. Refrigerate until serving time.
2. Just before serving, fold in the coconut and chopped pecans.

**WHAT'S HOT**

▶ Many different fruits and ingredients can be added to make delicious ambrosia. I usually top the fruit mixture with whipped cream, but you can also make a delicious ambrosia with equal amounts of sweetened whipped cream and sour cream mixed into the fruit. Bananas are another frequent addition, as are miniature marshmallows and maraschino cherries. If you aren't sure about sectioning oranges, replace the orange sections with canned, drained mandarin orange sections.

## Bananas with Rum Custard Sauce

SERVES 8

*This custard sauce is delicious served over sliced bananas, but you can also make the sauce to serve with a spiced bread pudding or other dessert or fruit.*

8 large egg yolks
2 ½ cups half-and-half
5 tablespoons sugar
¼ teaspoon salt
1 tablespoon dark rum
1 teaspoon vanilla extract
8 medium bananas, firm but ripe
Freshly grated nutmeg

1. In top of a double boiler over hot water, combine the egg yolks, half-and-half, sugar, and salt. Whisk until smooth. Continue cooking over low heat, stirring constantly, until mixture is thickened enough to coat a spoon. Strain and stir in the rum and vanilla. Cover and chill thoroughly.
2. Slice the bananas thin and arrange in dessert dishes. Spoon some of the custard sauce over the bananas and sprinkle each serving with a dash of freshly grated nutmeg.

## Apple Pecan Crunch

SERVES 6

*This is one of my favorite versions of an apple crunch or crisp.*

> 5 large apples, peeled, cored, and sliced
> ½ cup pecan pieces or halves
> 3 tablespoons water
> ¾ cup all-purpose flour
> 1 cup granulated sugar
> 1 teaspoon ground cinnamon
> ½ teaspoon salt
> ½ cup butter, softened

1. Heat oven to 350°F. Lightly butter an 8-inch square baking dish.
2. Arrange apple slices in the baking dish; sprinkle with pecans. Add water.
3. In a mixing bowl, combine the flour, sugar, cinnamon, and salt. Cut in butter with a pastry blender until mixture resembles coarse crumbs. Sprinkle the crumb mixture over the apples. Bake the apple crunch for 35 to 45 minutes, or until apples are tender.
4. Serve warm with ice cream or a vanilla sauce.

ASK YOUR GUIDE

**Is a particular kind of apple best for this recipe?**

▶ I use Golden Delicious or Granny Smith apples in apple crisps and crunches, but some other apple varieties that would work well are Cortland, McIntosh, Rome Beauty, Empire, Northern Spy, Gala, and Jonathan. There are many more varieties of apples you might use. The main thing to remember when choosing apples for pies, crisps, and similar baked desserts is that the apple should have good flavor and should be firm enough to hold its shape when baked.

## Fresh Strawberry Sauce
SERVES 8

*This is a delicious sauce for topping ice cream, or you can use it on pound cake, angel food cake, or as a topping for a cheesecake.*

> 1 pint fresh strawberries
> ½ cup granulated sugar
> ¼ cup water
> Juice and fine-grated zest of ½ lemon
> 2 tablespoons butter

1. Rinse the strawberries and hull. Cut small strawberries in half and slice large berries.
2. In a saucepan, combine the sugar, water, and lemon juice and zest; stir over medium heat until sugar is dissolved and the mixture just begins to boil. Add the butter and stir until melted. Add sliced strawberries and heat through. Do not cook the sauce.
3. Chill the sauce thoroughly before serving. This sauce is delicious on plain cheesecake, vanilla ice cream, pound cake or angel food cake slices, and other desserts.

**WHAT'S HOT**

▶ I have several popular strawberry shortcakes on my site, including the Old-Fashioned Strawberry Short-cake recipe at http://about .com/southernfood/sshort cake. The Deluxe Strawberry Shortcake is made with two 9-inch biscuit-like rounds that are filled with sweetened strawberries. Check it out at http://about.com/southern food/deluxesshortcake. My article on strawberry shortcakes, at http://about .com/southernfood/sshort cakearticle, has some history and a few more recipe ideas, including pound cake with strawberry topping and related recipes using strawberries.

## Old-Fashioned Butterscotch Sauce
MAKES ABOUT 2 CUPS

*This delicious butterscotch is wonderful on a bread pudding, or you could use it as a topping for ice cream.*

> 1 cup light brown sugar, packed
> ⅔ cup light corn syrup
> ¼ cup butter
> ⅛ teaspoon baking soda
> ⅔ cup evaporated milk
> 1 teaspoon vanilla

1. Combine sugar, corn syrup, and butter in a saucepan over medium heat. Bring to a full rolling boil, stirring constantly. Continue cooking, without stirring, at a full rolling boil for 1 minute.
2. Remove from heat and let stand for 5 minutes. Dissolve the baking soda in the milk and add the vanilla; stir into the sauce. Stir until smooth.
3. Pour into a 1-pint canning jar or two 8-ounce jars. Store the sauce in the refrigerator for up to 2 weeks.
4. To reheat the sauce, put the jar in a pan of warm water.

**WHAT'S HOT**

▶ Give a jar of this delicious butterscotch sauce as a gift and keep one for yourself! Decorate a half-pint jar with a square of gingham or calico cloth between the lid and seal and tie a bow around it with instructions on the tag. Make sure to add the refrigeration instructions to the tag, along with directions on heating and some of the great ways to use the sauce.

*How can I be sure the mixture is coating a spoon properly?*

▸ This method, which is used to test custards and some egg-based sauces, is easy to master. When the sauce mixture leaves an even coating on a wooden spoon, it is done. One way to be sure the sauce is done is to draw your finger across the coated spoon. If your finger leaves a track and the sauce is not running down into the track, the sauce or custard is ready.

# Bourbon Sauce
MAKES 2 CUPS

*This rich and delicious bourbon sauce is perfect for bread pudding. You can also substitute dark rum and use this sauce over bananas, ice cream, or other desserts.*

2 cups heavy whipping cream
⅔ cup granulated sugar
4 egg yolks
2 teaspoons vanilla extract
¼ cup bourbon

1. Combine the cream and sugar in a heavy medium saucepan. Heat over medium-low heat until the mixture is hot and it begins to steam.
2. In a small bowl or 2-cup measure, whisk the egg yolks. Whisk about a third of the hot mixture into the yolks, then stir the yolk mixture into the cream mixture in the saucepan. Reduce heat to low and continue cooking until mixture coats a spoon. Do not boil.
3. Remove from heat and stir in the vanilla and bourbon. Strain and serve warm.

# Vanilla Sauce
MAKES 1 ½ CUPS

*This makes a delicious sauce for berries, pudding, or gingerbread.*

2 cups water
1 cup granulated sugar or vanilla sugar
2 tablespoons cornstarch
4 tablespoons butter
1 tablespoon vanilla extract
Dash salt

1. In a medium saucepan, bring water to a boil over high heat. Combine the sugar and cornstarch, blending well, and then stir the mixture into the boiling water. Reduce heat to medium. Cook the sauce, stirring constantly, until thickened.
2. Remove from heat and add butter, vanilla, and a dash of salt. Stir until butter is melted.
3. Spoon warm sauce over dessert or berries. Store the sauce in a jar or tightly covered container in the refrigerator for 1 to 2 weeks.

**BEFORE YOU BEGIN**

▶ Vanilla sugar is wonderful to flavor coffee or other beverages, and it can be used in any recipe calling for granulated sugar. It also makes a wonderful, unique food gift. Cut 1 vanilla bean into 1-inch pieces and then combine them with 3 cups of sugar; cover and let stand for two weeks. Pour the sugar, with the pieces of bean, into ½-pint or 1-pint jars and give as gifts, or use it for desserts, beverages, or cookie decorating. Remove beans when using in a recipe.

## Get Linked

*I love dessert recipes, and you'll find many more fruit and dessert recipes on my Southern Cuisine site on* **About.com***. Here are some of my favorite dessert resources.*

**FRUIT RECIPES**

Here you'll find a broad range of fruit recipes, including pages of recipes devoted to specific fruits. You'll find recipes using bananas, blueberries, apples, raspberries and blackberries, oranges, rhubarb, muscadines, peaches, pears, pineapples, strawberries, melons, cherries, and many other fruits.

 http://about.com/southernfood/fruitrecipes

**PUDDING RECIPES**

Here are links to dozens of bread pudding recipes, banana puddings, and rice pudding recipes, along with sweet potato pudding recipes, basic vanilla and chocolate puddings, Woodford puddings, apple puddings, and more.

 http://about.com/southernfood/puddingrecipes

**COBBLERS AND FRUIT DUMPLINGS**

This is one of my favorite categories! You'll find peach cobblers, blackberry cobbler, sweet potato cobbler, apple cobblers, and many, many more, made with a variety of tops and crusts, along with some delicious fruit dumpling recipes.

 http://about.com/southernfood/cobblers

# Appendix A

# Glossary of Southern Food and Cooking Terms

**adjust seasoning**   To taste the dish near the end of cooking, before serving, to judge the need for salt and pepper, spices, herbs, or other seasonings.

**au jus**   A French term meaning "served with its own juice," used in reference to beef or other meat.

**bacon drippings**   Also known as bacon grease, this is the fat rendered from cooked bacon.

**bain-marie**   This French term, also known as a water bath, is a cooking technique used for sauces and custards, cheesecakes, and other egg-based dishes. The dish is cooked or baked in a larger pan of warm water, which helps keep the sauce from separating and helps to prevent cracks forming in cheesecake. A water bath is also used to keep some foods warm.

**baste**   To brush or spoon liquid, butter, or other fat over food as it cooks.

**batter**   The uncooked base mixture of most baked items and a mixture used to dip foods in before frying. Batter is usually made from a combination of flour, eggs, and liquid, and is thin enough to be stirred or whisked.

**beat**   Beating by hand is to rapidly stir in a circular motion; 100 strokes equals approximately 1 minute with an electric mixer.

**beignet**   A deep-fried New Orleans pastry, served hot with a generous dusting of powdered sugar.

**bisque**   A thick, creamy soup, often made with seafood.

**blacken or blackened**   A method of cooking in which meat, poultry, or fish is seasoned with a spicy seasoning mixture, then fried in a very hot iron skillet until crisp and blackened or very deeply browned on both sides.

**blanch**   Blanching is a cooking process in which food is briefly plunged in boiling water, and then submerged in very cold water to stop the cooking. Blanching peaches and tomatoes for 20 to 30 seconds makes them easier to peel.

**blend**   To mix two or more ingredients together until combined, using a spoon, whisk, blender, mixer, or other implement.

**braise**   To brown food in a small amount of fat, and then cover and cook it slowly over a long period of time in a small amount of liquid, such as water, wine, or broth, until done.

**broil**   To cook food directly under or over the heat source, usually in the oven under the top element, or on the grill. In the oven, the standard broiling temperature is usually 550°F unless the recipes specifies otherwise.

**brown**   To cook food over medium to high heat until the surface is browned. This can be done on the stovetop or under the broiler.

**butterfly** To cut a food, such as shrimp or pork tenderloin, down the center, but not quite through, leaving both sides attached. The food is then spread to resemble a butterfly.

**Cajun cooking** This is a blend of Southern and French cuisines; a country-style cooking method using animal fats and dark roux. Cajun seasoning blends tend to be spicier than Creole seasoning, but both Cajun and Creole cuisines typically use the "trinity" of chopped onion, celery, and bell peppers, and both use filé powder.

**capers** A small edible flower bud of a bush, usually grown in Mediterranean countries. Capers are dried then pickled in a vinegar and salt brine. Capers add piquant flavor to many sauces and condiments, such as remoulade sauce, and are sometimes used as a garnish.

**caramelize** To heat sugar until it melts, liquefies, and then turns golden brown. This technique is used to make candy, frostings, and topping for desserts such as crème brûlée.

**casserole** This term actually pertains to the baking dish as well as the ingredient combination it contains. Casseroles can be made with meat, poultry, vegetables, fish or seafood, and just about any combination, and they are often made with a bread crumb or shredded cheese topping.

**chili sauce** This is a ketchup-like sauce which is spicier and usually sweeter tasting. Often used in sauces, you'll find it near the ketchup in most supermarkets.

**chop** To cut into small pieces.

**chunk** To cut into bite-size pieces, usually 1 inch or larger.

**chutney** A condiment that usually contains fruit or vegetables, sugar, vinegar, and spices. Chutney makes a nice addition to various spreads and sandwich fillings.

**clarified butter** Butter that has been melted then skimmed of milk solids. Clarified butter is used to sauté foods and will withstand much higher heats than whole butter.

**cobbler** A baked dessert dish consisting of a fruit filling covered with sweetened soft dough, biscuit-like dough, or rolled pie pastry.

**country ham** Country ham is a distinctly Southern product, dry cured following federal guidelines that require at least 18 percent of the ham's weight be lost during the curing and aging process; the ham must also contain at least 4 percent salt.

**crawfish** Freshwater crustaceans that look like very small lobsters, with claws. About 3 to 6 inches in length, they're particularly popular in Louisiana and some other parts of the South. They are sometimes called crayfish in other countries and areas outside of Louisiana.

**Creole cooking** Creole cuisine, a cooking style found chiefly in New Orleans, is generally a blend of French, Spanish, and African cuisines. Creole cooking is thought to be somewhat more sophisticated than Cajun cooking, which uses more pork fat and spices compared with Creole cooking's emphasis on butter, cream, and tomatoes. One thing both cuisines have in common is the "trinity" of chopped onion, celery, and bell peppers, and both use filé powder. You'll find a variety of Creole seasonings on the market to give dishes a distinctive Creole flavor.

**croquettes** Ground or minced cooked food, such as chicken, salmon, or other meat, bound with a thick sauce then formed into shapes or patties and fried.

**cube** To cut into cubes, usually about ½ inch to 1 inch in size.

**cut in**   To incorporate solid fat into dry ingredients using a pastry blender, fork, or two knives. A food processor is sometimes used to cut in fats.

**dash**   A dash is a measurement less than ⅛ teaspoon.

**deep fry**   To cook in hot fat that is deep enough to cover the food.

**dice**   To cut food into small cubes, from ⅛ inch to less than 1 inch in size.

**dough**   A mixture of flour, liquid, and other ingredients that is too stiff to pour and is usually worked or blended with hands.

**drizzle**   To pour a liquid or thin mixture over something, such as a glaze for a cake or bread, or butter over a food just before baking.

**fatback**   The layer of fat found along the back of a pig. Fresh (unsalted) fatback is used to make lard and cracklings.

**filé powder**   A seasoning and thickener made of sassafras leaves. Filé is traditionally used to flavor and thicken Cajun and Creole dishes, such as gumbo.

**fillet**   a boneless piece of meat, poultry, or fish, sometimes spelled filet.

**fold**   To gently combine a light item or mixture with a heavier mixture, such as egg whites into a cake or pancake batter or berries into a batter. A rubber spatula is usually used to fold ingredients or egg white mixture into a batter. The spatula is cut into the batter then brought across the bottom of the bowl and up the side. The bowl is rotated slightly as the motion is repeated until ingredients are combined.

**fritter**   A sweet or savory deep-fried cake. A fritter may incorporate food into the batter, or single pieces of food may be dipped in batter.

**fry**   To cook food in fat over medium to high heat.

**garnish**   To decorate food or the dish on which the food is served. Examples of garnishes include lemon or citrus zest on a dollop of whipped cream, chopped parsley on a casserole, and lemon slices with cooked fish fillets or seafood.

**giblets**   The heart, neck, liver, and gizzards of poultry.

**glaze**   To coat food with a thin sweet or savory coating that becomes smooth and glossy after setting or cooking.

**grate**   To cut things into small shreds or pieces, using a hand grater or food processor grater attachment.

**grease**   To spread fat on a cooking pan or utensil to keep food from sticking. To grease and flour describes greasing a pan then dusting with a coating of flour, which is shaken to distribute evenly before inverting and discarding excess flour.

**grill**   To cook on a rack over hot coal, gas, or other heat source.

**grind**   To reduce food to very small particles, as in ground beef or sausage, spices, or coffee. Coffee grinders, a mortar and pestle, a food processor, meat grinder, and pepper mill can all be used to grind different types of foods.

**grits**   Any coarsely ground grain, but commonly used in reference to hominy grits, made from dried corn kernels.

**gumbo**   A Creole-style stew, usually made with tomatoes, okra, and other vegetables and meats. Gumbo usually starts with a roux as the thickener, and filé powder is often added just before serving.

**half-and-half**  A milk and cream mixture with about 11- to 18-percent milk fat. Substitute evaporated milk or equal amounts of milk and cream.

**ham hock**  The ham hock is the lower part of a hog's hind leg, usually cut in 3-inch lengths. Ham hocks are usually cured and smoked and make a good flavoring for beans, greens, and other dishes.

**headspace**  The amount of space left in the top of a jar of home-canned food or container of frozen food.

**heavy cream**  Cream with at least 36 percent fat content. Often labeled "heavy whipping cream."

**hog jowl**  From the cheek of a hog, this is cured and smoked, and can be cut into slices and used as bacon. Usually found only in the South, hog jowl is used to flavor beans, greens, and other dishes.

**Hoppin' John**  A dish of black-eyed peas cooked with pork fat and seasonings and usually served with cornbread. This is a traditional Southern New Year's Day dish, eaten to bring good luck.

**hush puppies**  A deep-fried cornmeal dumpling, often containing chopped green onions.

**jambalaya**  A very versatile Creole dish, jambalaya is a combination of cooked rice and a variety of other ingredients. It may include tomatoes, onion, green pepper, meat, poultry, a variety of spices, and/or shellfish.

**jus**  The French word for juice, as in *beef au jus*, or beef with natural juices.

**Key lime**  This lime, from Florida, is much smaller and yellower than the more common Persian lime.

**knead**  A baking technique used to mix and work dough using the hands. Dough is pressed with the heels of the hands while stretching it out, then it's folded over itself and the motion is repeated several times, as the recipe directs.

**lard**  Lard is rendered and clarified pork fat. The best lard is made from the fat around the pig's kidneys, called leaf lard. Lard makes tender and flaky pastry and biscuits.

**marinate**  To let food soak in a seasoned liquid to make it more flavorful or more tender.

**mince**  To cut food into very small pieces, using a knife, food processor, or other chopping utensil. Minced food is cut in smaller pieces than chopped food.

**mint julep**  A Kentucky specialty drink made with bourbon and mint, and usually with sugar syrup and crushed ice. The mint julep is a Kentucky Derby tradition and is sometimes served in a silver julep tumbler.

**nonreactive pan**  A nonreactive pan is made of a nonpourous material that does not produce a chemical reaction when it comes into contact with acidic foods. An aluminum pan is reactive, while stainless steel, glass, and enamel and enamel-lined pans are not.

**okra**  Okra pods, brought to the U.S. South by Africans during the days of slave trade, are green and tapered pods with ridges. Okra is often sliced and fried, pickled, or cooked with tomatoes. Sliced okra is also used for its thickening properties in stews and gumbo.

**Oysters Bienville**  A New Orleans dish, created in the 1930s by the famous Antoine's Restaurant, was named after the city's founder. The dish is made with oysters on the half-shell topped with a sherry sauce, along with garlic, mushrooms, and minced shrimp. The oysters are topped with a bread crumb and grated cheese mixture and baked on a bed of rock salt.

**Oysters Rockefeller**  Another famous New Orleans dish created by Antoine's, this dish was named after John D. Rockefeller. The dish is commonly made with oysters on the half-shell topped with spinach, butter, bread crumbs, and seasonings, baked on a bed of rock salt.

**pain perdu** A New Orleans French Toast, pain perdu literally means "lost bread," because it is a way to revive stale bread that would otherwise be lost.

**pilau** Also called pilaf and sometimes perloo, this dish is a combination of rice that has been browned in fat, along with chopped vegetables, meat, poultry, or seafood, and seasonings.

**pimiento** The pimiento is a large sweet pepper, about 4" × 3" in size, and chopped pimientos or strips are commonly used in pimiento cheese spread or other spreads and dips, and many casseroles. The pimiento is sweeter than red bell peppers, and stuffed green olives are stuffed with pimientos. They are found in supermarkets in small jars or cans, usually chopped or cut in strips.

**po' boy or poor boy sandwich** A New Orleans specialty sandwich made with split French bread rolls, mayonnaise, shredded lettuce and other vegetables, and sliced meat, fried oysters, and sometimes cheese or gravy.

**powdered sugar** Also called confectioners' sugar, powdered sugar is sugar that has been crushed into a fine powder and combined with a small amount of cornstarch to keep it from clumping.

**pulled pork** Barbecued pork roast, usually shoulder, which is slow cooked (usually in a pit or pit-type barbecue) until very tender and then shredded and mixed with sauce or served with a sauce. The sauce varies from one region to another.

**ramekin** A small baking dish, usually round, used to make custards, individual desserts, or individual servings of other dishes.

**reduce** To reduce a mixture is to boil a sauce mixture, juices, wine, or broth until reduced in volume through evaporation, making the sauce more flavorful and somewhat thicker.

**render** To extract the fat from meat or poultry by cooking over low heat. Rendered fat is strained after cooking.

**roast** As a verb, to cook a food in the oven in an uncovered, shallow pan with no liquid; much of the surface of the food is surrounded by heat.

**rolling boil** A fast boil that cannot be slowed by stirring or whisking.

**roux** A mixture of fat and flour that is blended and cooked slowly over low heat until the desired consistency or color is reached. Roux is used as a base for thickening stews, gumbos, and sauces.

**salt pork** Salt-cured pork that is essentially a layer of fat from the pig's belly or sides; it is similar to bacon but much fattier. Salt pork is used to flavor beans, greens, and other dishes.

**sauté** To cook food quickly in a small amount of fat, commonly in a sauté pan or skillet.

**scald** To heat a liquid such as milk to just below the boiling point. Scalding milk is not necessary these days, because of pasteurization, but you still might want to scald milk or heat it if you need to melt fat or dissolve sugar in it, or if you use raw milk. Scald also means to plunge a food into boiling water to loosen the peel.

**scallop** A dish cooked in a thick sauce, such as scalloped potatoes or corn scallop. A scallop is also a mollusk with fan-shaped shells, and can also mean to form a decorative "scalloped" edge along the edge of pie dough or other food.

**scant** A "scant" teaspoon, tablespoon, or other measurement is not quite full to the rim.

**score**  To cut shallow slashes, usually in a decorative pattern, in ham or other food. Scoring might be done to decorate, to allow excess fat to drain, or help tenderize a meat.

**sear**  To brown meat quickly over high heat. Meat, poultry, or fish might be seared under a broiler, in a skillet, or on the grill.

**shred**  To cut food into narrow strips or particles; shredding may be done using a knife, a food processor, a grater, or two forks.

**simmer**  To cook in liquid at a temperature just below the boiling point, when very small bubbles just begin to break the surface.

**skillet**  A long-handled pan, also called a frying pan, made with low sides. A skillet should have a heavy bottom for high heat.

**slow cooker**  An electric cooker with a crockery insert and a glass or plastic cover, made to cook foods at a low temperature for a long period of time using moist heat. The heating element is usually built into the sides of the cooker to surround the food with heat and avoid scorching.

**soften**  To make a food, such as cream cheese or butter, softer by letting it stand at room temperature or by wrapping it and submerging in warm or hot water.

**springform pan**  A round cake pan that is a little deeper than a standard cake pan. Springform pans have a clamp on the side which releases the sides from the bottom, leaving the cake undisturbed. Springform pans are commonly used for cheesecakes and tortes.

**succotash**  A Southern dish, usually made with a combination of seasoned lima beans and corn, sometimes with the addition of chopped onion, peppers, or cream.

**sweet onion**  Sweet onions have a higher amount of natural sugar, and can be found almost year-round. Varieties include a Southern favorite, Vidalia, from Georgia, along with the Hawaiian Maui, Washington's Walla Walla, Texas Sweets, Mayan, Grand Canyon, and others.

**Tabasco sauce**  A fermented hot sauce, made in Louisiana, which is commonly used to flavor a wide variety of dishes and beverages.

**vinaigrette**  An oil and vinegar sauce or dressing, usually used on salads or other vegetables. Vinaigrette might also contain seasonings, grated onion or shallots, garlic, mustard, or other ingredients.

**whipped topping**  An imitation whipped cream product, found frozen and ready to thaw and use, or made from a dry mix by adding milk. Many of these products are lower in fat and a quick substitute for whipped cream.

**whipping cream**  Whipping cream, also called light whipping cream, can contain from 30 to 36 percent fat.

**whisk**  A whipping utensil of varying shapes made with looped wires joined at the handle, used to whip or blend sauces, eggs, and other ingredients. As a verb, whisk means to whip or blend ingredients with a whisk.

**zest**  Zest is the colorful thin outer layer of citrus fruit, such as lemons, not including the white inner layer, or pith. Use a zester, sharp paring knife, vegetable peeler, or fine grater to peel or grate this aromatic layer from the fruit.

## Appendix B

# Holiday Meals and Special Occasions

**New Year's Eve**
Creamy Crab Dip (page 19)
Barbecued Chicken Wings (page 23)
Spicy Cheese Dip (page 17)
Cheddar Sausage Balls (page 22)
Dried Beef and Cheese Dip (page 20)
Pimiento Cheese Sandwiches (page 72)
Pecan Sandies (page 240)
Rocky Road Fudge (page 250)
Cranberry Party Punch (page 8)

**New Year's Day**
Spicy Hoppin' John (page 174)
Black-Eyed Pea Salad with Basil Dressing (page 67)
Spicy Shrimp and Grits (page 160)
Creamy Cabbage Slaw (page 62)
Savory Collard Greens (page 184)
Crispy Fried Okra (page 191)
Praline Cheesecake with Pecan Crust (page 228)
Lemon-Glazed Pound Cake (page 217)

**Game Day**
Creamy Crab Dip (page 19)
Barbecued Chicken Wings (page 23)
Spicy Beef Chili (page 96)
Beef and Barbecue Bean Stew (page 93)
Down-Home Pinto Beans (page 176)
Pulled Pork Barbecue Sandwiches (page 76)
New Orleans–Style Roast Beef Po' Boy (page 73)

Chili Beef Burgers (page 78)
Southern Skillet Cornbread (page 24)
Coca-Cola Cake (page 218)
Mom's Blonde Brownies (page 245)
Old-Fashioned Peanut Butter Cookies (page 241)

**Romantic Meal**
Eggs Benedict with Tomato Slices (page 44)
Baked Tilapia with Pecan Topping (page 157)
Chicken with Cajun Cream Sauce (page 136)
Herb-Pecan Crusted Rack of Lamb (page 104)
Savory Rice Pilaf with Green Onions (page 169)
Quick and Easy Broiled Tomatoes (page 192)
Red Velvet Cake (page 224)
Sweet Potato Crème Brûlée (page 256)

**Mardi Gras**
Pain Perdu (page 34)
Spicy Cheese Straws (page 14)
Chicken and Sausage Gumbo (page 50)
Crab and Shrimp Bisque (page 58)
Louisiana Red Beans and Rice (page 175)
Crab-Stuffed Mushrooms (page 15)
Shrimp Creole (page 162)
Crispy Fried Oysters (page 164)
Spicy Fried Eggplant Strips (page 186)
Spiced Bread Pudding (page 254)
Bourbon Sauce (page 264)
Bananas with Rum Custard Sauce (page 260)

# Appendix C

# Other Sites and Further Readings

## Other Sites

### Southern Foodways Alliance

The Southern Foodways Alliance, or SFA, is an institute of the Center for the Study of Southern Culture, which is located at the University of Mississippi in Oxford, Mississippi. The site contains membership and event information, along with an informative blog, aptly named Hot Off the Griddle, with the latest news and happenings.

www.southernfoodways.com

### The Culture of Southern Food

This is a study done by students of a 1996 applied anthropology course at the University of West Florida in Pensacola. It's a fascinating study that follows food contributions by the various cultural groups of different regions, including foods of the original Americans and those who came to the Southeast via the slave trade, along with information on Southern food in specific regions, including Virginia, Appalachia, and Louisiana.

www.uwf.edu/tprewitt/sofood/welcome.htm

### Hoppin' John's

This is the site of Southern cookbook author John Martin Taylor, with a nice selection of recipes, a link to his stone-ground grits, cornmeal, and corn flour, and links to his cookbooks.

www.hoppinjohns.com

### Emerils.com

Emeril Lagasse's site contains his restaurant menus, the latest news, cooking talk, recipes, menus, and more. It's a fun site to browse and read, and you'll copy more than a few recipes to try.

www.emerils.com

### The Gumbo Pages: The Creole and Cajun Recipe Page

Chuck Taggart's excellent Cajun and Creole food and recipe pages, with information and resources on both Creole and Cajun cuisines and ingredients, provide a great index of recipes.

www.gumbopages.com/recipe-page.html

### Chitterlings

A terrific soul food site with a wonderful collection of down-home recipes and a great daily newsletter.

www.chitterlings.com

## Further Readings

### Butter Beans to Blackberries, by Ronni Lundy

This is an excellent cookbook with an abundance of mouth-watering recipes and creative cooking ideas, along with resources for unique or hard-to-find Southern foods and seeds.

*Southern Food, At Home, on the Road, in History,* by John Egerton

> This entertaining food and recipe book is an excellent resource for anyone interested in Southern food and culture. It is a tour of the South, with stops at diners, barbecue joints, and restaurants, ending with a nice variety of essential Southern recipes.

*The Welcome Table,* by Jessica B. Harris

> A wonderful variety of African-American recipes, including recipes from the days of the slave trade in America, many classic Southern dishes, and family favorites.

*A Gracious Plenty,* by John T. Edge

> From the director of the Southern Foodways Alliance, this is a collection of treasured Southern recipes, along with essays on Southern identity.

*Damon Lee Fowler's New Southern Baking,* by Damon Lee Fowler

> This is an essential cookbook for anyone who loves to bake, with many updated Southern cakes, desserts, pies, and other goodies, from Savannah food writer Damon Lee Fowler.

*Cornbread Nation 2: The United States of Barbecue,* edited by Lolis Eric Elie

> This is a celebration of barbecue in Southern cuisine and culture, a compilation of articles, poems, columns, and other writings, with the focus on regional barbecue.

# INDEX